Visions in a Seer Stone

WILLIAM L. DAVIS

Visions in a Seer Stone

Joseph Smith and the Making of the
Book of Mormon

The University of North Carolina Press *Chapel Hill*

© 2020 William L. Davis
All rights reserved
Set in Arno Pro by Westchester Publishing Services
Manufactured in the United States of America

The University of North Carolina Press has been a member of the
Green Press Initiative since 2003.

Library of Congress Cataloging-in-Publication Data
Names: Davis, William L., 1968– author.
Title: Visions in a seer stone : Joseph Smith and the making of the
    Book of Mormon / William L. Davis.
Other titles: Joseph Smith and the making of the Book of Mormon
Description: Chapel Hill : The University of North Carolina Press, 2020. |
    Includes bibliographical references and index.
Identifiers: LCCN 2019037839 | ISBN 9781469655659 (cloth) |
    ISBN 9781469655666 (paperback) | ISBN 9781469655673 (ebook)
Subjects: LCSH: Book of Mormon. | Smith, Joseph, Jr., 1805–1844.
Classification: LCC BX8627 .D39 2020 | DDC 289.3092—dc23
LC record available at https://lccn.loc.gov/2019037839

Cover illustration of engraved plates by author.

Contents

Preface

My interest in the Book of Mormon began in childhood, though not initially from any personal desire or intense curiosity. Whenever I asked my mother to tell me bedtime stories, she almost never regaled me with magical fairytales. Much to my chagrin, she rather told me countless stories about our family's Mormon pioneer ancestors, interspersed with tales of ancient Christian prophets and warriors from the pages of the Book of Mormon. Nevertheless, though hobbits, elves, and wizards were more congruent with my youthful tastes, I began to appreciate the stories and messages in the Book of Mormon. Joseph Smith, the prophet of the Latter Day Saint movement, claimed that the ancient American epic was the "the most correct of any book on earth."[1] Such a confident declaration influenced me to embrace the work literally and wholeheartedly, to study its stories in painstaking detail, trusting that every passage, every verse, every word had the potential to unlock the mysteries of God. I examined the language, the turns of phrases, the rhythms, the stories, and the messages. I created my own timelines for narratives, traced out the sermon topics of ancient prophets, sketched maps of the cities and battles, built genealogy charts, and memorized select verses. Because my core beliefs ultimately anchored on the Book of Mormon, no other text was more important to me, and I dedicated my time and resources to understanding it to the best of my ability.

By the time I was in my mid-twenties, and though I continued my study of the Book of Mormon, I began to withdraw from active participation in the Mormon faith. A variety of reasons contributed to my decision, ranging from my own evolving spirituality to concerns about the leadership of the LDS Church (officially the Church of Jesus Christ of Latter-day Saints, commonly known simply as the Mormons) and the direction in which the institution was heading. Over the next several years, I moved from being an active and devout believer to a nonparticipant. Today, having now passed the half-century mark of age, I have spent more of my life on the far perimeter of the faith than within it. Even so, throughout all these developments, I have continued to read and examine the Book of Mormon. Such dedication ultimately derives from, and continues to reflect, a personal interest in the origins of my identity and how the Book of Mormon played a fundamental role during my formative years.

For me and many other people growing up in the faith, Mormonism represented much more than a religious organization. The church stood at the center of life, shaping one's sense of identity (for this life and the next), one's relationship to God and to other people, and one's values and beliefs. I saw the world through a very specific Mormon cultural lens, a lens so concentrating and all-encompassing that I was not aware of its ubiquitous presence framing every aspect of life. Neither was I aware that the paradigm was a cultural construct, comprised of a set of unquestioned premises that shaped how I viewed and interpreted the world. All facets of life ultimately revolved around the LDS faith and the culture it created, and the Book of Mormon sat at the center of that universe, anchoring and validating every aspect of life. For me personally, understanding the text therefore became a central preoccupation. Understanding how Joseph Smith produced the work directly correlated to understanding the construction of my own identity and how the specific spiritual and cultural inheritances of my childhood shaped my life and worldview.

I share this personal background for a reason. As Paul C. Gutjahr observes in *The Book of Mormon: A Biography*, the history of scholarship on the Book of Mormon has "largely fallen into two camps: Mormon educational and apologetic texts and Evangelical works attacking the book's veracity."[2] Thus, almost by default, scholars of the Book of Mormon, at least in the past, have often been shuffled into one of two opposing categories: "defenders of the faith" or "critics of the church." Given such circumstances, my past participation in the LDS Church will most certainly influence the ways in which some readers perceive this work and respond to this study. Nevertheless, this project is not a devotional effort; it is not invested in either proving or disproving religious claims. I do not aspire to participate in the former (and, unfortunately, sometimes still current) parochial and polemical battles between the "defenders" and "critics" of Mormon beliefs.

For my part, I am positioning this project within the rising academic field of Mormon studies, with a specific emphasis on evidentiary support for claims and a conscious avoidance of church doctrines and official beliefs. In recent years, many academic scholars—scholars who have no desire either to support or attack Mormonism's religious claims—have taken an interest in the Book of Mormon as a legitimate object of historical study, particularly when considering how the text informs (and is informed by) our understanding of religious history and various aspects of early American culture. As Laurie F. Maffly-Kipp argues, "For any reader wanting to learn more about the history of American religion, the Book of Mormon is an indispensable document."[3]

I see this work as part of that academic project. Regardless of what one believes about its historical or sacral authenticity, the Book of Mormon reveals important information about nineteenth-century American culture, particularly regarding oral culture and the formation of American literature among the non-elite classes of democratic-minded citizens, whose voices often emerged through the spoken word along religious avenues and byways.

Readers hoping for a study that debunks Joseph Smith and attacks the Book of Mormon will be disappointed with this work. This is not to say, however, that I will not be challenging some of the *un*official, nondoctrinal traditions and theories surrounding the text. In an effort to distance Smith from the authorship of the Book of Mormon, a segment of Mormon scholars has attempted to downplay or even erase nineteenth-century influences on the work. While such efforts might be understandable, at least from a religious point of view that seeks to limit inquiries into the nature and origin of one's sacred text, I believe such efforts are ultimately misguided and lead to faulty perceptions and self-imposed blind spots about the past. Some argue, for example, that Smith was too "illiterate," "unschooled," and "ignorant" to have composed the Book of Mormon. While Smith's formal educational opportunities were, in fact, limited and sporadic, a close examination of the evidence nevertheless reveals that such claims derive from anecdotal accounts and problematic representations, undermining the stability of such assertions as accurate depictions of his supposed lack of ability. Objectivity and impartial evaluations never appeared to be the goal in such accounts. The context of such claims inevitably reflects the desires and perceptions of the speakers describing Smith, rather than an attempt to provide objective information about his actual skills, knowledge, or capabilities.

Neither does Smith's purported ignorance stand as the sole example of pseudo-authoritative doctrine. Rather, it constitutes one piece of a larger matrix of nondoctrinal theories and proposals that, for some devotees, has assumed quasi-official status and overlaid the actual faith claims with a bristling crust of speculative theology. As a result, some individuals claiming to be "defenders of the faith" are actually "defenders of a cherished theory," while the faith itself has little to do with the discussion at hand. These presumably well-intentioned theories—the barnacles of faith encrusting actual doctrinal claims—run the risk of shutting down comprehensive discussions about the nature and origin of the Book of Mormon and the significant role it has played in American history, not to mention conversations within and among the various denominations of the Latter Day Saint movement—that is, the many churches that emerged from Joseph Smith's original organization, such as The

Church of Jesus Christ of Latter-day Saints, Community of Christ, The Church of Jesus Christ (Bickertonite), and Church of Christ (Temple Lot), among many others.[4] For Mormon studies to become a viable academic field, participants need to recognize the difference between speculative theories and core doctrines of the faith in order to create a space where scholars of all backgrounds, beliefs, and methodologies can discuss such issues in an impartial manner.[5]

Regardless of what one believes about the origin of the work, the Book of Mormon contains an enormous amount of nineteenth-century material that permeates both the content and structure of the work. These contemporary influences, however, do not (or should not) pose a problem for believers. Within the community of faith, several theories regarding Smith's translation process help to explain the presence of such modern elements. Some Mormon scholars, for example, propose that Smith did not actually translate the Book of Mormon but rather transcribed the text by peering into a "seer stone"—a stone used in crystal-gazing and folk magic—which provided a ready-made, preexisting English translation, either by projecting glowing letters on the surface of the stone or else catalyzing a vision of a written text (a theory referred to as "tight control").[6] In this view, according to Grant Hardy's formulation, "Joseph would have been using the seer stone to gain access to a previously existing translation, perhaps one done by God himself or by appointed angels."[7] For those who believe that the translation appeared on the surface of the seer stone or in a vision of the text, without Smith's input, the nineteenth-century anachronisms in the Book of Mormon can then be framed as God's alterations to the ancient record, which He transmitted to Smith via the seer stone or as a seer-stone-inspired vision in order to make the final text more accessible to Smith's nineteenth-century audience.

Alternatively, some believing scholars argue that Smith did, in fact, actually *translate* a text. In other words, through some process of visionary imagery, mental impressions, and divine inspiration, Smith produced the Book of Mormon by making use of his own vocabulary, frames of reference, training, and life experiences to articulate the work. Thus, for those who believe that Smith actively participated in a literal translation, the nineteenth-century elements can be understood as Smith's personal contributions to the translation project (a theory often described as "loose control").[8] How much or how little Smith contributed to the construction of the Book of Mormon is therefore left to the reader's personal determinations. Without commenting on the merits or failings of these competing theories, I invite those who believe in the historicity of the text to consider the ways in which their own religious and perceptual frameworks already provide a means to incorporate academic studies such as this one into their faith-based and faith-seeking paradigms.

Moreover, I would also encourage believing scholars and readers to recognize that this study addresses a readership that extends beyond the religious boundaries of the various denominations within the Latter Day Saint movement to include those who do not embrace the Book of Mormon as an inspired or authentic ancient text. This study represents an academic project, governed by evidence-based explorations of the connections between the Book of Mormon and the nineteenth-century environment in which it emerged. As such, I will be speaking about some of those specific nineteenth-century elements in the work as the product of Smith's compositional skill and creative imagination. Likewise, in order to avoid bogging down the work with constant clarifications of the differences between nineteenth-century textual elements attributable to Smith and elements that believing scholars attribute to ancient Book of Mormon authors, I will often streamline the discussion by referring to the work as the result of Smith's individual creative efforts.

This positioning, however, does not represent a tacit commentary on the validity of Smith's assertions about the divine origin of the text, nor does it aim to engage in polemical discourse regarding faith claims. Rather, this approach seeks to avoid the laborious repetition of disputed claims, while acknowledging a readership that extends well beyond the communities of faith. In any case, the historicity of the Book of Mormon and the validity of Smith's claims are not the focus of this study. Rather, I will be exploring how the textual phenomena and internal evidence within the pages of the Book of Mormon reach outside the text to engage with the pervasive oratorical training, practices, and concerns of Smith's environment in early nineteenth-century America. I believe that this information, for believers and nonbelievers alike, reveals valuable insights about the life of Joseph Smith, his background and religious experiences, as well as the cultural context in which he grew up. I invite the reader to join me in that journey of discovery.

Acknowledgments

My thoughts on Joseph Smith's production of the Book of Mormon have preoccupied much of my lifetime, and the development of my research has benefited from countless discussions with friends, mentors, teachers, librarians, and colleagues. Any attempt to identify all the people who have influenced my life and research must certainly be incomplete. While writing this book, I have benefitted from the insights of several scholars in English, history, and theater and performance studies. First and foremost is David Rodes, who spent countless hours discussing ideas, reading (and correcting) my drafts, and offering invaluable insights. Others providing crucial support include Michael J. Colacurcio, Michael Hackett, Patricia Harter, Henry Ansgar ("Andy") Kelley, V.A. ("Del") Kolve, Joseph Nagy, and Shelley Salamensky. I am also deeply grateful to those who reviewed the manuscript in its various stages of development, including William Deverell, Rick Grunder, H. Michael Marquardt, Brent Metcalfe, Colby Townsend, and the anonymous readers for the University of North Carolina Press. Elaine Maisner, my editor on this project, provided crucial advice, and I am deeply grateful to her and to the editorial committee for their support.

A network of friends, family, and supporters has also provided much-needed encouragement. I am indebted to the generosity of Michael Austin, Bob Baruch and Tom Knechtel, Linda Bourque, Joanna Brooks, John L. Bryant, Bronya and Andy Galef, William Handley, Doyle Harcrow, Nancy Hardin, Thomas Harrison, Jeremiah Ho, Marcia Howard, Sue and Jim Hurford, Judith Rodes Johnson, James Krauser, Barbara Levin, David Ligare and Gary Smith, Larry Luchtel, Mary McCafferty, Connell O'Donovan, Bob Owens, D. Michael Quinn, Boyd Petersen, Keith Peterson, Richard Rodriguez, Richard Schechner, Noel and Tanya Silverman and Audrey Andrews, James R. Sullivan, Dorothy Taylor, Steve Urkowitz, Paul Walsh, Sam Watters, and staff members of the UCLA Library, the William Andrews Clark Memorial Library, and the New York Public Library. My gratitude, of course, does not imply that these individuals or institutions share my views; any mistakes are my own. Finally, I want to offer special thanks to my family, and especially to my parents for their sustaining and unconditional love.

Introduction

In 1830 the young American Republic witnessed the publication of a new set of scriptures: the Book of Mormon. According to Joseph Smith, the young man who produced the work, these new scriptures represented an authentic history of ancient American civilizations and served as a companion volume to the Bible and as a second witness to Jesus Christ's life and mission. Smith did not claim, however, to be the sole originator of the work.[1] Rather, he asserted that he translated a preexisting ancient record, written in an unknown script called "reformed Egyptian" on a set of gold plates, which lay buried in a hill near his family's farm in Western New York. According to Smith's narrative of events, on the evening of 21 September 1823, an angel appeared to him in his bedroom and revealed the location of the gold plates. Smith did not immediately retrieve them but continued to meet with the divine messenger, called the angel Moroni, for the next four years to receive instructions on how to organize Christ's true church and "in what manner His kingdom was to be conducted in the last days."[2] Once he was prepared to perform the translation, Smith visited the nearby hill, the Hill Cumorah, and unearthed the gold plates, along with a few other ancient objects.

One of these objects, a set of "spectacles" known as "interpreters," and apparently attached to a breastplate, served as one of Smith's translation devices. Along with this implement, Smith also used one of his seer stones—mystical visionary objects commonly employed in contemporary folk magic practices—as another translation device. In addition to his use of such objects, Smith's production of the Book of Mormon differs from other traditional scriptural translations or written compositions in the methodology that he adopted for the work. Rather than studying the gold plates and writing down translations of the ancient script, Smith dictated the entire work to an attendant scribe in a process of revelatory translation, apparently without looking directly at the plates. Thus, through the sole medium of the spoken word, Smith unfolded the epic Christian narrative. Slowed only by the pace of his scribes, who busily tried to keep pace with his torrential flow of narrative production, Smith completed the work of more than five hundred printed pages within a ninety-day period (estimated at approximately fifty-seven to seventy-five actual full-time working days).[3]

The surviving, partial scribal manuscript of Smith's performance reveals that he did not return to revise the text for publication beyond relatively minor adjustments (mostly spelling and punctuation, though some alterations were consequential to doctrine) from the original outpouring of orally composed material.[4] In other words, the content of the oral transcription was nearly identical to the final printed form. Containing an estimated 269,510 words, the Book of Mormon stands as one of the longest recorded oral performances in the history of the United States, comparable in length and magnitude, as well as method and technique, to the classical oral epics of Homer's *Iliad* and *Odyssey* combined.[5]

Orality in Nineteenth-Century America

Smith's oral production of the Book of Mormon raises several questions about the role of oratorical culture in early nineteenth-century America. Smith lived in a time and place marked by a rich variety of oral presentations shaped by the technologies of the era, the dynamic relationship between orality and print culture, and the paramount role of public speaking in the cultural imagination of the people. Whether at home, school, church, work, or any number of other social and civic gatherings, cultural institutions in postrevolutionary America taught, developed, and encouraged oratorical skills at a level unparalleled in twenty-first-century American practices. And for ambitious young men who aspired to upward mobility as lawyers, politicians, educators, ministers, and leaders in society, acquiring fluency and skillfulness in the art of oral performance could spell the difference between notable success and abject failure.

Evidence of Smith's nineteenth-century oratorical culture emerges frequently in the pages of the Book of Mormon, prompting questions about the discursive dynamics that link Smith's performance to the historical milieu from which the text emerged. Because the key mode of its creation was the spoken word, the Book of Mormon might best be described as a script, or a transcript, of Smith's performative process—the artifact of a grander, multifaceted oratorical effort. And though Smith's original performance remains lost in time, the textual product of that performance reveals critical information about Smith's methods of oral composition. When the scribes wrote down Smith's epic narrative, they recorded his words nearly verbatim in the moment of utterance.[6] This precision in record keeping—a rare and verifiable account of a near verbatim recording of a live oral performance—therefore offers an opportunity for readers of the Book of Mormon to observe the specific oral performance techniques involved in its construction. Thus, the text, as a scriptural voice whispering out of the dust, invites us on a journey to retrace some of the most prominent cultural institutions and preoccupations that account for the textual phenomena that appear within its pages.

Focus of Research

The focus of this study is the oral performance techniques that Smith used to dictate the Book of Mormon, with specific attention to the methods of preaching in Smith's contemporary sermon culture. Thus, the central issues revolve around the methods of oral composition, rather than narrative content. As such, this study will only address matters of content—the stories, the messages, and the theology of the Book of Mormon—when they illuminate techniques of oral production. Abundant evidence throughout the work indicates that Smith made use of several techniques that facilitated the process of oral composition, including such methods as the semi-extemporaneous amplification of skeletal narrative outlines, the use of formulaic language in biblical and pseudobiblical registers, rhetorical devices common in oral traditions, and various forms of repetition (e.g., recycled narrative patterns), among other traditional compositional strategies. Viewing the Book of Mormon within the context of nineteenth-century oratorical training and techniques therefore offers a performance-based approach to understanding the text.

In the early nineteenth century children and young adults encountered many of these techniques, either by conscious study or direct exposure, through a variety of social venues: domestic worship and daily family Bible reading, domestic education, Sunday schools, church attendance, revivals, introductory composition lessons in common schools, and a variety of voluntary societies for self-improvement, such as juvenile literary and debate societies. Such skills were further reinforced within a culture that relied heavily on various forms of oral performance in social interactions, including household fireside storytelling practices, public orations at civic events, classroom recitation exercises, school exhibitions, exhortations and sermons in churches, and camp meeting revivals.[7]

Within this kaleidoscope of oral performances, Smith's exposure to the sermon cultures within his contemporary evangelical churches offers particularly important and relevant insights. Smith actively participated as a lay exhorter among the Methodists near his home in the Palmyra/Manchester region of Western New York, and he frequently attended the church services and revival meetings of several denominations in his surrounding area, including Baptists, Methodists, and Presbyterians. For young adults like Smith, who aspired to exhort and preach, exposure to the informal training among such evangelical groups involved the instruction in and regular practice of a robust set of oral performance techniques that figured prominently in the ambitious development of semi-extemporaneous oratorical skills.

A comprehensive study addressing all of these areas of influence lies well beyond the scope of a single monograph. Many of the oral techniques mentioned, for example, were integral components of introductory writing instruction in common schools, with lessons involving the composition of "themes," various imitation exercises, and a variety of short and expanded essays. As such, a thorough discussion on the topic of oral performance in early nineteenth-century education would, by itself, require a separate study. Even so, I have addressed some of these issues in greater detail in two preliminary works: "Performing Revelation: Joseph Smith and the Creation of the Book of Mormon" (2016), and "Reassessing Joseph Smith Jr.'s Formal Education" (2016). This present study contains material drawn from these two sources, which I have often silently revised and included in this work. Nevertheless, because Smith's own sermonizing and compositional styles follow common practices found among contemporary evangelical preachers, this study will focus on the relationship between Smith's works and contemporary sermon culture as the central topic of exploration.

Book of Mormon Narratives

Smith's epic story, perhaps better described as an episodic chain of dozens of narratives, contains fifteen books. The primary narrative begins around 600 B.C.E. in Jerusalem, where an ancient prophet named Lehi lives with his family. In a dire vision that foretells the destruction of Jerusalem and the Babylonian captivity, God warns Lehi to take his family and flee Jerusalem. Lehi obeys and leads his family into the wilderness. After years of journeying over land and sea, the weary travelers arrive somewhere on the shores of the American continent and establish a new civilization. Not all of Lehi's children, however, get along with one another. Lehi's oldest sons, Laman and Lemuel, perennial complainers and constant disobeyers of God's laws, grow jealous of their righteous younger brother, Nephi. Internecine strife tears the family apart, and the descendants of this original family clan realign themselves into two warring factions: the righteous, light-skinned Nephites against the wicked, dark-skinned Lamanites.[8]

Over the course of the next thousand years, these two civilizations engage in constant cycles of warfare, interspersed with religious awakenings and revivals. Finally, in the spiritual climax of the Book of Mormon, the res-urrected Christ appears to the people in the ancient Americas and estab-lishes a utopian society among them. This peace, however, does not last. As years pass and ensuing generations come and go, the descendants of this idyllic society forget their blessings and decline into wickedness. In time, the civilizations fall again into wars and strife, until the wicked Lamanites eventually destroy the unrepentant Nephites. In the final chapters of the book, the last Nephite prophet-warrior, Moroni, sees the end of his civiliza-tion looming and buries the historical and spiritual records of his people in a mound called the Hill Cumorah. Approximately 1,400 years later, the Smith family would establish their farm a few miles north of this same hill in West-ern New York, where young Joseph could unearth the records and translate them into English.

This study analyzes passages that contain the stories of several central Book of Mormon characters, such as Nephi's brother Jacob; King Benjamin; King Mosiah; Mosiah's missionary sons, Ammon, Aaron, Omner, and Himni; Ze-niff and his descendants; Abinadi; and Samuel the Lamanite, among others. Each analysis will provide a basic story context to help the reader locate the narrative within the overall work. In order to appreciate the techniques and structural relationships under discussion, however, readers are encouraged to read the entire work and to become familiar with the myriad characters and narrative episodes.

Western Esotericism and Folk Magic

Significantly, Joseph Smith's production of the Book of Mormon involved the use of a "seer stone," which inevitably leads to a discussion of folk magic prac-tices and Western esotericism in early America. Chapter 1 provides a histori-cal framework for understanding Smith's esoteric preoccupations, but I first want to alert the reader to my use of terminology. Terms such as "supernatural," "magic," and "occultism" can be highly problematic, especially when describing the beliefs and practices of earlier periods. Such terms carry cultural connota-tions and embedded value judgments, which, without being questioned, can reveal biases and false categorizations. My purpose in chapter 1 is to describe Smith's performative process within his own cultural context, according to the ways in which people in the early nineteenth century perceived and/or practiced a variety of esoteric activities. Critical to the appreciation of such beliefs is the understanding that many of the people engaged in various forms of mystical practices genuinely believed in their efficacy. This spiritual framework of belief therefore influenced the ways in which people perceived the world and all the events occurring within it.

To be clear, my use of such terms as "Christian occultism," "supernatural," and "folk magic" does *not* entail modern perceptions of "occultism" as being synonymous with "cult" or any form of satanic ritual.[9] Indeed, the practitioners of such arts were engaged in an emphatically different project that primarily concerned hopeful spiritual revelation and the discovery of God's mysteries. As such, I follow Arthur Versluis's broad description of Western esotericism as activities that involve "knowledge of hidden or invisible realms or aspects of existence," and that pertain to a system "either explicitly restricted to a relatively small group of people, or implicitly self-restricted by virtue of its complexity or subtlety."[10] My usage of such terms as "folk magic," "supernatural," "Christian occultism," and "Western esotericism" should therefore be understood within the broader context of practices that genuinely attempted to invoke mysterious, extraordinary phenomena that occur above and beyond the routine operations of the natural world.

The Text

Finally, unless otherwise noted, all quotations from the Book of Mormon refer to the 1830 first edition. Though the 1830 edition contains a number of typographical, grammatical, scribal, and other related flaws, I believe the text nevertheless offers a closer approximation to the language of Smith's original dictation than later editions. For ease of reference, however, I have included scriptural references to locate citations in the 1981 modern edition.

Regarding general bracket usage in citations, words <in angled brackets> indicate superlinear additions, while words [in square brackets] indicate missing letters or words, or provide clarifications of meaning. Page numbers in brackets indicate the location of a citation in a work, where the number was not written or printed in the source.

CHAPTER ONE

Seer Stones and Western Esotericism

In 1829 Joseph Smith Jr., the future prophet and founder of the Latter Day Saint movement, produced the Book of Mormon in an extended oral performance.[1] His process of spoken composition, however, was anything but usual: taking a mystical "seer stone," an object in Western esotericism that functioned much like a crystal ball (also described as "peep stones," "spectacles," "crystals," "glasses," and "show-stones," among other terms), Smith placed the stone into the bottom of his upturned hat, held the hat to his face to block out all light, and then proceeded to dictate the entire narrative to his attentive scribes. Smith would later describe the seer stone, along with another translation implement that he described as "spectacles" and "interpreters," by using the term "Urim and Thummim," endowing his instruments with a more prestigious biblical nomenclature.[2] As he proceeded with his project, Smith recited the text at a steady phrase-by-phrase pace, pausing only long enough for his scribes to repeat each transcribed phrase back to him in order to ensure the accuracy of the text.[3]

Eyewitnesses claimed that Smith never referred to notes, manuscripts, or books during the course of the actual dictation, though many scholars believe that he occasionally consulted a Bible.[4] The account of Emma Smith, Joseph's first wife, remains the primary source for this claim. In February of 1879, nearly fifty years after Smith finished the dictation in the summer of 1829, Emma provided a relatively detailed, though somewhat ambiguous and certainly belated, firsthand account of her experience with this process, recalling how Smith sat at their table "with his face buried in his hat, with the stone in it, and dictating hour after hour with nothing between us."[5] To his observers, Smith's prodigious flow of verbal art and narrative creation was nothing short of miraculous, and the seer stone represented an essential component of that ritualized oral performance.

Smith's use of a seer stone to produce the Book of Mormon raises a number of issues related to the origins of the Latter Day Saint movement, particularly with respect to Smith's worldview and the role of Western esotericism in his nascent church. The topic, of course, remains controversial and has understandably received a great deal of attention. Readers interested in pursuing such discussions and ramifications have an abundance of materials to explore.[6]

For the purposes of this study, however, this chapter will provide a brief historical context of Smith's use of a seer stone for readers who might be unfamiliar with the topic of folk magic and Christian occultism in the late eighteenth and early nineteenth centuries in America.

Esotericism in the Smith Household

Smith's use of a seer stone in the oral performance of the Book of Mormon immediately calls attention to the religious and esoteric preoccupations of the Smith family, particularly regarding their willingness to search for spiritual enlightenment by means of religious experimentation in both conventional and unconventional ways. No doubt the area where the family settled in Western New York fueled these preoccupations. In the nineteenth century the region "bounded by the Catskill Mountains on the east and the Adirondock [sic] Mountains on the north," and stretching to the far western edge of the state, encompassed a hotbed of religious fervor that surged with successive waves of revivalism.[7] The area would later become known as the "Burned-Over District" in reference to "the prevailing western analogy between the fires of the forest and those of the spirit." Rife with mixtures of religious ideologies and intensified religious expression, this "Burned-Over" region, with its "people extraordinarily given to unusual religious beliefs," provided an ideal environment for the Smith family's own religious searching.[8]

In their quest for religious truths, Joseph Smith's parents, Joseph Sr. and Lucy, investigated different religious ideologies as frequently and as restlessly as they moved from one farm to the next, without making permanent commitments to any of them. They were known as "Seekers," a form of Primitivism, which sought to restore Christ's church and all its practices to "the primitive or original order of things as revealed in Scripture, free from the accretions of church history and tradition."[9] For the Smiths, this meant that "both parents had broken out of the standard church orthodoxies while at the same time remaining pious and searching."[10] Over the course of their religious quest, their exposure to religious traditions included New England Congregationalists, Baptists, Methodists, Presbyterians, and Universalists, along with the religious ideologies of Primitivism, Millennialism, and Restorationism.[11] As Richard L. Bushman observes, "The Smiths were exposed to a conglomeration of doctrines and attitudes, some imported from Europe, others springing up in New England, none sorted or ranked by recognized authority, all available for adoption as personal whim or circumstances dictated. The result was a religious melee."[12] But these arguably conventional, though actively evolving, avenues were not the only sources of spiritual knowledge to which the Smiths turned for greater understanding of God's ways and mysteries.

The impulse to resist or embellish the dogmas and power structures of established religions encouraged eighteenth- and nineteenth-century Seekers to look outside the boundaries of traditional Christianity, where a panoply of philosophies and practices awaited the curiosity of those who sought alternative systems of belief among the various traditions of Western esotericism. Such alternatives included astrology, alchemy, versions of Christian Kabbalah, Rosicrucianism, Masonic philosophies and rituals, a variety of occult sciences (studies in secret knowledge, not to be confused with "cults"), mesmerism (and related ideas of "animal magnetism"), and a variety of folk magic practices.[13] Rather than looking to contemporary theologians or their immediate antecedents for answers to life's most pressing questions, inquirers after these philosophies attempted to reach back to the dawn of mankind "to recover the divine power and perfection possessed by Adam before the Fall, and indeed before Creation."[14]

This impulse was often driven by millenarian ideologies that predicted a restoration of God's knowledge and power to the earth before the last days. "Such knowledge, once possessed by Adam," Walter W. Woodward observes in his study on John Winthrop Jr.'s fascination with the occult sciences in colonial New England, "had been lost at the Fall, but it would be regained, many believed, through a process of research and discovery that would foreshadow Christ's Second Coming."[15] In postrevolutionary America, when the nation was entering uncharted waters of democratic institutions and wrestling with ideological displacements caused by radical and unprecedented changes, the steps toward a more perfect form of governance were often anchored in conceptions of a primordial past, when all the earth operated in perfect harmony. "From the perspective of many who lived during and following the [American] Revolution," Richard T. Hughes and C. Leonard Allen observe, "that event was the infinitely grand, cosmic battle that, now at last in these latter days, had begun the process of making the primordium contemporary." Moreover, they add, "the millennium typically constituted a restoration of the primordium, and all profane history that had intervened between these two end times was obscured, ignored, and transcended."[16] Within this grand teleological scheme, the search for hidden mysteries and secret knowledge played a significant role, and Christian occultism and Western esoteric practices represented some of the more intriguing avenues of discovery.

This conceptual framework of history and knowledge thus opened a critical space where the "supernatural" and the "miraculous" acted as highly charged manifestations of divine power and hidden (hence "occult") mysteries. Such knowledge had the potential to reveal how the natural world and all the operations of the universe existed in perfect harmony; how pure "Adamic" or "Angelic" languages held the Neoplatonic power to name accurately all creatures and substances according to their pure linguistic forms; and how unadulterated celestial knowledge could be harnessed to endow the righteous seeker with the power to foretell the future, exert control over the forces of nature, summon a variety of miracles, and communicate to God directly or through his ministering angels.[17] Moreover, as Samuel Morris Brown argues, "This pure language contained the possibility that humans could gain access to God's presence."[18] Evidence of such a mysterious ancient system of greater knowledge littered the Bible, providing Christian occult practitioners with examples of what they might seek to obtain.

If Moses and Aaron could become instruments in God's hands, using Aaron's rod in a conjuration duel with Egyptian sorcerers, turning rods to snakes, rivers to blood, or calling forth frogs and lice to cover the land, then a greater understanding of God's mysteries could potentially endow His righteous modern-day inquirers with similar power. If Moses had the power to part the Red Sea, then those with divine knowledge and "faith as a grain of mustard seed" could literally move mountains. If Hebrew high priests utilized oracular stones called "Urim and Thummim" to communicate with God, then mystical objects and the righteous power to invoke them were genuinely possible. And, if the appearance of a star revealed the birthplace of the Messiah, or if Jesus could proclaim that "the sign of the Son of man" would appear in the heavens to foretell his return, then it naturally followed that God revealed the future through astrological and earthly phenomena.[19] "Because God authorizes them," Brian Copenhaver observes, "extraordinary events that we might call 'magical' are not only real—meaning that they are factual, not illusory—but also legitimate."[20] The restoration of God's pure knowledge thereby made up one component of the restoration of His primordial order for all creation.

Thus, while the scriptures were rife with passages condemning evil magic, the texts also revealed an opposite form of God's virtuous power, which, shrouded in mystery, only the truly righteous could hope to discover. Within this system of knowledge, the history of mystical phenomena and the accounts of God's divine power intertwined, collapsing the distinction between "magic" and "miracle," between "occult" and "revealed," into an all-encompassing cosmology. To be certain, this brand of occultism was not nefarious, with a perverse aim to unleash the powers of darkness onto the world. Rather, this was enlightened Christian theurgy, with the goal of discovering God's hidden mysteries in order to harness greater spiritual knowledge and power.[21] For the lay religious seeker, delving into such secrets offered the opportunity to uncover and amalgamate new systems of personal belief that could potentially bring the believer closer to God's ancient undefiled religion, while simultaneously creating a space for liberated expressions of faith and self-determination. As David Hall observes, "Prophecy and magic were alike in helping people to become empowered, prophecy because it overturned the authority of mediating clergy and magic because it gave access to the realm of occult force."[22] Within this shifting milieu of mainstream faiths, popular culture, and fringe philosophies in Western New York, Joseph Sr. and Lucy developed their ideas and fostered their personal magical practices.

In an 1870 interview, Fayette Lapham, a farmer from a neighboring county, described his 1830 visit to the Smith family home, stating, "This Joseph Smith, Senior, we soon learned, from his own lips, was a firm believer in witchcraft and other supernatural things; and had brought up his family in the same belief."[23] Though a negative observation, and one remembered long after the time of the actual events, the comment was not unfounded. In the 1845 preliminary manuscript of her family history, Joseph's mother Lucy apparently confirmed the Smith family's preoccupation with mystical practices. When insisting that all the members of her family were hard workers and not, according to their critics, a group of lazy and shiftless people, Lucy informed the readers of her biography that they should not assume that the Smith family members "stopt our labor and went <at> trying to win the faculty of Abrac[,] drawing Magic circles or sooth saying to the neglect of all kinds of bu<i>sness[;] we never during our lives suffered one important interest to swallow up every other obligation but whilst we worked with our hands we endeavored to remmember [*sic*] the service of & the welfare of our souls."[24] Lucy's comment remains a point of debate among scholars: some argue that Lucy was admitting but downplaying the Smith family's involvement in magical practices, while others argue that she was denying their involvement altogether.[25] Moving beyond the context of her statement and its position within her biography, an abundance of corroborating evidence nevertheless confirms that the Smith family was involved in precisely the same activities that she described.

At the time Lucy wrote her history, the phrase "faculty of Abrac" had a somewhat ambiguous meaning that could either refer to unspoken Masonic mysteries or simply to the practice of folk medicine that involved charms and amulets made out of parchment to heal such sicknesses as the fever or the ague ("Abrac" being a shortened variant of "Abracadabra").[26] "Magic circles" were tied to the conjuration of and communication with spirits and were coupled with symbols, incantations, astrology, and magical implements (swords, daggers, witch hazel rods, magical parchments). Finally, "soothsaying" involved prophesying the future, telling fortunes, and creating "nativities" (intricate astrological horoscopes). Thus, this complex entanglement of religious and mystical ideologies became the Smith family's way of life, constructing a cultural and perceptual lens through which they would view and interpret the world.

Of all the magical practices that the Smith family pursued, treasure hunting—a widely practiced and relatively common obsession throughout the nation at the time—dominates the historical accounts of their activities. Searching for buried treasure involved more than the pedestrian manual labor involved in excavating sites for possible gold and silver: treasure-digging, also called money-digging, required elaborate mystical ceremonies. With a worldview that saw supernatural forces intermingling with the realm of nature, many early nineteenth-century Americans believed that hidden treasures— buried by ancient Native Americans, or Captain Kidd, or hidden in lost gold and silver mines—were protected by powerful spells and guardian spirits.[27] In order to obtain the treasure, the diggers therefore needed to neutralize the spiritual forces protecting them.

To that end, treasure seekers would engage in any number of magical rituals to counteract the powers of the guardian spirits, turning to astrology, binding spells and charms, magic circles overwritten with various mystical symbols, alchemical potions, witching rods, and religious texts, such as "the Bible, Prayer-book, and [John Bunyan's] Pilgrim's Progress."[28] After the Smith family moved to Manchester, Joseph Jr., often with the aid of his father, was involved in at least eighteen treasure quests "in the Palmyra/Manchester area, and later at various locations along the Susquehanna River running through Harmony, Pennsylvania, and the southern New York counties of Chenango and Broome."[29] Such ceremonies required several different magical practices to be performed properly, indicating young Joseph's advanced interest in supernatural gifts and esoteric rituals.

Within this panoply of esoteric practices, Smith family members appear to have gravitated toward favorite methods: Lucy was known to practice chiromancy, or palm reading (a form of soothsaying);[30] Joseph Sr. made use of a dowsing rod, which, apart from the task of locating minerals or water, could be used for telling fortunes, divining spiritual answers to yes-and-no questions, locating hidden treasure, or discovering ancient gold and silver mines;[31] and Joseph Jr., the most mystically talented child in the family, also used a dowsing rod and read palms, but eventually focused on his gift of "second sight" and gazing into seer stones.[32] In all, the magical implements and components of the Smiths' magical practices involved, "seer stones, astrology, a talisman, a dagger for drawing magic circles of treasure-digging and spirit invocation, as well as magic parchments ["lamens" that were "inscribed with magic words and occult symbols"[33]] for purification, protection, and conjuring a spirit."[34] Thus, taken altogether, the Smith family's investment in treasure-hunting quests and various magical practices revealed their deep concern with improving their dire worldly circumstances while simultaneously obtaining unmediated access to God and his greater mysteries.

Smith's use of a seer stone to produce the Book of Mormon therefore offers a view into the mystical and financial economies of ritualism, religious experimentation, and spiritual seeking among early Americans. Far from being unique to the Smith family, such magical practices emerged among all classes of society, appearing in a variety of forms that ranged from simple charms warding off sicknesses to full-scale treasure-hunting expeditions, complete with guardian spirits, magic circles, and incantations. For many families, such practices reflected the convergence of economic displacement and religious destabilization, disrupting traditional practices and refashioning new ideas and religious beliefs. Within the turbulence of the age and the frictions of ideologies, young Joseph accomplished more than mere survival: he confronted the times with a new formulation of belief, a syncretic cosmology pieced together from a constellation of destabilized fragments of multiple traditions. Once a village conjuror, Smith would rise above the bleakness of his circumstances to discover his own powerful and prophetic voice.

CHAPTER TWO

Laying Down Heads in Written and Oral Composition

Following the organization of the "Church of Christ" in 1830, Joseph Smith developed and refined the administration of his nascent church with a series of ongoing revelations. Included among these early directives was a command to keep historical records dealing with the rise and progress of the Mormon faith.[1] Subsequently, in 1832, Smith, with the help of Frederick G. Williams as a scribe, started working on a history of the church. The handwriting in the manuscript reveals that Smith alternated between dictating to Williams and writing in his own hand. This initial draft, however, was relatively short and soon abandoned. Even so, the manuscript remains instructive. Apart from being an important resource for understanding the ways in which Smith would develop and articulate his representation of the growing church, the text becomes significant for another, more fundamental reason: the manuscript reveals Smith's personal method and style of composition.

Smith's 1832 history begins with an opening paragraph that provides the reader with a sketch outline of the historical events that Smith wished to emphasize in his narrative. In order to highlight his ideas, I have inserted bracketed numbers that identify the topics and their order of arrangement (some spelling and punctuation modified for clarity):

> [1] A History of the life of Joseph Smith Jr. [2] an account of his marvilous experience [3] and of all the mighty acts which he doeth in the name of Jesus Ch[r]ist[,] the son of the living God of whom he beareth record [4] and also an account of the rise of the church of Christ in the eve of time[,] according as the Lord brought forth and established by his hand. [5] <firstly> he receiving the testimony from on high [6] seccondly[,] the ministering of Angels [7] thirdly[,] the reception of the holy Priesthood by the ministering of Aangels to administer the letter of the ~~Law~~ <Gospel—> <—the Law and commandments[,] as they were given unto him—>, and ~~in~~ <the> ordinencs [ordinance], [8] fo[u]rthly[,] a confirmation and reception of the high Priesthood[,] after the holy order of the son of the living God[,] power and ordinence from on high to preach the Gospel in the administration and demonstration of the spirit

[Joseph Smith's handwriting begins] the Kees [keys] of the Kingdom of God confer[r]ed upon him and the continuation of the blessings of God to him &c [etc.]_____[2]

After providing the reader with this introductory outline, Smith launched into his history by elaborating on each stage of his opening sketch, following the same sequence in the main body of the narrative that he established in the opening paragraph.

In other words, the opening phrase of the outline, "[1] A History of the life of Joseph Smith Jr.," corresponds with the opening section of Smith's narrative (the second paragraph of the manuscript), which details Smith's birth, up-bringing, and spiritual pursuits: "I was born in the town of Charon [Sharon] in the <State> of Vermont[,] North America," relates Smith, "on the twenty third day of December AD 1805[,] of goodly Parents." Smith goes on to mention his youthful concern about "the well fare [welfare] of my immortal Soul," because he had "become convicted of my sins," which, in turn, prompted him to scour the scriptures in search of spiritual relief.[3] In his distress, Smith "cried unto the Lord for mercy[,] for there was none else to whom I could go."[4] Smith's cry launches his narrative into the second stage, or "head," of the outline.

This second head in Smith's opening sketch concerns "[2] an account of his marvilous experience." This "marvilous experience" refers to Smith's "First Vision," in which he claimed that God the Father and Jesus Christ appeared to him (though Christ alone appeared to him in this early version).[5] Accordingly, the main body of the narrative provides a more detailed and elaborate account than the introductory outline: "while in <the> attitude of calling upon the Lord <in the 16th year of my age> a piller of fire light[,] above the brightness of the sun at noon day[,] come down from above and rested upon me and I was filled with the spirit of god and the <Lord> opened the heavens upon me and I saw the Lord and he spake unto me saying[,] Joseph <my son> thy sins are forgiven thee."[6] After relating this account of his divine visitation, Smith reflects briefly on the aftermath of the First Vision in his life and the lives of his family members, and then moves to the next step in the narrative.

The third stage in Smith's outline addresses "[3] all the mighty acts which he doeth in the name of Jesus Ch[r]ist, the son of the living God of whom he beareth record." In the corresponding expanded text, the narrative shifts to the events surrounding Smith's miraculous and supernatural translation of the Book of Mormon, beginning with the visitation of the angel Moroni, who revealed the location of the ancient buried plates of gold, and continuing through the early days of the translation process. At this point in the history, however, Smith abandoned the manuscript. The text does not reveal any further "mighty acts" by Smith, nor does it continue with the promised "[4] an account of the rise of the church of Christ in the eve of time," or the itemized list of important historical events ("[5] <firstly> he receiving the testamony ... [6] secondly, the ministering of Angels. [7] thirdly, the reception of the holy Priesthood ... [8] fo[u]rthly[,] a confirmation ..."). Yet, though incomplete, the manuscript nevertheless provides ample information to demonstrate Smith's approach to composition.

Laying Down Heads and Skeleton Outlines

Smith's method of using a preliminary outline, or, as more commonly termed, a "skeleton" of "heads" (an outline formed with key summarizing phrases) to organize and arrange his 1832 historical narrative, was a standard technique of composition in the early nineteenth century. The explicit use of the skeletal sketch in the opening of the history, marking each stage in the sequence of the narrative with a summarizing phrase, provides one of several expressions of the method commonly known as "laying down heads."[7] Both speakers and writers used this popular, widespread technique to designate and arrange the main topics of such compositions as sermons, public speeches, essays, narrations, and school lessons. In terms of application, this approach was quite simple and involved two basic steps: first, the speaker or author created a skeletal outline of his or her intended composition by using a sequence of key phrases ("heads") that concisely summarized each of the main topics, issues, or divisions of an idea contained within the overall passage that followed. Second, using this skeletal outline as a reference guide, the speaker or author would then elaborate on each key phrase, expanding it into a fully developed passage of oral address or text.

Smith's familiarity with this technique comes as no surprise, given the ubiquity of this organizational and mnemonic approach in the early nineteenth century. Schoolchildren taking beginning composition lessons received instruction on laying down heads to create skeletal outlines of essays of varying lengths and topics, as well as on creating narrative passages. Preachers sermonizing at church services, camp meetings, funerals, and special occasions regularly divided the subject of their orations into a number of "heads" to cover the main topics of their discourses. Authors and participants in debates, deliberations, editorials, letters, public orations, books, newspaper articles, government reports, and magazine essays frequently arranged and/or itemized their talking points by laying down heads. The common practice of laying down heads to organize compositions and to guide the performance of orations long predated Smith's nineteenth-century world, but it should be observed that during the period this method of composition was receiving a great deal of attention in educational circles.

While the technique of laying down heads was common in the eighteenth century (and much earlier), pedagogical approaches guiding students in a stepwise fashion from beginning compositional skills to advanced techniques were not yet prevalent.[8] At the turn of the century, however, educators began to focus on developing systematic and incremental approaches to implement the method. At the forefront of this shift, spearheading substantive changes in pedagogical strategies, was educational writer John Walker (1732–1807), popularly known by the moniker "Elocution Walker." Walker was a former actor and one-time member of David Garrick's acting company at Drury Lane in London, and he incorporated aspects of his former profession into his work in education.[9] In 1801 Walker published his highly influential book, *The Teacher's Assistant* (first American edition, 1804), which provided educators with a series of progressive exercises that aimed at bridging the gap between introductory texts and advanced models of imitation.[10]

Notably, Walker's central techniques for composing narratives reflect the same compositional strategies that Smith used for his 1832 history. Walker's method placed a heavy emphasis on memory, orality, and the use of mental outlines to guide the composition of essays. When advising teachers how to apply his method, Walker urged the following steps: first, teachers should read an essay to the students (students did not read the text themselves but listened intently to the instructor), discuss the essay's content and message, and then read the essay a second time, while alerting the students to each of the main points of the passage by repeating "distinctly the several heads of the Essay."[11] These "several heads" of succinct summarizing phrases formed the outline of the essay, just as Smith's preliminary summary of his 1832 history outlined his subsequent text.

Next, Walker advised teachers to have the students repeat from memory the number and sequence of heads in the outline in order to ensure that the students had the structure of the essay firmly in mind (in Walker's system, students were discouraged from writing down the skeleton and were required to memorize it as a mental outline). Next, using this memorized outline of heads as a blueprint, students rewrote the essay by expanding each of the heads ("abridged contents") back into a full-blown passage—a process commonly known as amplification.[12] Again, this is the same approach that Smith adopted for his 1832 history: he dictated a skeletal outline of summarizing heads to his scribe, after which he amplified (or planned to amplify) each of the heads into fully developed passages.

Whether or not he had direct exposure to Walker's manual, Smith nevertheless made use of this same method. Indeed, Smith's 1832 history provides a textbook example of the technique. Even so, by the time Smith would have been exposed to such exercises, several other authors on education had already started copying and reworking Walker's approach. The pedagogical shift that Walker instigated spread like wildfire through schools, and his highly influential work, as Robert J. Connors observes, would directly influence the composition instructions found in John Rippingham's *Rules for English Composition* (1811), Daniel Jaudon's *The Union Grammar* (1812), and William Russell's *Grammar of Composition* (1823).[13] "Certainly," Connors argues, "the seminal book for 'composition' as opposed to 'rhetoric' must be John Walker's *The Teacher's Assistant*."[14] Through such widespread borrowing and dissemination, Walker's system not only became popular, but it transformed into "the exemplar for a whole school of composition pedagogy."[15] By the time Smith was attending common schools in New England and New York, Walker's system, in one form or another, had become a central pedagogical model for teachers and schools across the young nation, primarily in secondary schools and academies but also in common schools and self-improvement venues.

Apart from composition instruction, the practice of laying down an opening summary of heads was also a popular print convention for tables of contents and chapter headings of books. Smith's 1832 history likewise mirrors such conventions. Consider, for example, the preliminary outline of heads that opens the first chapter in publisher John Ballantyne's widely distributed 1812 edition of Daniel Defoe's *The Life and Adventures of Robinson Crusoe* (followed by the opening line):

CHAP. I.

My Birth and Parentage—At Nineteen Years of Age I determine to go to Sea—Dissuaded by my Parents—Elope with a School-fellow, and go on board Ship—A Storm arises—Ship founders—Myself and Crew saved by a Boat from another Vessel, and landed near Yarmouth—Meet my Companion's Father there, who advises me never to go to Sea more, but in vain.

I was born in the year 1632, in the city of York, of a good family . . . [16]

Note how "*My Birth and Parentage*" in the summary corresponds with the opening line of the chapter, "I was born in the year 1632, in the city of York, of a good family." Smith's opening head in his 1832 manuscript, "A History of the life of Joseph Smith Jr.," launches a corresponding expansion in the opening of the main narrative: "I was born in the town of Sharon in the State of Vermont, North America, on the twenty-third day of December, A.D. 1805, of goodly Parents."[17] Indeed, the opening of the Book of Mormon reflects this same formulation with the head, "*An account of Lehi and his wife Sariah, and his four sons, being called, (beginning at the eldest) Laman, Lemuel, Sam, and Nephi,*" which corresponds with the first line of the narrative, "I, Nephi, having been born of goodly parents" (1 Nephi 1:1).[18]

Nevertheless, and in spite of the clear similarities between Smith's use of heads and the formatting of preliminary chapter headings in books, limiting the source of Smith's knowledge to his familiarity with printed works remains problematic. While juxtaposing Smith's 1832 history with contemporary print conventions might help to explain what Smith was trying to achieve in terms of his textual apparatus, the comparison falls short of explaining the origin of Smith's style. For example, several of Smith's prefatory heads in his 1832 history are far too long and excessively wordy for the concise phraseology modeled and usually required by print conventions (the phrase beginning with "Thirdly" contains thirty-two words, and "Fourthly" contains a whopping fifty-eight). More significantly, the presence of an itemized list of heads in the opening summary ("Firstly, Secondly, Thirdly, Fourthly") points to a different source of influence altogether. Such enumerated lists, decidedly atypical for chapter summaries and tables of contents, are extremely common in other oral and written sources. For the purposes of this study, and in light of the specific characteristics of Smith's style, the influence of contemporary sermon culture emerges as a primary factor in the formation of his approach. The following example offers an explicit illustration.

During a 29 January 1843 sermon on the Prodigal Son, Smith went on a brief tangent in his opening remarks to answer questions regarding information found in Luke 7:28 and Matthew 11:11 ("among those that are born of women there is not a greater prophet than John the Baptist: but he that is least in the kingdom of God is greater than he"). The previous Sunday, Smith had apparently been asked why John the Baptist was considered the greatest prophet, and he had further been asked to identity the person "that is least in the kingdom of God." Smith prepared his response and delivered it the following Sunday, while two members of the audience, Willard Richards and Franklin D. Richards (no relation), recorded Smith's answers in their notes. The precise wording differs between the two manuscripts, yet both sets of notes corroborate Smith's use of laying down explicit enumerated heads to restate the original questions and then to itemize his answers.[19] Franklin D. Richards notated Smith's discourse in the following way (formatting modified for clarity):

> the next sabbath he (Joseph) [had been] asked and [he] answered[:]
> 1st How was John the greatest prophet ever born of a woman[?]
> 2nd How ~~was Christ~~ [who] is the least in the Kingdom greater than he[?]
>   Ans[wer] to 1st [question] His greatness consisted in 3 things[:]
>   1st His appointment to prepare the way before the <u>Lord Jesus Christ</u>
>   2nd His privilege to Baptise him or induct him into his Kingdom
>   3d His being the only legal administrator in the affairs of the
>   Kingdom that was then on the Earth . . .
>   Ans[wer] to 2nd Query[:] Christ was least in the Kingdom in their
>   estimation.[20]

As Franklin's notes indicate, Smith prepared his response by treating each of the original questions as a main head (that is, the first asking how John was the greatest prophet, and the second asking for the identification of the person greater than John). After stating each main head of the overall outline, Smith then returned to the first question and divided his answer into an itemized list of three subheads (first, second, third) in the process of elaborating his response.

This opening portion of Smith's 1843 sermon on the Prodigal Son offers a clear and unambiguous example of laying down heads in sermon construction. Even so, such examples are infrequent in Smith's historical records. As the editors of the Joseph Smith Papers observe, "Joseph Smith rarely produced notes or outlines for his speeches, sermons, or prayers."[21] William V. Smith also notes that Smith "exercised little review for the generated texts of his sermons and he kept no extensive personal notes of his own sermons."[22] Moreover, Smith never published a formal collection of his discourses, which would have provided important clues to his methods; and more often than not the notetakers in his audience simply paraphrased the message with "rarely more than a sentence or two," rather than attempting to record his words verbatim.[23] As such, the opening of Smith's 1843 sermon on the Prodigal Son and his skeletal outline of main heads for his 1832 history offer rare glimpses into Smith's process of composition.

Nonetheless, however brief those glimpses might be, they offer enough information to identify Smith's methods of composition within the larger context of contemporary sermon culture. To that end, this chapter explores the role of "laying down heads" in the construction of sermon skeletons, along with a contextual review of common preaching methods in Smith's environment that ranged from preachers reading their orations from the pulpit to those who practiced extempore sermons. In particular, this chapter contextualizes Smith's compositional methods and spiritual register in relation to the sermon culture among the Congregationalists in the Connecticut River Valley, tracing a brief history of the dominant styles that existed in the region from the early eighteenth to the early nineteenth centuries.

Laying Down Heads and Sermon Skeletons

By explicitly identifying the main points in his 1843 sermon on the Prodigal Son, Smith was following a very common organizational, compositional, and performance convention among preachers. Laying down heads referred to the way in which preachers might explicitly inform their audiences about each of the main heads (main topics or points) of the oration, thus providing the listeners with a preview or a set of expectations about the topics that they were going to hear. Treatises on pulpit eloquence and sermon composition usually described this process in connection with the structure and arrangement of sermons, using such terminology as "dividing," "distributing," "cutting," and "dissecting" the main topic or scriptural text of the sermon into "heads," "points," "propositions," "parts," "divisions," "subdivisions," and "partitions," among other terms.[24] However the terminology might change from one author to the next, the basic process of choosing a text (a scripture, thesis, proposition, or gospel principle), deciding the main topics to address (the main heads), and then arranging the topics into a natural and cohesive order ("arrangement," "methodizing") remained fundamental across denominations in both preparation and delivery.

When observing the contexts of Smith's 1832 history and his 1843 sermon, we can make a few observations about Smith's use of this common technique in his own approach to composition. First, going back to Smith's 1832 history, we find that Smith dictated the majority of the opening skeletal outline to one of his scribes, Frederick G. Williams (though Smith also wrote the final phrase of the outline and continued writing in the opening portion of the history).[25] Such a process of dictation was standard for Smith, who regularly used scribes to compose letters, journal entries, church documents, and revelations. As Dean C. Jessee observes, Smith "seldom used the pen himself, dictating or delegating most of his writing to clerks."[26] In addition, there is no indication that Smith directly consulted notes to dictate either the opening outline or the main body of the 1832 history. This same method, it should be observed, is consistent with Smith's production of the Book of Mormon. Eyewitnesses to the project, such as his wife, Emma, insisted that Smith "had neither manuscript nor book to read from."[27] This presumed lack of notes during dictation sessions, however, does not necessarily equate to a lack of preparation. When examining Smith's outline for his 1832 history and 1843 sermon, we find clear sequences of events and topics, complete with enumerated lists of significant points. This ordering indicates that Smith's process, on one occasion or another, involved carefully crafted outlines emerging from thoughtful preparation and premeditation that lent themselves to extensive expansion.

In addition, when he composed the main body of his 1832 history, Smith followed the same sequence of events that he had established in the opening outline (as, on a smaller scale, he would do with his 1843 sermon). In order to achieve this result, without apparently using notes, Smith would have obviously needed to dictate the work by following a familiar or memorized outline, using it as a mental guide during both oral composition and dictation. Thus, Smith's mental outline anchored and guided his oral expansion of each predetermined head to articulate the main body of the history. And while this approach also mirrors composition exercises in school classrooms, which would have informed and reinforced this method, there is one central and critical difference: in classroom exercises, the memorized outlines resulted mainly in *written* assignments, while Smith's mental outline guided the *oral performance* of his 1832 historical narrative and his 1843 sermon. This distinction yields further clues. The process of moving directly from mental outlines to spoken orations, bypassing the written components taught and practiced in writing instruction, emphasizes techniques that are fundamentally oral in nature and geared toward the dynamics of spoken delivery, rather than any form of literary exercise.

This consequential difference between written and spoken performances refocuses attention away from the specifically literary exercises in school classrooms to the various forms of semi-extemporaneous oral performances in Smith's environment that made use of the same technique of laying down heads to create and follow skeletal outlines. Moreover, given that he used this method to compose his initial church history and some of his spiritual discourses, Smith clearly associated this technique with religious content. That specific association offers additional insight into the origins and influences of Smith's approach. The method of laying down heads to create skeletal outlines of orations, which the speaker fleshed out extemporaneously in the moment of performance, was one of the most common approaches to sermon construction and oratorical delivery found among evangelical preachers in Smith's immediate environment. Smith's application of this approach for his own religious works therefore suggests his awareness of, and participation in, the contemporary methods and practices found in the vibrant sermon cultures of several evangelical denominations in his immediate historical context.

Preaching Methods in Smith's Milieu

In the early nineteenth century, preachers across multiple denominations composed and delivered their sermons in a handful of different ways. For our purposes, David Williamson (1763–1831), a Scottish Presbyterian (Secession Church), offers a useful summary of five contemporary practices in his *Reflections on the Four Principal Religions* (1824). In his first category of preaching methods, Williamson describes ministers who "read their sermons from their notes."[28] Such "notes," in spite of the terminology, were not usually brief comments. Rather, they often consisted of meticulous outlines of entire sermons, filling up several handwritten manuscript pages and ranging in detail from highly developed skeleton outlines, with fleshed out main heads and detailed subtopics, to manuscripts approaching fully composed texts.[29] Preachers following this method took their extensive notes to the pulpit, where they read them aloud to their audiences, with little or no language left for the spontaneous inspiration of the moment.

Williamson's second category also describes ministers who composed exhaustive outlines and drafts of their entire sermons, but, instead of reading their sermons, they would memorize them and then preach "from notes fully written and committed to memory" (a style of delivery often described as "*memoriter*").[30] Next, his third category describes ministers who, once again, composed detailed outlines or entire sermons in their notes, yet they would only commit the "train of ideas" to memory, "without overwhelming it [the sermon] with the load of words, trusting that the ideas will clothe themselves, with proper words in proper places."[31] In practice, a preacher following this third method would memorize the main points and key phrases of a fully (or largely) composed sermon and then attempt to deliver the actual oration semi-extemporaneously, though adhering closely to the original written draft or outline. Even so, he would still write out the majority of the sermon in lengthy notes, and then take the notes with him to the pulpit in order to glance at them periodically, if necessary, to remember his main points and to keep the sermon on course.

With Williamson's fourth category we arrive at a method of composition and delivery that mirrors most closely the same approach that Smith used to compose his 1832 history. This "fourth mode" depicts preachers who prepared their sermons by laying down heads to create a skeletal outline of their sermons (also called a "plan," "brief," or "short notes") without writing out the sermon in full. Preachers then used these outlines in one of two ways, "either carrying them to the pulpit in short notes, that at the different pauses of the sermon they may meet the preacher's eye, or in fixing them on the memory, without carrying notes to the pulpit, and filling up the illustrations in such words as present themselves on the spur of the occasion."[32] Preachers using this semi-extemporaneous method trusted more information to their memory and experience than those who used regular notes or fully written-out sermons. Rather than detailing each step in the sermon, preachers using "short notes" merely outlined the main talking points ("chief heads"), allowing themselves the flexibility to respond to the audience's reactions by expanding or contracting certain points, as well as inserting new information spontaneously into the sermon. Because Smith adopted various forms of this style of semi-extemporaneous preaching, chapter 3 goes into further detail about this technique.

For now, however, the last and final method that Williamson discusses is a form of extempore preaching that involved little or no immediate preparation on the part of the preacher, "either in his mind or committed to paper."[33] In theory, the preacher simply stood before an audience, opened his mouth, and said whatever came to mind. Preachers who adopted this approach often cited scripture to justify the practice. "Take no thought beforehand what ye shall speak," Christ advised his apostles, "neither do ye premeditate: but whatsoever shall be given you in that hour, that speak ye: for it is not ye that speak, but the Holy Ghost" (Mark 13:11). Indeed, Smith would advise his followers to do the same. In an 1832 revelation, one of many such examples, Smith, speaking for the Lord, instructed his lay preachers and missionaries on how to preach the gospel: "Neither take ye thought beforehand what ye shall say; but treasure up in your minds continually the words of life, and it shall be given you in the very hour that portion that shall be meted unto every man."[34] Indeed, this particular approach, valorized among Baptists, Methodists, and Presbyterians, among several other denominations, would become a calling card for Mormon evangelists.

"As with other outsider groups," Brian Jackson observes, "Mormon preachers, in both attitude and practice, demonstrated a clear preference for letting the Holy Ghost make up for what an unlearned, unprepared, ostracized preaching force lacked, i.e., explicit rhetorical literacy."[35] Nonetheless, this category of the "extempore" contained a spectrum of methods and performances, ranging from pure unpremeditated exhortations to sermons preached by experienced ministers, who, in spite of approaching the pulpit without neces-sarily having a specific or fully developed plan in mind, drew upon the language, topics, and scriptures of prior sermons and religious studies. Smith's directive to "treasure up in your minds continually the words of life" specifically echoes common eighteenth- and nineteenth-century admonitions to engage in a life-long study of the scriptures, to pay close attention to sermons and exhorta-tions, to read religious works, and to meditate daily on gospel principles. In doing so, preachers could develop a mental storehouse of doctrinal teachings and rhetorical patterns, which the Spirit could presumably draw upon when the preacher delivered extempore exhortations and sermons.

As such, the boundaries between Williamson's categories of preaching styles are inevitably artificial. Rather than distinct styles with fixed and well-defined borders, the actual sermon practices contained a complex mixture of styles in a nuanced continuum of preaching methods, particularly when considering the fungible borders between the semi-extemporaneous and unpremeditated extempore categories. Furthermore, in all of Williamson's five categories, to one degree or another, in one form or another, the process of laying down heads played a substantial role in the creation, delivery, and reception of sermons.

Sermonizing in the Connecticut River Valley

As previously noted (yet deserving special emphasis), any attempt to situate Smith's style of oral composition within the context of his life and the religious traditions that he avidly explored in his youth results in multiple potential ave-nues of influence. Identifying the specific religious traditions that would have participated in shaping Smith's style of oral composition confronts the inves-tigator with an overdetermined field of possibilities—the practice of preach-ing from short notes and concise skeletal outlines was simply too ubiquitous to pinpoint its source in a single religious tradition. As a boy in the Connecti-cut River Valley, Smith grew up in a region saturated with extemporaneous styles of preaching among lay itinerants and exhorters, as well as among university-trained evangelical ministers.

And later, after the Smith family moved to the western region of New York, into the area infamously known as the "Burned-Over District" for its intense religious fervor and sweeping evangelical innovations, Smith would be even more deeply exposed to the extemporaneous and semi-extemporaneous forms of preaching and exhorting among Baptists, Methodists, and Presbyterians. Thus, throughout his childhood and early adulthood, Smith grew up in some of the most spiritually dynamic (and spiritually inflamed) regions of the country, where theological innovation and dramatic oral performances, delivered in both unpremeditated extempore exhortations and semi-extemporaneous sermons, dominated the religious soundscape. A review of these various resonant traditions therefore provides a geographical and temporal context for Smith's exposure to such methods.

In the Connecticut River Valley, one of the most famous advocates of a long-established semi-extemporaneous style was Congregationalist preacher Solomon Stoddard (1643–1729). As an influential (and controversial) minister in Northampton, Massachusetts, Stoddard famously decried the practice of reading notes from the pulpit in his well-known sermon *The Defects of Preachers Reproved* (1724). Stoddard's method of preaching without notes was not an innovative move among early Congregationalists in New England, where ministers, depending on their personal preferences, had preached from long notes, short notes, or without any notes at all.[36] Rather, Stoddard's admonition appealed to a time-honored method, which, as Stoddard explained, "has been the manner of worthy men both here and in other Places, to deliver their Sermons without their Notes."[37] Though he was otherwise spare in details about the precise method used by those unnamed "worthy men both here and in other Places," Stoddard offered a depiction that would have nevertheless resonated with his contemporary readers, pointing to the semi-extemporaneous techniques advocated by such theologians as William Perkins (1558–1602), Richard Bernard (1568–1641), John Wilkins (1614–72), and Gilbert Burnet (1643–1715), whose prominent works were used as preaching manuals in New England and often cited by advocates of pulpit eloquence.[38]

In addition, when tracing the heritage of preaching techniques in colonial America, it is important to recognize that Stoddard's carefully prepared method of semi-extemporaneous preaching differed from the popular styles of unpremeditated extempore sermons that would shortly emerge during the First Great Awakening (1730s–40s). As Meredith Marie Neuman cautions, "Puritan ministers often spoke *ex tempore*, a style of delivery that might suggest the enthusiasm and spontaneity associated with later trends in evangelical preaching from the Great Awakening through current-day revivalism, but such a comparison is misleading."[39] Stoddard was certainly not advocating an *unpremeditated* extempore style, in which the preacher approached the pulpit without any form of conscious preparation whatsoever.[40] Rather, as Sandra Gustafson observes, "Behind the Puritan preacher's semi-improvised sermon were hours of thought and preparation. Theirs was an art that disguised its own artifice, producing an effect of immediacy and transparency that became the performative sign of authentic spiritual power."[41] Indeed, even a cursory review of Stoddard's sermon *The Defects of Preachers Reproved* reveals that the entire work is carefully organized, arranged with explicit heads that follow the common Puritan format of introducing a text (in this case, Matt. 23:2–3), followed by laying out the divisions, a listing of "instances" (reasons, examples, proofs), and ending with "uses" (applications). Though he argued for the delivery of sermons "without notes," Stoddard clearly invested a great deal of time and preparation in the composition of his orations, a process fundamentally different from "extempore" sermonizing.

The methods practiced by the earliest generations of Congregational ministers in New England and in the Connecticut River Valley, while influenced by Perkins, Bernard, Wilkins, and Burnet, would not stay frozen in time but undergo radical new developments during the First Great Awakening. In particular, one preacher emerged as the most charismatic among his energetic and voluble contemporaries: George Whitefield (1714–70), a young Anglican itinerant from Britain who helped John and Charles Wesley promote Methodism in the early portion of his career. Whitefield's expansive views and religious commitments, however, reached beyond the early Methodist movement, and his passionate efforts to established Christ's kingdom on earth extended to people in all denominations. "O for a mind divested of all sects and names and parties!" Whitefield proclaimed. "I think it is my one simple aim to promote the kingdom of JESUS, without partiality and without hypocrisy, indefinitely amongst all."[42]

Whitefield's popularity drew crowds from all denominations and all walks of life, whether for spiritual renewal or sheer entertainment, and his preaching style would exert enormous influence on the methods of sermon delivery across multiple denominations in both England and the North American colonies. Though clergy could certainly be at odds with Whitefield's controversial doctrinal tenets, ministers among the Congregationalists, Baptists, Methodists, Presbyterians, and Unitarians, among others, found inspiration in his striking style of preaching. As such, any examination of the history of Smith's semi-extemporaneous method inevitably finds a common precursor in the towering figure of Whitefield and his style of semi-extemporaneous preaching, whether as a direct or indirect source of influence.

According to Harry S. Stout, Whitefield's arrival in colonial America, first "in 1738 in the Middle and Southern Colonies" and later in New England in 1740, became "the most sensational event in the history of New England preaching."[43] While the structural organization of his speeches often reflected traditional sermon patterns, Whitefield's innovative style of delivery was an abrupt departure from standard contemporary methods.[44] In sharp contrast to the styles of preaching that dominated New England pulpits, where a large number of clergymen had fallen into the habit of reading their sermons or sermon notes, Whitefield's performances were astonishing: he engaged his full body in theatrical gestures and postures normally reserved for stage plays; he fully committed his resounding voice to the affective features of his message, thundering over the audience with God's wrath in one moment, while flooding the pulpit with tears in another; and he deployed a penetrating style of direct address that demanded active participation from the audience, focusing all his attention on his auditors' responses. He also regularly preached without notes of any kind, delivering both recycled sermons and unpremeditated orations; and, perhaps most significantly, he invoked the audience's imagination with intense visual imagery, inviting the audience to conjure up key moments in biblical narratives in their minds—a vision-inducing strategy that prompted many spectators to *see* the events of biblical stories unfold before their spiritual eyes.[45]

Key to Whitefield's preaching was the conviction that the Holy Ghost guided his extemporaneous performances. "I find I gain greater light and knowledge by preaching extempore," Whitefield recorded in his journal, "so that I fear I should quench the Spirit, did I not go on to speak as He gives me utterance."[46] Nevertheless, Whitefield's precise method(s) of extempore delivery remained (and still remains) elusive to pin down. In a heated debate with members of the Harvard College faculty, who had accused Whitefield of advocating unpremeditated extempore preaching, Whitefield argued, in his most extensive exposition concerning his personal method, that his approach was *not* entirely spontaneous but rather involved study and meditation: "But *Gentlemen*, does extempore Preaching exclude Study and Meditation? . . . Now you say, 'Mr. *W*[hitefield] evidently shows, that he would have us believe his Discourses are *Extempore.*'—And so they are, if you mean that they are not wrote down, and that I preach without Notes—But they are not extempore if you think that I preach always without Study and Meditation—Indeed *Gentlemen*, I love to study, and delight to meditate, when I have Opportunity, and yet would go into the Pulpit by no Means depending on my Study and Meditation, but the blessed Spirit of God, who I believe now, as well as formerly, frequently gives his Ministers Utterance, and enables them to preach with such Wisdom that all their Adversaries are not able to gainsay or resist."[47] Whitefield's response, for all its fervor, nevertheless remains ambiguous and perhaps contradictory: he claimed to prepare himself with study and meditation, while simultaneously asserting that he did not depend upon his preparations when he ascended the pulpit.

By claiming reliance on both sides of the "extempore" argument, Whitefield was practicing modesty by deferring to a higher power: these outpourings were the work of "the blessed Spirit of God," and not, ultimately, the work of men. His striking evangelical style proved controversial, spurring divisions between preachers and congregations into "New Light" and "Old Light" factions. "The term *New Light* emerged in New England during the Great Awakening (1740–1743)," indicates Stout, "to describe the evangelical supporters of George Whitefield and the mass revivals he inspired."[48] In contrast, the Old Lights were "the socially and theologically conservative opponents of George Whitefield," who "denied that the Great Awakening was a work of God, claiming instead that it destroyed the peace and unity of the church by pitting enthusiastic lay people and itinerant preachers against the established clergy of New England."[49] Clergy agreeable to Whitefield's style and message often observed his performance techniques firsthand and adopted similar methods, and his reputation for preaching extempore destabilized the longstanding practice of delivering memorized sermons (*memoriter*) or reading sermon notes. In the years following Whitefield's tours, the number of ministers using only short notes (or no notes) for semi-extemporaneous sermons notably increased, as well as the number of graduate ministers who embraced New Light theology.[50]

Such transitions in style had a direct effect on the sermon culture in the Connecticut River Valley, where Smith spent his earliest years. "From Yale," Stout observes, "evangelical pastors entered the homes of New Light pastors for postgraduate study in the new methods of preaching, and from there they poured into the Connecticut countryside and the towns along the Connecticut River Valley."[51] Among Whitefield's best-known friends and associates, Eleazar Wheelock (1711–79) would play an especially prominent role in the training and development of semi-extemporaneous preachers in the Connecticut River Valley.[52] At the height of the revivals, according to two of his early biographers, Wheelock, in the "space of a year," preached "a hundred more sermons than there are days in the year."[53] Wheelock's style of preaching was heavily influenced by his developing friendship with Whitefield, and he actively employed the method of using short notes and extempore language: "Usually he [Wheelock] wrote only short notes, and sometimes his preaching was extemporaneous."[54] William Allen, who married Wheelock's granddaughter Maria Wheelock and gained control of Eleazar's private papers, observed, "Very few of Dr. Wheelock's sermons were written out at length. His manuscripts in general exhibit only short notes of the heads of his discourses, especially after the first few years of his settlement, when the pressure of a multitude of cares gave him little leisure for writing sermons."[55] Wheelock's busy schedule after his settlement in Hanover, New Hampshire, was, of course, a result of his ambitious project to set up a permanent location for his Moor's Indian Charity School, along with the creation of the adjacent institution that would become Dartmouth College.

Moor's Charity School (as it would later be called) became a nationally recognized institution for training new generations of ministers within the New Light tradition, retaining a reputation for placing a sympathetic emphasis on preaching to Native American populations.[56] Wheelock laid the groundwork by drawing upon his extensive network of contacts to recruit faculty members and tutors for his school. With respect to the curriculum aimed at teaching the skills of rhetoric and oral performance, Wheelock often selected teachers who, perhaps more by association than intent, had witnessed Whitefield's preaching tours and/or had personal experience in the semi-extemporaneous methods of sermonizing.

For instance, Benjamin Pomeroy (1704–84), Wheelock's brother-in-law, who taught for a time at Moor's and later became a trustee of the school, "often preached without notes, and with great fluency and pathos. As an extempore preacher he held a very high rank."[57] Chandler Robbins (1738–99), a theological student who worked for a time at Moor's as a tutor, tended not to write out his sermons, "but the outline was committed to paper, and he could safely trust to his extemporaneous powers for the filling up."[58] Robbins was also described as preaching "chiefly without notes, having only a skeleton of his sermon before him."[59] Indeed, Robbins likely learned his techniques from his father, Philemon Robbins (1709–81), who, having also been inspired by Whitefield's tours, "preached from short notes, and had a ready command of language in extemporaneous speaking."[60] Wheelock's decision to establish his institution in the same river valley and cultural region where Solomon Stoddard insisted on ministers preaching without notes seems hardly a coincidence.

Nonetheless, Wheelock's connections and communications were not isolated to the Upper Connecticut River Valley. As John Fea amply demonstrated, Wheelock's prolific correspondence positioned him as a prominent hub of communication among Congregational ministers throughout New England, allowing him to create "a regional network of New Lights that would become foundational to the economic and religious support of his Indian schools."[61] Wheelock's vast network of friends and associates included such Congregationalists as Joseph Bellamy (1719–90), whose "preaching was generally from short notes"; Samuel Hopkins (1721–1803), who "usually preached

from short notes"; Joseph Huntington (1735–94), who "spoke extemporaneously, seldom writing more than a skeleton, or the principal topics, of his discourse"; and Stephen West (1735–1819), who wrote his sermon skeletons "on
one-fourth of a sheet of foolscap," which contained "all the important points,
arguments, and illustrations. In the delivery of his sermons, he expounded
these notes in a happy extemporaneous manner."[62] In all, such samplings
of Congregational ministers offer only a glimpse into the pervasive practice
of semi-extemporaneous preaching by ministers who used short notes and
skeletal outlines for their orations. The method was ubiquitous, and it would
persist well into the nineteenth century, both as a common practice in local
churches and as part of the rhetorical training that occurred at Moor's Charity School and Dartmouth College.

The rhetorical and homiletic training at Moor's Charity School therefore
alerts us to one of several possible avenues of Smith's exposure to the sermonizing method of laying down heads for semi-extemporaneous composition and
oral performance, because one of Smith's older brothers, Hyrum Smith, attended Moor's Charity School before the Smith family moved to New York
State.[63] When Hyrum entered Moor's, John Walker's *Rhetorical Grammar*
(1785) was the first schoolbook on rhetoric, oratory, and composition that he
and his new classmates would have studied in their freshmen year.[64] From its
pages, Hyrum would have been taught the basics of oral and written composition, learning how to choose a subject and divide it into its central topics, followed by literary exercises and training in oratorical delivery.[65] As a
supplement, many students would also turn to Walker's *The Teacher's Assistant* to aid in the development of compositional skills, reinforcing the method
of laying down heads and the use of memorized mental outlines.[66] And in the
latter part of his sophomore year, Hyrum would have continued his studies
with Hugh Blair's enormously popular *Lectures on Rhetoric and Belles Lettres*
(1783), which, among numerous other lessons, would have exposed Hyrum to
the fundamental techniques of sermon composition and pulpit eloquence,
including explicit instructions on the method of laying down heads.[67]

Hyrum's curriculum, though indirectly linked to Joseph, offers one of the
few documented cases of advanced rhetorical training and formal instruction
in the detailed mechanics of sermon composition and delivery received by a
member in the immediate Smith family household. Nevertheless, whether or
not Hyrum shared what he was learning with Joseph remains a matter of con-
jecture. Even though the culture of domestic education normally required
older siblings to participate in the instruction of their younger brothers and
sisters, such an injunction does not guarantee that Hyrum ever shared his

knowledge with Joseph. Yet, by the same token, the question of Hyrum's potential influence on Joseph needs to be raised. While definitive answers may remain
elusive and lacking "direct evidence," it would be irresponsible for historians to
dismiss such a potential avenue of influence, particularly if the motive for such
negligence was part of an effort to preserve hagiographical accounts based on
anecdotal evidence of Joseph's purported ignorance and lack of education.

Regardless of what information may or may not have been shared between
Hyrum and Joseph, Moor's Charity School was certainly not the only venue
that showcased Congregationalist preaching in the region, nor would it have
been the only exposure that Smith family members had to Congregationalism.
As historian Richard Lloyd Anderson has repeatedly demonstrated in his work
Joseph Smith's New England Heritage, Congregationalism figured prominently
in the lives of the Smith's extended family. At the time of Joseph's birth in 1805,
and for several years afterward, the Smith family lived in close proximity to several members of their extended family in Vermont. And though the family
moved several times during this period, they always remained within a stone's
throw of relatives. "Between 1803 and 1811," Bushman indicates, "all the moves
were in a tiny circle around Tunbridge, Royalton, and Sharon, immediately ad-
joining towns, and probably never involved a distance of more than five or six
miles."[68] Within that circle of towns lived Joseph's grandparents on both sides
of the family, along with several aunts, uncles, and cousins, all of whom had
current or former ties to the Congregational Church.[69]

Young Joseph's childhood in the Upper Connecticut Valley, surrounded
by immediate and extended family members with extensive ties to Congregationalism, would have exerted some measure of influence on the future
prophet. Through the means of domestic worship, the likely attendance at
Congregational services, the religious influences of extended family members (particularly his devout Congregationalist grandmother Lydia), and
Hyrum's attendance at Moor's Charity School, young Joseph would have
started out life with an intimate exposure to the religious culture of his immediate and extended families. No matter how much these influences may
have informed his future skills as a preacher, however, they were not the only
source for his religious experiences. Indeed, the exposure to evangelical revivalism in his later years would likely prove even more profound. In the winter
of 1816 to 1817, young Joseph's immediate family moved from the Upper Connecticut Valley to the growing village of Palmyra in Western New York, and
this move dropped the Smith family into the heart of the Burned-Over District, one of the most spiritually inflamed and religiously combustive regions
in all the nation.

CHAPTER THREE

Revival Sermons in the Burned-Over District

When the Smith family moved to Western New York in the winter of 1816–17, the Second Great Awakening (ca. 1790 to 1840) was well underway, and the region had long been experiencing periodic and increasingly powerful waves of intense religious revivalism that would surge and retreat, only to surge again. In his influential study on the Burned-Over District, Whitney R. Cross described how "the series of crests in religious zeal begun by the Great Revival [of 1799–1800 in Western New York] formed the crescendo phase of a greater cycle. Strenuous evangelism mounted irregularly from the 1790's to reach a grand climax between 1825 and 1837."[1] Within this larger cycle of spiritual outpourings, the period "following the War of 1812 surpassed all previous experiences," and the Smith family settled in the Palmyra/Manchester area when "western New York was more intensively engaged in revivalism than were other portions of the Northeast."[2] Within this whirlwind of religious activity, Joseph Smith would experience a range of revivalist preaching unlike anything he had previously encountered. Preachers among the Baptists, Methodists, and Presbyterians frequently swept through the region, delivering fiery sermons that spurred their audiences to awaken from the sleep of indifference, repent of their sins, change their hearts, and become humble followers of Christ.

Such performances would have introduced Smith to a variety of sermon styles and traditions, not only across denominations but also from one preacher to the next. In time, Smith would eventually show interest in learning how to preach by joining a Methodist class meeting and participating as an unlicensed lay exhorter. In order to place Smith's preaching skills and compositional techniques within his cultural context, I focus in this chapter on three areas: Smith's early interest in the Methodist faith and his involvement as a lay exhorter; the kind of training and practice that he would have likely experienced among the Methodists; and how those experiences would have related to the sermon styles and oratorical practices of revivalist preachers in other denominations.

Smith's Spiritual Quest and Methodism

When composing his history, Smith would recall how "there was in the place where we lived [Manchester, New York] an unusual excitement on the subject of religion. It commenced with the Methodists, but soon became general among all the sects in that region of country."[3] In his description of events, Smith further identified the major denominations involved in the revivals that he witnessed: "Some were contending for the Methodist faith, some for the Presbyterian, and some for the Baptist."[4] And though he did not formally join any of the churches, he nevertheless "attended their several meetings as often as occasion would permit."[5] Joseph was not alone in his participation in the meetings and revivals of the several local churches. William Smith, one of Joseph's younger brothers, recalled how the interest in the revivals started as a family effort, noting how their mother, Lucy, had "prevailed on us to attend the meetings, and almost the whole family became interested in the matter, and seekers after truth."[6] As a result, Joseph's mother and three of the Smith children joined the Western Presbyterian Church in Palmyra, New York: Lucy, Hyrum, Sophronia, and Samuel.[7]

Whatever his exposure to the Presbyterians, however, Joseph chose not to join. Neither did he join the Baptists, though he also attended their meetings and revivals. Baptist historian Mitchell Bronk (1862–1950), born and raised in Manchester, New York, mentioned Smith's participation in a historical account, which Vogel observes as being "partly based on his memory of conversations with his grandfather and other old Manchester townsmen."[8] Bronk noted how "Joe occasionally attended the stone church [The First Baptist Church of Manchester]; especially the revivals, sitting with the crowd—the 'sinners'—up in the gallery. Not a little of Mormon theology accords with the preaching of Elder [Anson] Shay."[9] Nevertheless, among the churches Smith visited in his search for spiritual truth the Methodists made the deepest impression on his mind.

When asked, "What caused Joseph to ask for guidance as to what church he ought to join," William claimed that Joseph had been motivated by a sermon on James 1:5 ("If any of you lack wisdom, let him ask of God"), which a Methodist preacher, the Reverend Mr. George Lane, had delivered during "a joint revival in the neighborhood between the Baptists, Methodists and Presbyterians."[10] Lane's sermon on James 1:5 had a long and significant history in Methodism. In one of the first publications of his collected sermons, John Wesley spoke to his readers about his personal journey to discover "*the naked Truths of the Gospel*." Confronted with a history of contradictory religious literature, Wesley chose to set it all aside (with the exception of those authors he felt were inspired) and to start at the beginning, "*as if I had never read one Author, Ancient or Modern*," in order to avoid "*intangling myself with those* [thoughts] *of other Men*." In a characteristically Protestant move, Wesley bypassed mortal authorities and looked to the Bible for answers ("*Here is Knowledge enough for me*"). In his *sola scriptura* search for truth, Wesley turned to James 1:5 and John 7:17 for answers, praying to God for guidance: "*Lord, is it not thy Word*, If any Man lack Wisdom, let him ask of GOD? *Thou* givest liberally and upbraidest not. *Thou hast said*, If any be willing to do thy Will, he shall know. *I am willing to do. Let me know thy Will*."[11] Smith's journey to discover divine truth would follow a similar pattern.

While attending the services and revivals of the several churches in his area, Smith became confused by some of the contradictory teachings he observed and turned to the scriptures for help. "While I was laboring under the extreme difficulties caused by the contests of these parties of religionists," Smith recalled, "I was one day reading the Epistle of James, first chapter and fifth verse, which reads: If any of you lack wisdom, let him ask of God. . . . Never did any passage of Scripture come with more power to the heart of man than this did at this time to mine."[12] George Lane's sermon on James 1:5 in a Methodist revival, undoubtedly influenced by Wesley's personal and foundational narrative, may well have been the catalyst that would eventually lead to Smith's "First Vision" of God the Father and Jesus Christ.

Apart from William Smith, Oliver Cowdery, the primary scribe for the Book of Mormon, also mentioned George Lane's influence on young Joseph.[13] Lane, whom Cowdery described as "a presiding Elder of the Methodist church" and "a tallented man possessing a good share of literary endowments," preached in a forceful and moving style: "Mr. Lane's manner of communication was peculiarly calculated to awaken the intellect of the hearer, and arouse the sinner to look about him for safety." Cowdery later added, "and in common with others, our brother's [Joseph's] mind became awakened."[14] Whatever Lane's role in rousing Joseph's interest, the young prophet's heart inclined toward the Methodists. When reflecting on this period in his young adult life, Joseph noted, "In process of time my mind became somewhat partial to the Methodist sect, and I felt some desire to be united with them."[15] Two local residents in Palmyra confirmed Joseph's interest.

According to Pomeroy Tucker, Joseph "joined the probationary class of the Methodist church in Palmyra, and made some active demonstrations of engagedness, though his assumed convictions were insufficiently grounded or abiding to carry him along to the saving point of conversion, and he soon withdrew from the class."[16] Tucker's observation suggests Smith's attendance did not last very long. After preliminary acceptance into a local class meeting, potential new members started their probationary period, receiving "notes of admission" and then remaining "on trial for six months."[17] At the end of the six-month trial, the leaders would review whether or not the applicant was sincere in his or her convictions before accepting the new member into full fellowship.

Tucker's description suggests that Smith withdrew from the probationary class sometime within this initial six-month period. Yet, in spite of this relatively brief time, Joseph's participation was evidently sufficient for him to absorb a measure of Methodist preaching and exhortation techniques. Orsamus Turner, another Palmyra resident, claimed that Joseph attended long enough to participate as a lay exhorter. "After catching a spark of Methodism in the camp meeting, away down in the woods, on the Vienna road," Turner recalled, Joseph became "a very passable exhorter in evening meetings."[18] Turner's description of Smith not only suggests multiple attempts at exhortation but further implies a level of skill that Turner, who was decidedly antagonistic toward Smith, still acknowledged as sufficiently impressive to warrant favorable comment.

Smith's exhortations in Methodist class meetings, whatever his level of participation and whatever his reasons, did not ultimately lead to a formal calling as an ordained exhorter. As H. Michael Marquardt notes, "Joseph did not become a licensed exhorter because such persons had to be members in full standing with the denomination."[19] Smith's level of experience, however, suggests the circumstances in which he delivered his oral performances, as well as the type of exhortations that he would most likely have delivered to his fellow class members. When he attended such meetings, Smith would have been exposed to a variety of extempore and semi-extemporaneous oral performances, including prayers, exhortations, conversion narratives, and sermons.[20] During such gatherings, Methodist leaders were encouraged to identify and select exhorters from among the participants, who, in the course of class meetings, revealed "an extraordinary gift of prayer and some gift for exhortation."[21] Smith's participation as a lay exhorter reveals his success in meeting the basic criteria to exhort fellow members.

As to matters of style, Smith's efforts would have involved two primary forms of semi-extemporaneous orations. If delivering a standalone exhortation, Smith would have been limited to generic appeals, such as urging the audience members to obtain a conviction of their sins, recognize their fallen state, awaken themselves to the necessity of Christ's atoning sacrifice, and embrace Christ into their lives.[22] If performing in tandem with a preacher, Smith would have exhorted after the sermon, reaffirming the main topics of the minister's message, along with more generic appeals to repent and seek Christ.[23] Exhortation skills thus involved active listening to and repetition of the minister's message, the performance and repetition of formulaic patterns, and improvisational techniques that could respond to the immediate concerns of any given sermon or audience.

Smith's participation as an exhorter also suggests his religious aspirations. The engagement of unlicensed exhorters in repeated performances during class meetings inevitably indicated their growing desires to become fully licensed preachers. Apart from being an instrument in God's hands to awaken souls to their spiritual condition, exhortations functioned as entry-level sermons that revealed the speaker's talents, providing a way for aspiring preachers to develop their oratorical skills. Methodist leaders encouraged such candidates to exhort fellow members in order to gain experience; yet, the leaders were also advised to "let young preachers often exhort without taking a text [that is, without interpreting a passage of scripture]."[24] Sermons based on scriptural texts involved doctrinal interpretations, which were reserved, understandably, for ordained preachers. Thus, the prohibition had a two-fold purpose. First, it created a measure of quality control, reining in the exuberance of new exhorters, who, with their lack of knowledge and experience, might otherwise espouse doctrines at odds with the principles of the wider movement. And second, Methodist preaching valorized the dynamic, affective appeals to an audience over the less effective, pedantic styles—"the fine metaphysical reasoning" and "the philosophical disquisitions"—that often emerged when young ministers learned how to preach by focusing exclusively on intellectual and rationalist analyses of scriptural texts.[25]

Dynamic exhortations thus prepared aspiring Methodist preachers in the art of delivering stirring and impassioned sermons, as well as being initiation exercises, or "trials," that revealed a preacher's "gift" of oral performance. "It is exceedingly useful for young preachers," advised Bishop Francis Asbury and Bishop Thomas Coke, the first bishops of the Methodist Episcopal Church in America, "to habituate themselves to the giving of warm exhortations [that is, dynamic and lively], otherwise they may get into a formal way of preaching [that is, rigid formality, devoid of the Spirit] without a due application of the subject."[26] Methodist preaching aimed to motivate souls with emotionally poignant orations that would convert the unregenerated heart.[27] Requiring aspiring preachers to begin their oral performances with emotionally charged exhortations thus reinforced a hierarchy of preaching modes, in which learning how to deliver sermons with affective power and penetrating force took precedence over the necessary but potentially pedantic, stale, and cerebral interpretations of a text.[28]

Treasuring Up the Word of God

In a May 1829 revelation to his brother Hyrum, Joseph Smith articulated his framework for the preparation process involved in speaking with divine inspiration. Hyrum, anxious to participate in building the kingdom of God, apparently asked Joseph to enquire of the Lord about becoming a preacher. In response, the revelation exhorted Hyrum—an exhortation that would be extended to include "all who have good desires" to preach—to prepare for such a calling by first studying the scriptures and becoming deeply familiar with the principles of the gospel: "Seek not to declare my word, *but first seek to obtain my word*, and then shall your tongue be loosed."[29] Joseph's concept of treasuring up the word of God through study and preparation in order to fill the preacher's mind with material for the Holy Spirit to draw upon was not a novel approach among early nineteenth-century preachers. Indeed, Joseph would have come into contact with this philosophy during his exposure to all the major denominations that he studied in his quest to find gospel truths. His ventures into Methodism, however, particularly his participation as a lay exhorter, would have certainly introduced him to this concept during the basic instruction that he would have received, even if only participating for a limited time. A look at how Methodists approached this concept helps to situate Joseph Smith's preparation and delivery styles.

Methodist exhorters and preachers were the direct inheritors of the extempore and semi-extemporaneous methods of oratorical delivery favored by George Whitefield, the "Grand Itinerant," and Methodist founder John Wesley, whose respective concepts of speaking according to divine inspiration involved a systematic approach to study, meditation, and preparation. In particular, Methodist training was heavily influenced by Wesley's ambitious system of informal education and self-improvement. As Vicki Tolar Burton observes, Wesley had long espoused a program of diligent reading and preparation for his preachers that included the study of "Scripture, Greek, Hebrew, texts of the early Church fathers, secular history, science, logic, metaphysics, natural philosophy, mathematics, human nature, and manners."[30] Moreover, to direct lay preachers in such studies, Wesley "edited and published the fifty-volume *Christian Library* [1750] with the idea that the preachers would read these works volume by volume, thus gaining the background in Christian history and theology they needed for the work."[31]

Of course, it is unlikely that all of Wesley's exhorters and preachers read every book and every section in his vast multivolume work. Nevertheless, Wesley's *Christian Library* became a prominent resource for answers to theological and devotional questions. Moreover, Wesley's admonitions for dedicated reading and study provided clear guidance for self-improvement. Indeed, the memoirs and biographies of Methodist preachers frequently include entries that portray regular and sustained habits of scripture study, devotional reading, meditation, and prayer.[32] The impetus behind such preparation was no doubt pragmatic: even though preachers were instruments in God's hands, divine promptings and spiritual inspiration were meaningless if the Holy Spirit had nothing to draw upon except empty minds and empty vessels.

Treasuring up knowledge, both secular and sacred, thus created a storehouse in the preacher's mind, which the Holy Spirit could ideally use to produce informed and vivid orations that would respond to the immediate needs of the audience. "Read the most useful Books, and that regularly and constantly," Methodists preachers and exhorters learned from *A Form of Discipline for the Ministers, Preachers, and Members of the Methodist Episcopal Church in America* (1787). "Steadily spend all the Morning in this Employment, or at least five Hours in four and twenty." Anticipating the possibility that some aspiring preachers might complain of such a rigorous program and argue that they had "no Taste for reading," the Methodist leaders who considered and approved *A Form of Discipline* urged their advice with a blunt response: "Contract a Taste for it by Use, or return to your former Employment."[33] In days when they were not working or traveling, ministers were encouraged "from four to five in the Morning, and from five to six in the Evening, to meditate, pray and read," and "from six in the Morning till twelve (allowing an Hour for Breakfast) read in Order, with much Prayer, the Christian Library, and other pious Books."[34] If he had not already developed personal habits of study and meditation, Smith's attendance at Methodist class meetings and his efforts as an unlicensed exhorter would have exposed him to a religious environment dedicated to the principles of rigorous education and systematic self-improvement.

The concept of filling the mind for extempore orations was not, of course, confined to the Methodists. In his enormously popular *A Guide to Prayer* (1716), Isaac Watts (1674–1748), the famous Nonconformist hymnodist, argued that the Holy Spirit inspires those who engage in diligent *"Reading, Hearing, Meditation, Study, and Attempts of Prayer"* in order to "treasure up a Store of Matter," which, among other blessings, assists preachers "in the holy skill of Exhortation, in order to become able Ministers."[35] In his widely read book *Cardiphonia: Or, The Utterance of the Heart* (1781), John Newton (1725–1807), the well-known Anglican minister who wrote the words for the hymn *Amazing Grace* (1779), offers advice to a young minister on how to "speak extempore as a clergyman."[36] Newton counsels, "As to speaking without notes, in order to do it successfully, a fund of knowledge should be first possessed." More specifically, "you must use double diligence in study: your reading must not be confined to the scriptures; you should be acquainted with church-history, have a general view of divinity as a system, know something of the state of controversies in past times and at present, and indeed of the general history of mankind."[37] Though less popular than Watts's *A Guide to Prayer*, Newton's *Cardiphonia* (frequently described as "Newton's Letters") was often advertised for sale in the local Palmyra newspaper during the same period when Smith would have attended the Methodist probationary class meetings and the services of other denominations.[38]

As these references indicate, treasuring up the word of God was not a passive activity. It involved sustained, systematic study that often included regular note-taking during daily Bible reading, sermon construction, scripture memorization, referencing scriptural commentaries and published concordances, the construction and memorization of homemade concordances, and the study of sermons and devotional treatises. "Though the bible be infinitely preferable to all other books," admonished Methodist Bishops Asbury and Coke, "yet we are, even on that very account, to study the writings of those spiritual and great divines, who have by their comments, essays, sermons, or other labours, explained the bible: otherwise, we ought not to attend the preaching of the gospel."[39] In a church filled with preachers who often had little formal education, Asbury and Coke, following directly in the footsteps of Wesley, nurtured a sermon culture within Methodism that framed intense curiosity, dedicated study, and concentrated personal preparation as religious imperatives.

Some specific methods of preparation offer additional insights into the kinds of exercises that some preachers pursued in their studies. For instance, in his pamphlet *A Letter to a Methodist Preacher* (1800), Adam Clarke (ca. 1760–1832), a Methodist minister and prominent theologian, urged young clergy to read the Bible with concerted effort and strategic study: "But while you read the Bible as the revelation of God and the fountain of divine knowledge, don't let your reading *end* there. . . . read much; but take care that all your reading be directed to the increase of your knowledge and experience in the things of God."[40] In order to focus the attention of new preachers on the text, Clarke suggested that they make a list of all the scriptures on which they felt confident to preach: "Read the book of God. Read it regularly through, at least once in a year; and take down in order, every text [scripture] you think you have light [knowledge] sufficient to preach from."[41] Preachers following Clarke's suggestions would engage in constant acts of scriptural analysis, self-reflection, and record keeping. And in order to identify possible sermon texts, they would consider their ability to address such texts effectively, and then produce a tailored list of scriptures and topics for future reference material.

Clarke was also adamant that young preachers become familiar "with every branch of science," arguing that no one could fully explain the scriptures "who has not a tolerable knowledge of history, chronology, geography, astronomy, anatomy, and chemistry."[42] Drawing on the familiar language of treasuring up the word of God, Clarke warned preachers against the limitations that would come with a lack of diligence: "The *indolent* preacher is soon known by his preaching; he has little or no *variety*. He cannot bring out of his treasury things both *new* and *old*—alas for him! *treasury* he has none—*his* coffers are all empty."[43] It should be remembered that Clarke's advice was aimed at "the Junior Preachers (Both Local and Travelling) in the Methodist Connexion," meaning, of course, that his instructions were specifically tailored to an audience of developing semi-extemporaneous preachers.[44]

Long before Clarke, authors of manuals on pulpit oratory offered similar exercises to help preachers internalize the scriptures. In *The Arte of Prophesying*, for example, William Perkins advised preachers to use blank commonplace books to record any material they might need for a future time: "those things, which in studying thou meetest with, that are necessarie and worthie to be observed, thou must put in thy tables or Common-place books, that thou maiest alwaies have in a readines both old and new."[45] One of the exercises Perkins suggested was the creation of a personal concordance of related scriptures, or, as he described it, "The collation or comparing of places together." By collecting scriptures with similar themes, topics, and wording, the preacher could thus interpret the meaning of scriptures more effectively, "whereby places [in scripture] are set like parallels one beside another, that the meaning of them may more evidentlie appeare."[46] Simply recording such parallels in a personal commonplace book, however, was not enough.

After suggesting ways that preachers could format their commonplace books and record their material, Perkins admonished them on the importance of committing the information to memory: "It is not sufficient to have a thing written in thy booke, unlesse it be also diligentlie laid and locked up in thy memorie."[47] The advice was consistent with his approach to performance and delivery. Without such internalization, preachers would not be able to follow Perkins's method of semi-extemporaneous preaching, in which preachers followed their short notes or a memorized mental outline but left the actual spoken words to the moment of performance (that is, the words would "not unwillingly follow the matter that is premeditated").[48] Perkins was not alone in this opinion. When advising preachers on their preparations, Bishop Burnet offered the same advice, urging preachers to "read the Scriptures very exactly" and to "have great Portions of them by Heart," along with making "a short Concordance of them in his Memory; that is, he must lay together such Passages as belong to the same Matter; to consider how far they agree or help to illustrate one another, and how the same Thing is differently expressed in them." Neither did preparation consist of casual reading for Burnet. "Upon this a Man must exercise himself much, draw Notes of it, and digest it well in his Thoughts."[49] Thus, for Perkins and Burnet (among others), all the notes, observations, and lists of parallel scriptures should be well "digested" through memorization and internalization.

Along with the creation of homemade commonplace books and the construction of personal concordances, church leaders and authors of manuals on pulpit eloquence advised preachers to consult published concordances, commentaries, essays, and sermons. When Smith was exploring Methodism and participating as a lay exhorter, Bishops Asbury and Coke had already been reinforcing longstanding traditions by advising Methodist preachers to reference the works of commentators during study and preparation. But the advice, of course, was not limited to Methodism. Asbury and Coke's instructions, for example, specifically echoed the admonitions contained in popular preaching manuals, such as the Reverend Jean Claude's *An Essay on the Composition of a Sermon*, which recommended that preachers "avail yourself of criticisms, notes, comments, paraphrases, &c. and, in one word, of the labours of other persons."[50] Over a century earlier, Bishop Wilkins had already provided readers with exhaustive lists of publications in his work *Ecclesiastes; Or, a Discourse Concerning the Gift of Preaching*, which included biblical dictionaries; multiple translations of the Bible; concordances; commentaries on specific biblical passages; interpretations of doctrine; gospel commonplaces; and manuals on preaching, church polity, Jewish history and culture, and "Heathen Moralists" (Plato, Aristotle, Seneca, and so on), among numerous other categories.[51]

In the period when Smith was investigating Methodist exhorting, another widely available resource was Adam Clarke's multivolume Commentary on the Bible (1810–25). Clarke, described as "the greatest name in British Methodism in the generation which succeeded Wesley" and "the first great representative commentator of Methodism," started work on his Commentary on 1 May 1798, and finished the massive project on 28 March 1825, though portions of the Commentary were published along the way.[52] As D. W. Riley observed, "Adam Clarke's Commentary on the Holy Bible was first published in parts between 1810 and 1825, and in America from 1811 to 1825."[53] Appearing under the titles *The Holy Bible, Containing the Old and New Testaments* and also *The New Testament of Our Lord and Saviour Jesus Christ*, the Commentary was an instant success. "Few commentaries have had a greater sale," historian Maldwyn Edwards observes. "Butterworth, the publisher, had to strike off eleven thousand eight hundred copies before the first demand could be supplied and successive editions were printed both in England and America."[54] Stan Larson also notes that there were "at least ten American printings and editions in New York from 1811 to 1829."[55] Moreover, the Commentary would remain in demand throughout the nineteenth century. "The Commentary most popular and most widely read in England during this century," mused John Beauchamp in his 1884 essay on Methodist literature, "has perhaps been that written by Dr. Adam Clarke."[56] Such admiration reflected the popularity of Clarke's Commentary, which circulated widely in Methodist circles and well beyond.

Clarke's Commentary holds particular interest in relation to Smith and Methodist sermon culture. Some scholars believe that Smith may have consulted Clarke's Commentary when he created a partially revised version of the King James Bible, known as the "Joseph Smith Translation," or simply the "JST," and that he may also have possibly referred to the Commentary during the production of the Book of Mormon.[57] In addition, an anecdotal account from the period when Smith started his dictation of the Book of Mormon also suggests Smith may have been aware of Clarke's Commentary, even if only in passing. When Smith began working on the Book of Mormon, he and his wife, Emma, were living in Harmony, Pennsylvania, where several of Emma's immediate and extended family members lived, many of whom were Methodists. One of Emma's uncles, the Reverend Nathaniel Lewis, a local Methodist preacher, lived in their neighborhood. "I have been acquainted with Joseph Smith Jr. for some time," Lewis stated, "being a relation of his wife, and residing near him, I have had frequent opportunities of conversation with him, and of knowing his opinions and pursuits."[58] During one of those conversations, the Reverend Lewis purportedly asked Smith if he could use Smith's translation device (described as "spectacles") to perform his own translations of ancient texts in order to verify Smith's claims.

The Reverend George Peck, a Methodist itinerant preacher, friend, and colleague of Lewis, described what purportedly happened. After listening to Smith's "story of the golden bible and the miracle-working spectacles," Reverend Lewis asked, "Joseph, can anybody else translate strange languages by the help of them spectacles?" "O yes!" was the answer. "Well now," said Mr. Lewis, "I've got Clarke's Commentary, and it contains a great many strange languages; now, if you will let me try the spectacles, and if by looking through them I can translate these strange tongues into English, then I'll be one of your disciples."[59] According to Peck, Smith "was much offended, and never undertook to convert 'uncle Lewis' afterward."[60] The accuracy of the details in Peck's account of this exchange, however, needs to be questioned. Clarke's Commentary, for instance, provides immediate translations of foreign words and phrases in his footnotes, rendering the use of the "spectacles" entirely unnecessary. Rather than an objective historical account, Peck's story comes off as a well-rehearsed anecdote, shaped into the framework of tavern tales and neighborhood lore.

Nevertheless, the widespread popularity of Clarke's Commentary, combined with the close proximity of Emma's Methodist relatives—particularly in light of her uncle Nathanial Lewis's standing as a local Methodist preacher—provides a set of circumstances that could easily have resulted in Smith's exposure to Clarke's work before and/or during the time of his dictation of the Book of Mormon. If his first encounter with Clarke's Commentary occurred among Emma's relatives, or even earlier, when participating as a Methodist exhorter in the Palmyra/Manchester area, Smith would not have been alone. For Methodist preachers in the early nineteenth century, Clarke's Commentary was a popular and widespread godsend. Rather than aiming his work at formally trained biblical scholars, Clarke specifically sought to make biblical criticism—interpretations of passages, translation issues, historical contexts, and so on—accessible to everyone. As he stated, "Because, having designed my Notes not for the learned, but for comparatively simple people, or those whose avocations prevent them from entering deeply into subjects of this kind, I thought it best to bring every thing as much as possible, within *their* reach."[61] By making biblical scholarship accessible to nonexperts, Clarke singlehandedly raised the intellectual bar and quality of devotional apologetics among Methodist preachers. And for those with limited funds and few educational opportunities, Clarke's work provided access to scholarship that would otherwise require a substantial library and a measure of formal training to duplicate.

Exposure to Methodist Sermon Culture

Smith's exposure to Methodist sermon culture would not merely have been limited to instruction on study and meditation but would have included exposure to the delivery of exhortations and the basics of sermon composition.

As suggested by William V. Smith, "Methodist practice and ideas had a profound influence on Mormonism throughout Joseph Smith's lifetime and later, perhaps especially with regard to sermon traditions."[62] In order to appreciate how this influence operated in detail, however, it is essential to differentiate between stereotypical representations of Methodist performances and the actual practices of study, preparation, and delivery. Though critics accused Methodist preachers of delivering sermons purely extempore, without any thought or preparation whatsoever—a claim further complicated by some Methodist preachers, who similarly claimed that everything they uttered was unpremeditated and entirely inspired by the Holy Spirit—the performances were nevertheless the result of sustained preparation, devoted study, and repeated practice.

In his apologia of Methodist sermon culture in the introduction of his work *Christian Holiness* (1800), Disney Alexander (ca. 1795–1825), an English surgeon and physician who "had become a Methodist and a local preacher," defended Methodist preaching from critics who accused the preachers of engaging in spontaneous, unpremeditated sermons.[63] In his introduction, Alexander expressed the hope that his work would "tend to lessen some of the prejudices which any, who are not in the habit of hearing us, entertain against our preaching; who seem to take it for granted, that we pay not the smallest attention to order, argument, or consistency [specific sermon techniques]; but imagine, that because we preach without notes, we are at no pains to arrange our ideas, or to meditate beforehand upon the passage we mean to discuss."[64] In his attempt to clarify Methodist doctrine and practices, Alexander thus offered critical insights into late-eighteenth-century and early nineteenth-century Methodist sermon culture. Preaching without notes and being guided by the inspiration of the Holy Spirit did not mean preaching without preparation.

In *A Form of Discipline* (1787; revised and retitled *The Doctrines and Discipline* in 1798), Methodist preachers in America were advised to "Chuse [choose] the plainest Texts you can" in preparation for sermons and to "Take Care not to ramble, but keep to your Text, and make out what you take in Hand [that is, organize any notes taken to the pulpit]."[65] In their annotations upon these specific recommendations, Bishops Asbury and Coke revealed some of the widespread practices of sermon construction that preachers adopted throughout the Methodist movement in America. The approach they outlined followed the common sequence of choosing a scriptural text, arranging the primary heads of discussion, composing an introduction, and finishing with a section on practical applications. "When the preacher has fixed upon the subject which he judges most suitable to the states of the souls he is going to address," Asbury and Coke advised, "he must keep to his point. He must labour to arrange his ideas.... He must first endeavour fully to explain, and then to apply."[66] *The Doctrines and Discipline* was one of the central texts of Methodism in America, a work that Coke and Asbury wished to see "in the house of every Methodist," and a resource for aspiring Methodist exhorters and preachers.[67]

Moreover, because the work functioned as a manual on church polity, beliefs, and practice, church leaders used the text as a standard introduction to Methodism for new and probationary members. Every meeting would normally have time devoted to the reading and discussion of teachings contained in the text, while every quarter each Methodist society was required to read through the entire work together. Elders, deacons, and preachers in charge of circuits were obliged "to read the rules of the society, with the aid of the other preachers, once a year in every congregation, and once a quarter in every society."[68] With such a resolute program of instruction for new and potential members in the doctrines and practices of Methodism, Smith undoubtedly would have encountered some aspect of this text in virtually every meeting of the probationary class that he attended.

In his pamphlet *A Letter to a Methodist Preacher* (1800), Clarke also offered a fundamental program outlining the expectations for budding ministers that ranged from the composition and delivery of sermons to the basics of proper behavior in public and the maintenance of good health. Specific to sermon construction, Clarke urged preachers to select texts appropriate for their skill level and understanding ("Never take a text which you do not fully understand"), to arrange the main points and divisions appropriately, and to commit the outline to memory: "Be sure to have the matter of your text well arranged in your own mind before you come into the pulpit, that you may not be confused while speaking." Moreover, Clarke admonished preachers to keep their sermon outlines clear and simple by limiting the number of heads in each discourse: "beware of too much *dividing*, and *subdividing*." Too many unnecessary heads created an overly complicated mental outline, argued Clarke, that "rather fetters than enlarges the mind: and that which is ominously called the *skeleton*, i.e. a system of *mere bones*, is in general but ill clothed with muscles, worse strung with nerves, and often without the breath either of a spiritual or intellectual life."[69] Publishers in Britain and North America regularly reprinted Clarke's popular work, usually offering it as a standalone pamphlet in order "*to render the work as cheap as possi-*

ble," thereby making it widely available to anyone with a shilling to spare and a desire to preach.[70]

Wesley's Influence on Methodist Sermon Culture

Smith's exposure to Methodist sermon culture, which owed much of its heritage to the dramatic and theatrical performances of George Whitefield, was also deeply influenced by John Wesley's approach to preaching. Though often remembered primarily for his teachings and organizational skills, Wesley was also well known for his sermons. "He preaches without notes," observed the author of *Pulpit Elocution; Or, Characters and Principles of the Most Popular Preachers* (1782), "and there is something in his pathetic [emotionally moving] delivery at once original and engaging, nervous, sublime, and beautiful."[71] Indeed, early historians of the movement often attributed the practice of preaching extempore among Methodists to Wesley, rather than Whitefield. "In the beginning of the year 1735, he [Wesley] for the first time preached extempore, in All-hallow's Church, Lombard-street, London. He went with a view of hearing Dr. Heylin, but he not coming, the Church-wardens requested Mr. Wesley to preach. He complied, though he had no notes. This is now universally practised by all the Methodist Preachers, and also by many Ministers of the Established Church [Anglican], especially those who are considered as *Gospel Ministers.*"[72]

Wesley's method of preaching "extempore" and "without notes" was often the result of careful preparation, and, if his printed sermons offer any indication, he was particularly inclined to lay down the heads of his sermons explicitly to his audiences. Caution must be exercised, however, in equating his printed sermons—the result of revisions, emendations, and an editorial process—with his performances in the pulpit. As William Gibson observes, "John Wesley certainly published sermons which bore little or no resemblance to those he delivered."[73] Nonetheless, for young Methodist exhorters and preachers born in early nineteenth-century America, who never had the opportunity to see Wesley or to witness any of his pulpit performances, the printed sermons and stories of Wesley's style would have been all that remained to study and imitate.

In terms of his composition process, Wesley appears to have followed the common practice of selecting a scriptural text and dividing his message into primary heads, all of which he arranged into a "skeleton" outline. In a July 1747 letter to his brother Charles (1707–88), a renowned preacher in his own right,

Wesley spoke about the need to address the issue of "justifying faith" in Methodist doctrine. Wesley presented a draft outline of his thoughts, stating, "A skeleton of it (which you may fill up, or any one that has leisure) I have roughly set down." Wesley's "skeleton" included the proposal (the text), "Is justifying faith, *a sense of pardon? Negature,*" followed by four main heads: "I. Every one is deeply concerned to understand this question well. . . . II. By justifying faith I mean, that faith, which whosoever hath it not, is under the *wrath* and the *curse* of God. . . . III. Because, if justifying faith *necessarily* implies such an explicit assurance of pardon. . . . IV. If you object, [here, Wesley breaks down the main head into four sub-topics]."[74] Wesley's letter offers insight into his process of sermon composition, particularly his tendency to lay down explicit heads, which frequently appeared in the final versions of his lectures and discourses.

For eighteenth- and nineteenth-century Methodist preachers and exhorters, Wesley's sermons not only provided models for study and imitation, they also provided examples of structural form. His sermons displayed textbook examples of methodical arrangement, clarity of message, comprehensive coverage of key issues, and forceful applications. The concentrated preparation he invested in his orations was self-evident. Yet, at the same time, his presentations were deceptively simple in format and expression. Wesley was careful to limit the number of his main points, averaging only two to four heads per sermon. He then placed special emphasis on those central topics of his outline in order to help his audiences remember the information he shared.[75] Wesley's works circulated widely in England and America, appearing as individual sermons, articles in Methodist magazines, and collected works. One of his most popular collections, *Sermons on Several Occasions* (1746), appeared in multiple editions well into the nineteenth century, and the work was readily available in local bookstores near the Smith family farm.[76] For neophyte Methodist preachers, such works contained a rich trove of subject matter, effective techniques, and sermon patterns.

Among the techniques young ministers might encounter, the method of laying down heads featured prominently. Wesley's discourse on the doctrine of justification offers a typical example. After starting with his text (Rom. 4:5, "To him that worketh not, but believeth on him that justifieth the Ungodly, his Faith is counted to him for Righteousness"), Wesley stated the issue he wished to address: "How a Sinner may be justified before God, the Lord and Judge of all, is a Question of no common Importance." Following a brief introduction, Wesley then set down the heads of his argument,

First, What is the general Ground of this whole Doctrine of Justification.
Secondly, What Justification is.
Thirdly, Who they are that are justified. And,
Fourthly, On what Terms they are justified.[77]

Wesley's structural format derives from the same tradition that Smith would later adopt for his 1832 history and his 1843 sermon on the Prodigal Son, though this observation does not suggest that Smith learned his method exclusively from Wesley or Methodist sermon culture. The approach of explicitly laying down heads, as already noted, was simply too ubiquitous to be traced to a single source of influence. Though he spent time training as a Methodist exhorter, Smith could have easily learned about this technique, or, at the very least, had his knowledge reinforced, when he attended meetings and revivals with Baptists and Presbyterians—if not earlier, from the Congregationalists in the Upper Connecticut River Valley.

Situating Smith's 1832 history and 1843 sermon within his cultural milieu therefore necessitates a wider scope of inquiry than an isolated look at Methodism. While Smith's experiences among the Methodists offer insights into some of the events and circumstances he likely encountered, the Baptist and Presbyterian preachers would have exerted their own particular influence. And when searching specifically for the semi-extemporaneous style of oral composition that Smith employed for his dictated works—that is, preparing a skeletal outline in advance and expanding it extemporaneously in the moment of dictation, or speaking extempore and following the impulses of spiritual impressions in the moment of utterance—we find that many preachers, within all of the denominations that Smith visited in his search for spiritual truths, made regular use of the same basic techniques in the construction and delivery of sermons and exhortations.

Semi-Extemporaneous Preaching Styles

In the previous chapter, we reviewed the major categories of sermon practices in the nineteenth century that David Williamson outlined in his *Reflections on the Four Principal Religions* (1824). Among these methods, Williamson identified a "fourth mode," in which preachers prepared a brief outline of their sermon and used it as a guide to deliver a semi-extemporaneous sermon.[78] In order to understand better Smith's varied applications of this technique, we need to take a closer look at this particular method.

In the descriptions of their semi-extemporaneous styles, revivalist ministers described four basic yet overlapping applications of this "fourth mode" of semi-extemporaneous preaching: (1) preparing written short notes and taking them to the pulpit; (2) preparing written short notes, memorizing the notes, and then going to the pulpit without them; (3) preparing a mental outline, without ever writing down notes, and expanding and delivering the memorized sermon skeleton from the pulpit; and (4), relying exclusively on a mental storehouse of past sermons, habituated sermon patterns (text, introduction, divisions, applications), and personal preparations (scripture study, debates, memorized scriptures), in order to deliver what appeared to be unpremeditated sermons. In actual practice, preachers often used a nuanced mixture of these approaches, rather than following a single style. In order to contextualize Smith's uses of this method, the following descriptions and examples provide greater detail.

The first semi-extemporaneous approach noted above involved the preparation of a written skeletal outline of a sermon ("short notes," "plan," or "brief"), which preachers then took to the pulpit for easy reference during the course of the sermon. Presbyterian Charles Grandison Finney (1792–1875), one of early nineteenth-century America's most famous preachers, who crisscrossed upstate New York with his sermons and revivals, made regular use of short notes in the pulpit. In fact, his popular work, *Lectures on Revivals of Religion* (1835), was based on sermons he delivered with short notes. The book was the result of efforts by Joshua Leavitt (1794–1873), an author and Congregationalist minister, who sat in the audience and recorded Finney's lectures. In his description of Finney's performances, Leavitt observed "that Mr. Finney never writes his sermons; but guides his course of argument by a skeleton, or brief, carefully prepared, and so compact, that it can be written on one side of a card."[79]

Methodist Henry Chase (1790–1858), who was born in upstate New York and spent part of his career in the New York East Conference, "was an extemporaneous preacher, never taking any other evidence of preparation into the pulpit than a slip of paper containing the heads of his discourse. He, however, did make special preparation for the pulpit by prayer and study." Methodist James Covell (1796–1845), who, as a teenager in Poughkeepsie, New York, began delivering extempore prayers and exhortations in Methodist class meetings and later served part of his career in upstate New York, "generally preached without a manuscript before him, though he sometimes had a brief outline of his discourse, written on a piece of paper scarcely larger than a man's hand." Baptist Ebenezer Rodgers (1788–1854) used the same technique: "His sermon was *extempore*, except that he had before him a narrow slip of paper about four inches long, written upon one side."[80] This technique of composing short notes and taking them to the pulpit was nearly identical, and certainly interchangeable, with the next category of preaching.

The second semi-extemporaneous approach involved the preparation of a written sermon skeleton, which preachers then memorized prior to performance and delivered without any notes in the pulpit. Methodist founder John Wesley, as mentioned earlier, preached "extempore" and "without notes," though his preparations involved laying down explicit heads and sketching out meticulous outlines of his sermons.[81] Baptist John Stanford (1754–1834), who spent most of his career in New York, "was accustomed to arrange his thoughts for the pulpit on paper, and to make himself master of his subject, committing the outline, thus prepared, to memory, and then to preach without any manuscript before him." Presbyterian William Paxton (1760–1845) followed the same approach, preparing for sermons by selecting a subject, sketching an outline, meditating on his message, but then leaving his notes behind. "I am not aware," recalled his colleague the Reverend David McConaughy, "that he ever used, in the delivery of his sermons from the pulpit, even this summary outline."[82] The practice of writing and memorizing short notes during sermon preparations, however, might further evolve into a process in which some ministers would skip the writing component altogether, as described in the following variation of the method.

The third semi-extemporaneous approach involved the preparation of a mental outline during study and meditation, which the preacher retained in his memory and used as a guide during performance, *without ever committing anything to paper*. Methodist William Capers (1790–1855), for example, joined the Methodists in 1808 at the age of eighteen and was soon invited by itinerant preacher the Reverend William Gassoway to accompany him on his circuit. Throwing Capers into the proverbial deep end, Gassoway called upon Capers, apparently without notice, to deliver his first exhortation to a waiting audience. Capers "obeyed the command, but not without great embarrassment." Such a traumatic formative experience might well have prompted Capers to create a mental storehouse of material to draw upon at all times. "He always preached extemporaneously," recalled the Reverend William M. Wightman, "without manuscript or brief [short notes] of any kind before him. His preparations were exclusively mental. I never knew him to write an outline but once."[83]

Seasoned preachers, such as Presbyterian Drury Lacy (1758–1815), often abandoned the use of short notes later in their careers, no longer needing them for preparation: "During the last fifteen years of his life, the period of his greatest ministerial success, he rarely, if ever, wrote his sermons, and but seldom prepared even short notes for the pulpit. His preparation was almost exclusively mental and spiritual. He thought intensely upon his subject, arranged the matter carefully in his mind, and then trusted to the occasion to suggest the appropriate language." Methodist George Dougharty (ca. 1772–1807), who spent much of his career in South Carolina, adopted a similar approach by meditating on his subject and constructing a mental outline for his sermons. "His discourses, though delivered extempore, were well elaborated in his own mind, and his words seemed to flow forth as the effect of a constantly kindling inspiration."[84] The repeated creation of such mental outlines could also result in habituated formulaic patterns, allowing preachers to plug new material into preexisting templates. Such regular construction of mental outlines during meditation serves as a transition to the next category of oratorical technique within the rich spectrum of extemporaneous performances.

The fourth and most radical semi-extemporaneous approach involved unpremeditated preaching (or the appearance of such), when, without apparently planning or meditating on a particular sermon in advance, the preacher ascended the pulpit and seemed to rely exclusively on the impulses of the moment to select and preach upon a topic of discourse. Presbyterian James Ives Foot (1796–1840), for instance, was known as "a fluent extemporaneous speaker, and could speak on any subject or any occasion with little previous notice, or no notice at all." Methodist Samuel Parker (ca. 1774–1819) "was strictly an extemporaneous preacher,—rarely, if ever, even using notes." Baptist Jeremiah Vardeman (1775–1842), whose "opportunities for education were limited indeed" and whose skills "did not reach beyond reading, writing, and arithmetic," may well have preached purely extempore throughout his entire career. Vardeman's "training," like so many other frontier itinerant preachers with modest educational opportunities, was probably limited to his observations of fellow itinerants and the development of his own personal style through the repeated delivery of exhortations and sermons. According to the Reverend James E. Welch, a preacher converted by Vardeman and trained as a minister under his care, Vardeman's "manner of preaching was ready [that is, he could preach at a moment's notice], and always without notes before him, and apparently extempore."[85]

As noted previously, however, the various methods of extempore sermonizing practiced among Baptists, Congregationalists, Methodists, and Presbyterians were complicated by the fact that many seasoned preachers who pursued this course of delivery had already established formulaic templates and well-worn habits of sermonizing. Therefore, the concepts, ideas, interpretations, instructions, and applications in sermons and exhortations rarely (if ever) emerged *ex nihilo*, without prior appearances in a speaker's vocabulary or in the familiar patterns of former orations. Moreover, whether described in anecdotal narratives or written in historical reflections, the biographical and autobiographical accounts of revivalist preachers do not always provide sufficient details to determine each individual's specific approach—or, more accurately, *approaches* (again, preachers often followed more than one style)—to these common methods of semi-extemporaneous delivery. Descriptions of preachers who prepared short notes during their study and meditation, for example, do not always indicate whether or not the preacher took his notes to the pulpit or simply memorized the outline in advance and spoke without written aids.

Nonetheless, such nuances are merely individual expressions of the same underlying technique of semi-extemporaneous performance, and this same fundamental method operated as the most pervasive mode of sermon composition and delivery among evangelical preachers. Indeed, this observation requires special emphasis. These techniques were not limited to a small subset of ministers. Rather, the various manifestations of this underlying semi-extemporaneous approach dominated the styles of evangelical preachers in every location where the Smith family lived. Smith's methods were by no means unique, but rather part and parcel of the same pervasive oral strategies practiced widely by the evangelical sermon traditions in his immediate environments. Because Smith inherited his oral techniques directly from this compositional and rhetorical milieu, even a brief snapshot of ministers and their methods proves instructive.

Along with the Methodist preachers already mentioned, William Ward Ninde (1810–45), born and raised in Lyons, Wayne County, in Western New York (approximately sixteen miles east of Palmyra and Manchester, the locations where the Smith family once lived), "generally wrote a brief sketch, thoroughly studied the thought of his discourse, and then trusted to the inspiration of the occasion for the diction which gave it expression and power." John Summerfield (1798–1825), who spent part of his career in the New York Conference and whose "short" notes appear to have been actually rather long, "rarely wrote his sermons at length; but generally made a tolerably full outline, and spoke with that before him, though apparently making but little use of it." Charles Sherman (1803–44), who also spent part of his career in upstate New York, prepared for his sermons by "meditating carefully and devoutly on his subject, and writing a brief outline of his discourse; but for the language he trusted entirely to the impulse of the moment."[86]

Methodist Clark T. Hinman (1817–54), born in Harpersfield, Delaware County, in upstate New York, delivered his first impromptu exhortation at the age of nine at a local Baptist meeting. One of his colleagues, the Reverend Francis A. Blades, observed Hinman reusing a sermon skeleton, recalling, "Though I had heard him [Hinman] preach from the same outline, the filling up [that is, the language in the moment] was quite different from anything that I remembered." Joseph Aplin Waterman (1798–1852) delivered his sermons "from a skeleton." James Smith (ca. 1783–1826) "was strictly an extempore preacher," recalled his acquaintance Philemon B. Hopper, "though his subject had always been thoroughly studied, and, with this preparation, he could speak better than he could write."[87]

Methodist Joseph Lybrand (1793–1844) "never wrote his sermons out, nor delivered them *memoriter* [memorized]. They were well matured as to the matter [subject], but extemporaneous as to the language." Charles Pitman (1796–1854), who started his career as a licensed exhorter, trained himself to compose sermons by writing them out in full, though in actual performance he was "uniformly an extemporaneous preacher." Henry Bidleman Bascom (1796–1850), who began his ministry as an exhorter in Ohio, was described as having "the *action* [gestures] of an impassioned extempore speaker, unfettered by manuscript or brief [short notes]."[88] As part of a cross-denominational technique of performance in sermon culture, these same variations of styles also appeared among the Presbyterians.

When young Smith participated in joint revivals involving Presbyterians, along with attending the local Sunday school at the Western Presbyterian Church in Palmyra—the same congregation that his mother and several siblings joined for a period of time—he would have been exposed to a similar range of vibrant preaching styles.[89] Presbyterian Seth Williston (1770–1851), who preached extensively in upstate New York, wrote out many of his sermons for publication. Apart from such printed works, however, many of the sermons he actually delivered "were either not written at all, or were delivered from short notes." William Hill (1769–1852) "seldom wrote his sermons. Like most of his brethren in Virginia, he preached from brief notes." George Duffield (1732–1790), who "sympathized with the friends and followers of [George] Whitefield," did not usually write out his entire sermons, "but, having made a skeleton, and arranged his thoughts, awaited the inspiration of the occasion for the filling up." John Holt Rice (1777–1831) preached "almost uniformly *extempore*. He used notes, (often very brief,) sometimes covering perhaps a sheet of *foolscap* paper."[90]

Presbyterian Matthew Lyle (1767–1827) "uniformly preached without notes,—rarely, if ever, taking even a skeleton of a sermon with him into the pulpit." George Addison Baxter (1771–1841) "was what is usually termed an *extempore* preacher," according to his colleague, the Reverend John Leyburn: "He probably never had a manuscript sermon in the pulpit in his life; and in all the preaching which I ever heard from him, I never saw him with even the briefest outline committed to paper. His pulpit preparations were nevertheless thorough." Baxter's biographer also notes, "His sermons were extemporaneous, in the sense of not being written, but were nevertheless carefully premeditated." Robert Henderson (1764–1834) "preached extempore, and without even short notes." John Blair (1720–1771) "sometimes wrote his sermons in full, yet his common mode of preaching was by short notes, comprising the general outlines." Samuel Taggart (1754–1825), an early graduate of Dartmouth College who spent a short time in Western New York, delivered sermons that "were marked by vigorous thought, were extremely methodical [that is, precisely arranged], and abounded in Scripture quotations. . . . He preached generally from short notes, but he seemed to make little use of them."[91] This catalog of preachers and their techniques offers a mere sampling of a much wider group of Presbyterian preachers following these methods.[92]

Smith's attendance at Baptist meetings and joint revivals would have further exposed to him the same set of semi-extemporaneous techniques. Thomas Baldwin (1753–1825), for example, "rarely wrote his sermons in full; and not generally, at least in the better part of his life, did he even furnish himself with a copious skeleton. His preparation most commonly consisted in studious reflection upon his subject, and writing merely the leading divisions." In his funeral sermon for Baldwin, the Reverend Daniel Chessman added, "He sometimes wrote his sermons; but generally, having reflected on the subject, delivered his discourses extempore." William Batchelder (1768–1818) "seldom wrote out a sermon. There are among his papers numerous skeletons of sermons which show that he premeditated what he delivered; but his fluent eloquence required no previous writing out in detail."[93]

Baptist Hezekiah Smith (1737–1805) "never wrote his sermons. . . . [but] He left a large number of skeletons of sermons, which supply a general idea of his method." William Palmer (1785–1853) "left no fully written sermons, but a great number of briefs or skeletons, for he never preached without careful preparation." Aaron Leland (1761–1833) "spoke extempore without any apparent effort, and, so far as I know, during his whole ministry, never made use of written discourses." John Kerr (1782–1842), whose extemporaneous sermons "were often protracted to three hours' length," relied upon "the extemporaneous resources of his mind, and the momentary inspiration of the pulpit."[94] Again, such a sampling only hints at the pervasive use of semi-extemporaneous techniques among Baptist preachers.[95]

In this vast range of sermon styles and practices, an effective and highly individualized balance between preparation and inspiration, rhetorical patterns and formulaic variations, seemed to attract the greatest admiration among preachers themselves. And audience members, anticipating the inspired delivery of gospel messages, responded to the immediacy of the semi-extemporaneous presentations with zeal and approbation. Thus, systematic and devoted preparation (preferably hidden from the audience's view and awareness) made the speaker an effective and admired instrument in God's hands. Such groundwork allowed the Spirit to draw upon the treasures in the preacher's mind and to inspire the delivery of God's word in manifestations of power that seemed to extend well beyond the preacher's humble talents and ability.

With such divine aid (and not a little showmanship), the words of even an unlettered and "illiterate" preacher could move an audience to repentance and conversion more effectively than the stale sermons of university-trained ministers who simply read their sermons from a prepared text. Wherever he turned, from Congregationalists to Methodists, from Presbyterians to Baptists, the young Joseph Smith was surrounded by these creative, God-driven performances. And the methods of preaching that occurred in his environments— with private preparation and inspired delivery—would forever mark his method of narrative production and oratorical style.

Print Culture, Performance, and the Semi-Homogenization of Style

The similarity of semi-extemporaneous preaching techniques shared among preachers of the various evangelical denominations in the late eighteenth and early nineteenth centuries was no coincidence. Even though each tradition would develop distinctive characteristics in their styles of *delivery*, such as the Baptist "whine" or the Methodist "groan," and though they would also focus on topics and scriptures most relevant to the beliefs of their particular sects, the underlying *techniques* involved in semi-extemporaneous composition remained relatively consistent across revivalist traditions.[96] These similarities arose from multiple factors.

All of these evangelical denominations in America, for example, traced various aspects of their performance techniques back to the methods embraced by itinerant preachers during the First Great Awakening. Joint revivals involving preachers from multiple denominations, such as the "joint revival" that Smith attended involving "the Baptists, Methodists and Presbyterians," were also common during the Second Great Awakening and further contributed to the cross-pollination of ideas and techniques shared among preachers.[97] And in a related dynamic, much like George Whitefield in the previous generation, popular orators in the late eighteenth and early nineteenth centuries, such as Charles Grandison Finney, Lorenzo Dow, Harriett Livermore, Dwight L. Moody, and Charles Spurgeon, drew audiences from all religious backgrounds, thereby influencing a rising generation of preachers from multiple denominations who sought to imitate and extend their success.

Among the primary factors contributing to the similarities of semi-extemporaneous sermons across denominations, the unprecedented availability of pamphlets, books, and instructional manuals on pulpit eloquence also exerted tremendous influence. Such texts complemented the formal and informal training that occurred within the sermon cultures of each denomination, providing both teachers and learners with comprehensive programs that started with the basics of sermon composition and delivery, and then moved toward more advanced techniques. For a young aspiring preacher in the early nineteenth century, a short walk to the nearest bookstore or printing office, along with any number of public, private, circulating, or Sunday school libraries, would be all that one needed to find hundreds of printed sermons and dozens of works on the techniques and styles of effective preaching.

Groundwork

Between the Upper Connecticut River Valley and the Burned-Over District of Western New York, Smith grew up in regions of the country where the semi-extemporaneous delivery of sermons was the most pervasive and influential method of pulpit performance. Given his repeated exposure to this style of composition and delivery in his immediate environments, Smith's technique of laying down heads to form skeletal outlines for both his 1832 history and the opening of his 1843 sermon on the Prodigal Son reflects his historical circumstances, arising as a natural manifestation of the same fundamental methods used by Baptist, Congregationalist, Methodist, and Presbyterian preachers that he witnessed in his spiritual quest for gospel truths. Moreover, as a neophyte Methodist exhorter, Smith's knowledge of this technique would certainly have been informed by the intense culture of self-improvement found among aspiring Methodist preachers, who treasured up the Word of God by regularly studying the scriptures, taking systematic notes, constructing personal concordances, referencing the commentaries and works of authorities, reading and imitating sermons, memorizing scriptures, composing and memorizing sermon skeletons, and applying their skills in semi-extemporaneous exhortations.

The creative tension between study and preparation on the one hand, and inspired exposition on the other, would have been evident before Smith in Methodist class meetings, church attendance, and participation at revivals. Though the historical records addressing Smith's habits of reading, study, meditation, and exhortation are spare and contested for his pre–Book of Mormon years, Smith's works nevertheless clearly demonstrate his familiarity with the techniques and practices of contemporary sermon composition and delivery. Such skills in Smith's repertoire of oral composition and performance should come as no surprise: for an aspiring exhorter and preacher in the sermon culture of early nineteenth-century America, exposure to the method of laying down heads as a fundamental organizing principle and a compositional strategy would have been inescapable.

CHAPTER FOUR

The King Follett Sermon

On Sunday, 7 April 1844, less than three months before his murder at the hands of an angry mob at Carthage Jail in Illinois, Joseph Smith delivered one of his most profound and influential discourses, the King Follett funeral sermon. King Follett (1788–1844), an early member of the Mormon movement, had recently died from injuries sustained during the construction of a well; and his family, distressed by his untimely demise and in search of consolation, asked Smith to speak on the subject of death and the loss of loved ones. Smith responded with an oration that not only provided comfort to the family but also elevated the minds of his auditors to a new understanding of the human soul's potential. The occasion for Smith's sermon was a church-wide five-day conference held in Nauvoo, Illinois, where thousands had gathered together to commune with one another and to receive counsel and instructions from their religious leaders. Delivered to an audience estimated at somewhere between eight thousand and twenty thousand observers, the sermon lasted approximately two hours and fifteen minutes, and the entire recorded discourse (at least what the reporters were able to document) amounted to approximately 6,800 words.[1] No other sermon by Smith received such detailed recording and treatment. Moreover, Smith adopted strategies of oral composition and delivery both similar to, and different from, his 1832 history and the opening of his 1843 sermon on the Prodigal Son. The King Follett sermon thus offers additional insights into Smith's personal style of sermon composition and methods of oral performance.

Reduced to its essence, Smith's sermon centered on the potential progress of the human soul in eternity, and how an awareness of that potential could provide comfort to those who were mourning. According to Smith, if people would cast their minds back to the beginning of time in order to understand the first principles and doctrines of the gospel, they could discover the origin and nature of God and their relationship with Him. People would understand that God the Father was once a man, like themselves: "God Himself who sits enthroned in yonder heavens is a Man like unto one of yourselves—that is the great secret!" Moreover, sometime in the distant past, God "*once* dwelled on an earth the same as Jesus Christ himself did in the flesh *and like us*," the same as all other mortal human beings. In His pre-deified state, God had "power in

Himself" that gave Him the ability "to lay down His body and take it up again." The stages of mortal life, death, and resurrection thus formed essential steps in a grand pattern of eternal progression, whereby Jesus Christ was also able "to lay down my [Christ's] life as my Father laid down His body that I might take it up again," and whereby all righteous human beings could do the same: "though *they lay down this body and* all earthly tabernacles shall be dissolved, that their very being shall rise in immortal glory."[2] And for righteous human beings, the story would not end with the resurrection.

Smith informed his audience that the souls of righteous men would also have the potential to become "heirs of God and joint-heirs with Jesus Christ," whereby they would "inherit *and enjoy* the same glory, powers, and exaltation [as God and Christ] until you ascend a throne of eternal power *and arrive at the station of a God*, the same as those who have gone before."[3] Smith admonished his attentive audience, proclaiming, "You have got to learn how to make yourselves Gods in order to save yourselves and be kings and priests to God, the same as all Gods have done—by going from a small capacity to a great capacity, from a small degree to another, from grace to grace, until the resurrection *of the dead*, from exaltation to exaltation—till you are able to sit in everlasting burnings and everlasting power and glory as those who have gone before, sit enthroned."[4] Thus, Smith's message offered considerable consolation: not only would mourners have the opportunity to reunite with loved ones in the eternities, they might also continue to grow, learn, and progress in the afterlife, until they attained the lofty heights and eminent status of eternal godhood.

Logistics

However controversial the theological content of the discourse, Smith's King Follett funeral sermon offers an unparalleled opportunity to analyze his personal method of composition and delivery within the context of nineteenth-century sermon culture. Such performances involve any number of analytical factors, as we can examine not only the recorded text of the sermon but also the circumstances surrounding the performance. The speaker's level of experience, the size and responsiveness of the audience, the amount (or lack) of speaker preparation, the location and space of the performance (indoors, outdoors, weather conditions), among many other possible influences, all exert shaping forces on oral performances. In terms of analyzing Smith's sermon, a brief look at some of the key factors surrounding his performance offers additional insights into Smith's production of this work—insights that reveal important characteristics of Smith's habits of oral creativity. These issues include Smith's description of his own performance, his amount of forethought and preparation on the subject, and the nature and size of his audience.

Smith's Method

In a fortuitous move for modern researchers, Smith conveniently described his method of delivery in the introduction of his discourse. Adopting language commonly used to describe semi-extemporaneous orations, Smith announced that he would address the topic by combining (1) his own thoughts on the subject with (2) the immediate spiritual promptings of the Holy Ghost: "I feel disposed to speak on the subject in general and offer you *my ideas* as far as I have ability and as far as I will be *inspired by the Holy Spirit*."[5] Within this framework, Smith approached the sermon with his own premeditated ideas, while simultaneously allowing for spontaneous elaborations and digressions, dictated according to the spiritual impulses of the moment.

Further evidence of Smith's forethought on the issues that he addressed comes from several sources. In the opening of the sermon, for example, Smith mentioned that he would be commenting "on the subject which was contemplated in the fore-part of the conference," revealing how, at least in some aspects, his sermon was not wholly improvised but contained a response to earlier pronouncements on the same subject.[6] More importantly, the fundamental message of the sermon was not new to Smith, though likely new to many members of his audience. "The sermon was almost entirely a summary and expansion of a number of Smith's sermons over the previous four years," observes William V. Smith, "but those sermons were largely unpublished and therefore . . . unknown."[7] Indeed, as early as 1832, as Van Hale has demonstrated, Smith had already started to reveal such key concepts as the potential of the human soul to attain deification in eternity (1832), the existence of a hierarchy of gods in the heavens (ca. 1839), and the idea that God was once a mortal man (1841).[8] Smith's thoughts on those topics had been fermenting over a long period of time, rather than emerging in a spontaneous and unpremeditated effort.

Smith's Audience

Another significant circumstance involved the nature and composition of Smith's audience. Apart from a sizeable contingent of Nauvoo residents, "many spectators were present from Quincy, Alton, Warsaw, Fort Madison, and other towns."[9] And though the audience was mainly composed of faithful members of the sect, a number of disenchanted and antagonistic observers stood in the crowd, ranging from those wavering in the faith to dissenters, non-Mormon critics, and outright apostates. All was not well in Zion. In fact, as historian Donald Q. Cannon observes, "in the weeks immediately preceding April conference, a conspiracy developed against the Prophet. Those involved in the intrigue claimed that Joseph Smith was a fallen prophet, citing as evidence the practice of polygamy, the monopolistic economic policies of the Church, and the increase in his personal power."[10] Smith was highly conscious of the mixed nature of his audience, and his sermon, though it never directly confronted any of his detractors by name, reflected his awareness of the current challenges in the nascent sect and the tensions surrounding his leadership. Even though the discourse was a funeral sermon aimed at consoling the bereaved members of the Follett family, Smith nevertheless made frequent and apparently extemporaneous digressions throughout the speech to assert his authority as a prophet and to criticize doubters and apostates of the church. These tangential and likely improvised excursions further suggest that Smith was not preaching from a fixed, prewritten text but was rather responding directly to the people in the crowd and to his perceptions of their concerns and reactions.

Smith's Notetakers and Sermon Culture

Another important factor involves the detail of the notes taken by recorders who witnessed the performance. Unlike most of Smith's sermons, which observers usually only documented with brief summaries and personal responses, the King Follett discourse benefited from four different recorders, who, with varying degrees of precision, detailed Smith's oration. The notes by Thomas Bullock, William Clayton, and Willard Richards were taken during Smith's speech. The original notes by Wilford Woodruff, however, are missing, though he apparently used them to write a clean copy of the sermon in his journal at a later time (thus making his account the result of a combination of memorial reconstruction and references to notes).[11] In addition, Bullock and Clayton attempted to record the sermon word-for-word (a comparison of the notes, however, indicates that neither of them was successful at a verbatim account), while Richards merely recorded a sketch outline of the speech.

Yet, in spite of the different note-taking habits of each recorder, the four accounts, as Stan Larson observes, "have no irreconcilable parts—no contradictory statements" and contain "a high degree of agreement and harmony."[12] As a result, the King Follett discourse provides the best-known and most detailed account of Smith's semi-extemporaneous style of sermon delivery. "Of all the speeches given by Joseph Smith," Larson further observes, "this one has the greatest contemporary manuscript support, which certainly strengthens claims of its reliability and authenticity."[13] The degree of corroboration among the multiple accounts therefore provides important documentation that confirms the shape and progress of the sermon, complete with digressions and rhetorical strategies.

King Follett Sermon Structure

Unlike his 1832 history and the opening of his 1843 sermon on the Prodigal Son, Smith did not explicitly lay down the heads of the King Follett sermon to his audience. Moreover, the frequency of digressions from his main topic tends to diffuse the focus on the central subject matter (the potential deification of the human soul) and to obscure the basic sermon format and mental outline that he adopted for the oration. Nonetheless, these excursions provide important insights into Smith's spontaneous train of thought in the moment of performance. Such tangents from the main subject include, among a number of brief asides, an opening invocation for prayers of support, a digression on religious freedom, diatribes against apostates, (semi)-irrelevant proofs, a short narrative on the origin of the devil, and a doctrinal tangent about the state of children in the resurrection.

In spite of such departures from the central topic, however, Smith would consistently (or eventually) return to his main subject throughout the course of the sermon, indicating that Smith had, on some level, a mental outline of the primary issues that contained the central points of his discourse. When commenting on Smith's overall approach to sermons, Calvin Smith similarly observed this method, arguing, "At best, he [Joseph] seemed to have in mind only a mental checklist of topics he intended to cover. However, he always felt free to revise even that to vent ideas which came to him while delivering his addresses."[14] Joseph's preparations, however, reached beyond a mental checklist of ideas to include the structural schematics of a basic and popular preaching format.

Looking beyond the extraneous detours and focusing on the core structure of Smith's King Follett sermon, we find a conventional four-part framework: (1) a subject, or the "text"; (2) a lengthy introduction with preliminary principles and a contextualizing preamble; (3) points of doctrine with proofs, confirmations, reasons, and applications; and (4) a conclusion with further applications and a short exhortation. This collection and sequence of elements in the over-all pattern of the sermon indicate that Smith was following, however loosely, a traditional "doctrine, reasons, and uses" format (that is, the pattern for "plain style" sermons), often depicted as either a three-part or four-part structure, and described by William Perkins as "THE ORDER AND SUMME of the sacred and only methode *of Preaching*," and by John Wilkins and Richard Bernard as simply "*Doctrine and Use*."[15] The descriptions of this method appeared in a variety of ways, with an assortment of terms, labels, and categories. Yet, differing terminology aside, they all described the same set of basic structural elements. Moreover, the main headings of this format could contain a seemingly countless number of subdivisions, often coinciding with the central purpose of each sermon, which in general terms might be categorized as explanatory, polemical, morally instructive, or any number of specific applications (including some mixture of them all). Contextualizing Smith's King Follett funeral oration, however, requires a closer look at this traditional pattern and the different ways in which preachers applied it.

In general, the basic four-part sermon pattern consisted of a *text*, which was usually but not exclusively a passage of scripture. Others "texts" might appear as a proposition, a doctrine or principle of the gospel, a theological claim or argument, or simply the main subject of the discourse. Next, the sermon contained an *introduction*, which usually served as an expository preamble, offering important contextual information for the audience to understand the purpose of the sermon and the preacher's line of reasoning. Introductions might include such additional elements as invocations, various appeals to an audience for their support and prayers, and an optional announcement of the main heads of the discourse (explicitly laying down heads). Next came what might be best described as the *doctrines and proofs* section, which involved any number of categories and strategies of rhetorical invention that served to elaborate and to expound upon the topic. Some of the most common elements and descriptions of this section included proofs, arguments, inferences, connections, confirmations, points of doctrine, and reasons.

Finally, the sermon ended with a *conclusion*, which, apart from reiterating and reinforcing the central message, contained "applications" or "uses," as well as possible "exhortations" and summaries. The applications offered specific instructions to the audience on how to apply the message of the sermon to their daily lives. These instructions frequently appeared in the form of specific exhortations related to the main subject, though generic exhortations—general admonitions that could be appended to virtually any sermon—were also common. It is important to note that these categories—particularly doctrines, proofs, applications, and exhortations—were not necessarily fixed into a rigid template but could appear anywhere throughout the sermon, depending on the personal preferences of the minister.

One preacher, for example, might deliver all the "applications" at the end of his sermon, while another might propose individual applications after every "proof" or "confirmation" at each stage throughout the course of the oration. Indeed, such variations had characterized New England preaching styles from the colonial period. As Phyllis Jones and Nicholas Jones observe, the doctrine and use pattern "was not mechanically predictable," and it was common "for a large unit of preaching to deviate from the standard four-part presentation or for the parts to be mingled."[16] These expressions of personal preference continued well into the nineteenth century, with countless individualized variations. In the King Follett funeral sermon, for instance, Smith regularly moves back and forth between categories in this pattern—that is, stating principles, offering proofs, and occasionally adding applications, and then repeating the pattern—prior to arriving at his conclusions.

Because of the simple but highly utilitarian nature of the three- and four-part sermon patterns, they enjoyed immense popularity and dominated the sermon styles in English-speaking pulpits. Whether delivering a sermon within the walls of a church or in the open fields of a camp meeting, preachers of every stripe and denomination, from dissenters to established clergy, relied on this tradition and regularly used these centuries-old patterns to frame their discourses. Perkins, one of the earliest and most popular writers to explain and advocate this approach, summarized the method with the following oft-quoted steps:

1. To read the Text distinctly out of the Canonicall Scriptures.
2. To give the sense and understanding of it being read, by the Scripture it selfe.
3. To collect a few and profitable points of doctrine out of the naturall sense.
4. To applie (if he have the gift) the doctrines rightly collected to the life and manners of men, in a simple and plaine speech.[17]

Later, Wilkins provided his own version of this pattern, dropping the self-evident category of the "text" and describing the method as consisting of three parts: "*Explication. Confirmation. Application.*"[18] Even ministers trained in five- and six-part classical rhetorical models (e.g., Introduction, Statement, Division, Narration, Argument, and Conclusion) might nevertheless simplify their actual sermons into this "doctrine and use" format.[19] Among itinerant preachers with no formal training and limited education, the three- and four-part structure streamlined the classical models into a simple format that could be easily and readily adopted into their sermons. Apropos to Smith and his training as a Methodist exhorter, for example, "the American [Methodist] itinerants were careful to adopt the three-part form—preamble, points of doctrine, and application—favored by Wesley."[20] This simplified format provided preachers with a general structure to organize their orations, while simultaneously providing a high degree of flexibility that allowed for extemporaneous excursions throughout the course of a sermon.

Comparing Smith's Compositions

The similarities and differences among Smith's 1844 King Follett sermon, his 1832 history, and the opening of his 1843 Prodigal Son discourse also offer an opportunity to consider some additional issues related to Smith's semi-extemporaneous production and common strategies of sermon composition. For example, Smith's introduction for the King Follett sermon suggests that he had some form of an outline in mind prior to delivery. "Before I enter fully into the investigation of the subject that is lying before us," Smith announced, "I wish to pave the way, make a few preliminaries, and bring *up* the subject from the beginning in order that you may understand the subject when I come to it."[21] Thus, Smith did not approach the pulpit unprepared, trusting exclusively in the promptings of the Spirit to guide him. Rather, Smith followed a common strategy for "explanatory" sermons by providing a simple introduction before moving into more advanced issues. "That which is simplest and plainest ought generally to be begun with," remarked George Campbell in his lectures on pulpit eloquence, "and from this we ought to advance to that which is less obvious and more complex."[22] As the text of the sermon indicates, Smith had previously arranged his subject matter into such a sequence so as to teach a few introductory principles first, before launching directly into the more complicated doctrines in the main body of his discourse.

In these opening stages, Smith's King Follett sermon falls within the same pattern as his 1832 history and 1843 Prodigal Son sermon: he studied and premeditated on the topics he wanted to share, followed by the division and arrangement of his central ideas into a sketch outline to guide his performance. In the next stage, however, Smith chose to follow a "concealed" method for the Follett sermon. Rather than explicitly announcing the main heads of his sermon to his audience, providing the listeners with an outline that tracked the trajectory of his oration, Smith simply progressed from one topic to another at his own pace and in his own time.

As a semi-extemporaneous technique, this method of "concealing" the outline offered the speaker great flexibility. Without providing the audience with a structured list of enumerated heads, Smith could adhere to, or depart from, any preliminary outline that he had prepared, thereby allowing him greater freedom to extemporize in the moment of performance. In other words, Smith did not explicitly "lay down heads" to his audience in the Follett sermon, even though some form of an unspoken outline continued to guide the shape of his oration. This style of performance calls our attention to three additional issues: first, the different meanings of the phrase "laying down heads" in the context of composition and delivery; second, the use of "concealed" heads or a "concealed" method; and third, the relationship between laying down heads and memorization, both for the speaker and the audience.

Laying Down Heads during Composition

When he provided his readers and his audience with explicit preliminary outlines in his 1832 history and 1843 Prodigal Son sermon, Smith was using one form of "laying down heads"—specifically, the open announcement of the order and sequence of forthcoming material. But the concept of laying down heads did not exclusively refer to the explicit announcement of an address's structure to an audience. Instead, laying down heads had two primary meanings, or, rather, two distinct but related applications: one described *the act of announcing* the primary divisions of a sermon to an audience, but the other merely described *the process of composing* an outline for a sermon during prior preparations (regardless of whether or not the outline would be expressly stated to an audience). Thus, Smith's premeditated arrangement of a core outline for the King Follett sermon, though largely unspoken during delivery, reveals another form of "laying down heads" that Smith employed during his preparations and meditation. Understanding this process helps to situate Smith's methods within his contemporary sermon culture.

When annotating the Reverend Jean Claude's discussion on the division of a text into its component parts in *An Essay on the Composition of a Sermon* (1782), editor and dissenting Baptist preacher Robert Robinson (1735–90) stressed the point that preachers divided their sermons during preparatory study (i.e., privately laying down heads to create a skeletal outline), as well as announcing the divisions, or laying down the heads, during the actual delivery of the oration: "We should distinguish between the *composition* of a sermon in private, and the *delivery* of it in public. The composing, or the putting together of a sermon, implies a previous distinction of parts [i.e., laying down the main heads during preparatory composition]."[23] The examples in the previous chapter of semi-extemporaneous methods contain several references to the creation of sermon skeletons during private study and meditation, but a closer look at the process provides greater insight into this prevalent approach to composition.

In his autobiography, Congregationalist and Harvard College–trained minister John Barnard (1714–66) described this common (and commonsensical) approach to preparation, which reveals a typical process of sermon construction. After choosing a subject and a complementary scripture for his sermon, Barnard studied the Bible and various books on the topic, and then considered the main points he wanted to share: "Sometimes, not always, I penned the heads of the discourse. Then I took the first head, and thought over what appeared to me most proper to confirm and illustrate it, laying it up in my mind; so I went through the several heads; and when I had thus gone over the whole, in its several parts, then I went over all in my meditation."[24] After preparing a detailed outline of his sermon and committing the framework to memory, Barnard took his notes to the pulpit for easy reference during delivery, though he claimed that he rarely referred to them.

As Barnard's reflections indicate, laying down heads referred to the process of composition, the initial stage of choosing a subject and identifying the main topics for discussion (the "heads" or "divisions"), along with arranging the heads into a skeletal outline of the oration. Barnard does not indicate, however, if he explicitly announced the heads during his sermons. He might have stated them openly to his audience, or he might have kept silent about them and merely used them as a personal guide for his oration. In the latter case, Barnard would have been making use of "concealed" heads.

Concealed Heads

"Concealed" heads refer to divisions of an oration—certain main topics or points—that the preacher does *not* explicitly announce to the audience.[25] As Charles Simeon advised in his *Helps to Composition: Or, Six Hundred Skeletons of Sermons* (1801 London; first American edition, 1810–11), "the *divisions may be either mentioned or concealed, as the writer shall choose.*"[26] In other words, a preacher might "lay down heads" during the composition of a sermon, but not "lay down heads" during the actual delivery of it from the pulpit. Preachers had any number of reasons to use concealed heads, such as a desire to avoid sounding overly pedantic and programmatic, or to keep an audience in suspense by not revealing the final outcome of the sermon from the outset of the oration.[27]

For instance, Hugh Blair describes this approach as "a concealed method," which he recommends for occasions "when the Discourse, perhaps, is to be short, or only one point is to be treated of; or when the Speaker does not chuse to warn his hearers of the method he is to follow, or of the conclusion to which he seeks to bring them."[28] John Quincy Adams, when discussing the explicit and concealed methods of laying down heads ("partitions"), provided a list of six common objections against the announcement of formal divisions, including such issues as "the speaker is liable to forget some of the points, which he has laid down"; "it gives an air of stiffness and premeditation to the discourse"; "it necessarily and invariably discloses the whole design of the speaker, when his object often requires that he should bring his audience to conclusions unawares even to themselves"; and "it counteracts and interferes with all powerful appeals to the passions."[29] The last issue, in particular, could be deadly for evangelical preachers relying on "warm" exhortations and passionate deliveries to move their audiences. Revealing the affective climax of a sermon in the opening introduction, long before the actual climax occurred, risked the appearance of emotional manipulation and artificial theatrics.

In other words, the explicit announcement of the main heads of a sermon immediately alerted the audience that the discourse was premeditated and calculated, rather than a spontaneous eruption of words guided by the immediate influence of the Holy Spirit. "As nothing can be more opposed to emotion than calculations," Adams further advises, "so a minute and scrupulous dissection of parts [explicitly laying down heads to an audience] is utterly irreconcilable with those great, sudden, unexpected touches, which extort the suffrage of the hearer from his feelings."[30] The use of concealed heads thus offered semi-extemporaneous preachers a way to study and prepare the overall structure of their sermons in advance, while keeping the eventual performances open to the inspiration of the moment. They could meditate on a topic or text, select main points for discussion, arrange them into a skeletal outline as a guide for performance, and yet allow for a great deal of freedom to extemporize in the moment of speaking.

This flexibility could result in situations in which audience members might perceive the preacher to be speaking purely extempore, even though he or she might actually be following a well-prepared mental outline. Moreover, semi-extemporaneous preachers regularly delivered sermons that fluctuated between following a premeditated outline and taking extempore excursions as a standard mode of performance, so that even their colleagues might not be able to differentiate between prepared and improvised material. "Whether he sometimes preached memoriter [memorized text], or always trusted to the inspiration of the moment for his language," observed the Reverend Dr. Andrews of the sermons by Presbyterian minister James Grier, "I have never been able to ascertain."[31] Identifying preachers regularly using a "concealed method" or "concealed heads" could be difficult and elusive. But in a sermon culture that valorized speaking by the guidance of the Holy Ghost, that ambiguity was, of course, precisely the point.

Moreover, in the late eighteenth and early nineteenth centuries the historical trajectory, in the main, reveals a movement toward concealed heads and concealed methods in order to emphasize the presence of divine inspiration in sermons. This shift, it should be noted, did not come from preachers alone. The demands and expectations of audiences spurred the transition along. For instance, in a May 1812 letter to a colleague, Baptist preacher David Rathbone (1763–1823?), writing from Scipio, New York (approximately fifty miles east of the Smith homestead in Manchester), described the expectations that Baptist congregants had of their ministers: "*The Baptists generally in this Western Country . . . are of the opinion, that Ministers should take no thought how, or what they should speak . . . for it is not they that speak, but the Spirit which speaketh in them*."[32] For many preachers, learning how to perform their sermons with the appearance of inspired and unpremeditated delivery became a central focus of training and development, regardless of their actual preparations in private. Concealing one's methods of study and preparation, as well as the silent but pervasive structures of delivery, became increasingly popular among groups that valorized performances driven by the Holy Spirit. This conscious transition in sermon culture toward a concealed method proves especially relevant when considering Smith's thoughts concerning the Book of Mormon and the context in which he made his preparations to perform its text.

Memory and Oral Milestones

The prevalence of laying down heads resulted from factors that went beyond a simple matter of preachers embracing longstanding traditions within their sermon cultures—indeed, the method was not a style without specific functions. Advocates of this approach were quick to point out the pedagogical advantages of the technique. Blair, in one of the most comprehensive defenses of laying down heads, argued that the method made sermons "more clear, more easily apprehended, and, of course, more instructive to the bulk of hearers, which is always the main object to be kept in view." Adopting the metaphor of taking a journey, Blair continued, "The heads of a Sermon are great assistances to the memory, and recollection of the hearer. They serve also to fix his attention. They enable him more easily to keep pace with the progress of the Discourse; they give him pauses and resting places, where he can reflect on what has been said, and look forward to what is to follow."[33] Blair borrowed his journey metaphor from Quintilian, the famous Roman rhetorician, who argued, "The conclusion of each head is a relief to the hearers: just as, upon a journey, the mile-stones, which are set up on the road, serve to diminish the traveller's fatigue."[34] The method of laying down explicit heads to the audience thus provided the listeners with an oral roadmap to track the progress of the sermon, where the chief heads acted as oral guideposts, alerting the audience to the main topics and themes of the sermon, along with the order and sequence of ideas.

The method of laying down heads thus assisted the memory, both for the listeners as well as the speaker. As Wilkins had long ago argued, this method could "be a great advantage" to "Our Selves" and to "Our Hearers," as a pedagogical tool and for the development of the memory. For the audience, the active memorization of the heads would instill the message of the sermon in their hearts and minds. People listening to a sermon, argued Wilkins, "may understand and retain a Sermon with greater ease and profit, when they are before-hand acquainted with the general heads of matter that are discoursed of." And for preachers, Wilkins urged the method of laying down heads, because it would assist them with "*Invention* and *Memory*," or the ability to discover systematically any number of arguments and topics related to the issue at hand, as well as the ability to "more easily *retain them*" in the mind. And in terms of performance, the speaker's memorization of the main heads within "such a regular frame, wherein every part may have its due place and dependence," had the obvious advantage of embedding the structure of the sermon in the preacher's thoughts, providing habitual reference points and delivery patterns to guide the course of the oration.[35] Whether a minister announced the heads of his sermon to the audience, or merely kept the heads "concealed" to himself, the skeletal outline thus furnished the preacher with a blueprint for performance.

The heads of a sermon, all arranged within a skeletal outline, therefore acted as *mnemonic cues* for the preacher to anchor his discourse. "Every one who speaks," advised Blair, "will find it of the greatest advantage to himself to have previously arranged his thoughts, and classed under proper heads, in his own mind, what he is to deliver. This will assist his memory, and carry him through his discourse, without that confusion to which one is every moment subject, who has fixed no distinct plan of what he is to say."[36] For the semi-extemporaneous speaker, who relied on the impulses of the moment to depart onto excursions from premeditated thoughts, the memorized outline functioned as an indispensable central guidepost for the oration.

For instance, in *Hints on Extemporaneous Preaching* (1824), Henry Ware admonished that, "the whole subject [of the sermon], with the order and connexion of all its parts, and the entire train of thought, [should] be made thoroughly familiar by previous meditation." Adopting the familiar journey metaphor, Ware continued, "There must be no uncertainty, when he rises to speak, as to what he is going to say; no mist or darkness over the land he is about to travel; but conscious of his acquaintance with the ground, he must step forward confidently, not doubting that he shall find the passes of its mountains, and thread the intricacies of its forests, by the paths which he has already trodden [i.e., previously studied material]."[37] Much like Quintilian's milestones for travelers along a road, the heads of a sermon became milestones in the preacher's memory to keep the sermon on track.

The frequency and length of a semi-extemporaneous preacher's excursions would, of course, differ from one orator to another. In his personal copy of Ware's *Hints on Extemporaneous Preaching*, for example, Presbyterian James Patriot Wilson (1769–1830) wrote, "I have preached twenty years, and have never written a full sermon in my life, and never read one word of a sermon from the pulpit, nor opened a note, nor committed [memorized] a sentence, and have *rarely wandered five minutes at a time from my mental arrangement previously made*."[38] Wilson's desire to stick closely to his mental sermon skeleton reflected one end of a spectrum of extemporaneous departures from a premeditated plan. At the other end, preachers regularly used skeletons as loose guides, making frequent and lengthy departures whenever the impulses hit them.

In his biography of Methodist preacher and former president of Dickson College John Price Durbin (1800–76), the Reverend John A. Roche described Durbin's "system" of preparation and performance: "Early in the week, we have seen, he digested his subject and had his sketch [short notes outline] in readiness for the pulpit. When he began to speak the current of his language flowed on in the channel of previous thought, and words were extemporized as they were wanted. If on some occasions a text, a theme, a division came to him as by inspiration, then every thing was extemporized. Theme, thoughts, terms, sentences, were seized."[39] However much or little a semi-extemporaneous preacher might adhere to a sermon skeleton, the practice of laying down heads into a written or mentally arranged skeleton emerged as a common denominator in the technique.

The memorized sermon skeleton thereby acted as a safety net. With a "well digested" sermon outline in mind, speakers could have the assurance that anytime they felt inspired to deviate from their initial plan—by introducing new scriptural proofs, topics, arguments, examples, elaborations, applications, or any other impromptu addition—they could always find their way back to the central focus and outline of their oration. Expounding on the writings of Cicero and the Archbishop of Cambray, the Anglican Reverend James Glazebrook (1744–1803), in his work *The Practice of What Is Called Extempore Preaching Recommended* (1794), added, "that though all the parts of a discourse should be ranged [arranged] exactly in the memory, &c. yet that we are so to use this preparation, as to be ready off hand, to add whatever may be occasionally suggested, from a view of the audience, or unexpected accidents."[40] Moreover, the regular use of mental outlines ingrained formulaic templates of sermon patterns that the preacher could evoke and utilize in a perfunctory or fluent manner, with little or no conscious effort.

Thus, even when a speaker might momentarily forget an idea or the trajectory of a sermon, the habits developed from prior experience could save the performance. "It is not denied that extemporaneous speakers sometimes lose the train of thought. . . . But the extemporaneous speaker has an alertness and fruitfulness of mind that greatly lessen the risk of utter failure," observed Roche. "When the train of his thought is broken the mental locomotion continues, and there is some idea to carry him on till the *train returns*, and then he accepts it, unless he thinks his diversion was for a good end. The mind puts on strength and shows its treasures."[41] These "treasures," of course, refer to the practice of regular study and meditation to treasure up the word of God in preparation for inspired extemporaneous performances.

Ware made a similar observation in his work on extemporaneous speaking, noting how the habitual practices of speakers could save them from the embarrassment of having their minds go blank in front of a crowd. The habits, in fact, could be so automatic that speakers might feel as though everything they said had come directly from the inspiration of the Holy Spirit, without any conscious effort on their part. "Many men have thus continued speaking in the midst of an embarrassment of mind which rendered them almost unconscious of what they were saying, and incapable of giving an account of it afterward," observed Ware, "while yet the unguided, self-moving intellect wrought so well, that the speech was not esteemed unwholesome or defective by the hearers. The experience of this fact has doubtless helped many to believe that they spoke from inspiration."[42] Ware's observation alerts us to a critical issue: habituated patterns and repeated practice could result in performances that appeared—*even to the speaker*—to materialize from the pure inspiration of the Holy Spirit, resulting in coauthored performances that seemed to originate from both the mind of the speaker and the divine influence of God.

Guideposts and Resumptive Repetition

Smith's use of a mental outline to anchor the central ideas of the King Follett discourse reveals additional information about his habits of oral composition, specifically in terms of his style of repetition. His preamble to the discourse offers an opportunity to observe these characteristics in detail. After introducing the subject and appealing to his audience for their prayers and faith to support him in his sermon, Smith initiated a preamble "to pave the way" with "a few preliminaries" to contextualize his topic. By tracking Smith's repetitions through this preamble, we can identify the central concepts that anchored this opening portion of his sermon. These mental (and oral) guideposts, which allowed Smith the freedom to extemporize, centered on Smith's pedagogical strategy to lead his audience "back to the beginning of creation" in order to "understand something of God Himself in the beginning."[43] When removing the material extraneous to the core outline for this section, but leaving the primary heads that form the central anchors to the passage, we can observe Smith's insistent return to the concept of understanding God's character and nature by returning to the beginning of time and the creation of the world (the words in *italics* do not indicate special emphasis but rather words unique to the auditor notes of Wilford Woodruff):[44]

> *King Follett Discourse, Introduction*
>
> [MAIN CONCEPT]: ". . . bring *up* the subject from the beginning in order that you may understand the subject when I come to it."
> [30-word tangent on his intentions]
> [REPEAT CONCEPT]: "In the first place I wish to go back to the beginning of creation . . . For us to take up beginning at the creation it is necessary *for us* to understand something of God Himself in the beginning."
> [191-word tangent on correct knowledge]

[REPEAT CONCEPT]: "I want to go back, *then*, to the beginning *that you may understand* . . . . What kind of a being is God? Ask yourselves! I again repeat the question: What kind of a being is God? [81-word tangent on the importance of knowing God]

[REPEAT CONCEPT]: "My first object is to *go back and* find out the character of the only wise and true God *and what kind of a being He is.*" [441-word tangent on religious freedom]

[REPEAT CONCEPT]: "What kind of a being was God in the beginning, before the world was? *I will go back to the beginning to show you.*"[45]

Smith's dynamic style of preaching, switching between his adherence to a central guiding concept in his mental outline and several tangential excursions (likely improvised), demonstrates a common feature of semi-extemporaneous performance.

When following their short notes or premeditated "skeletons," semi-extemporaneous preachers, using the main heads of their outlines as guideposts, could fall into a specific pattern of delivery: they might state the main head of an outline, elaborate on the head or diverge onto a tangent, and then return to the main head as a way of reconnecting to their outline and keeping their sermon on track. This form of repetition can result in a pattern, which, among scholars studying biblical editorial practices and the influence of orality in biblical texts, is known as "resumptive repetition."[46] Brant Gardner offers a helpful observation on this relationship between resumptive repetition and oral performance, describing how such repetitions are "a technique well suited to oral presentations: the original line of thought being refreshed by the repetition of words that were used prior to the aside."[47] Gardner's focus rests on the comparison of compositional techniques among Old Testament redactors with the ancient prophet named Mormon in the Book of Mormon narrative, but the observations equally apply to Smith's oral compositions, as well as to the semi-extemporaneous sermons delivered by his contemporaries.

Gardner further observes, "As the Old Testament is known to have been a written document from a primarily oral culture, it suggests that this is a structural technique developed in oral presentations to make it easier for a listener to return from the aside to the original thread."[48] Thus, the practices of semi-extemporaneous preachers in Smith's cultural milieu confirm Gardner's theory about the connection between resumptive repetition and oral performance, a relationship that further demonstrates the presence of orally derived techniques appearing in literary texts, revealing the permeable boundaries between oral and written works.

Amplification and Mnemonic Cues

In the interplay between premeditated outlines and extemporaneous expressions of core concepts and digressions, Smith's repetitions also provide insight into his ability to expand a central idea into a lengthy passage. As noted earlier, Smith's explanations and digressions in the preamble of the King Follett sermon orbit around a single concept: going back to the creation to discover the nature of God. At the end of this section of the sermon, Smith finally answers his rhetorical question, declaring, "First, God Himself who sits enthroned in yonder heavens is a Man like unto one of yourselves—that is the great secret!"[49] Thus, the opening of the sermon, which consists of the announcement of the subject, a perfunctory and formulaic appeal for the audience's prayers, the repeated statements of the core concept, and the eventual answer that God was once a mortal man, all emerged from the extemporaneous expansion of a *single* premeditated concept. From this lone concept, Smith produced a passage of approximately 1,420 words in an oral performance. In the parlance of sermon culture, this example demonstrates Smith's skills in the "amplification" of a single "chief head" of his sermon skeleton.

Smith's ability to amplify the heads of skeletal outlines into extensive passages began long before the 1844 King Follett sermon. His dictation of the 1832 history reveals the same technique of expansion. Without including the words and phrases that form the opening sketch outline, the 1832 history contains more than two thousand words. Smith, it will be recalled, abandoned the project before completion. Instead, he only expanded the first three heads: "[1] A History of the life of Joseph Smith Jr. [2] an account of his marvilous experience; [3] and of all the mighty acts which he doeth in the name of Jesus Ch[r]ist, the son of the living God of whom he beareth record."[50] Nevertheless, these forty-one words provided Smith with sufficient information to expand the opening heads into the entire unfinished draft of his two-thousand-word history. In her study *Revelatory Events*, Ann Taves suggests that Smith "had a marked ability to elaborate a big picture from minimal cues," and the composition of his 1832 history offers ample proof of this.[51]

Smith's use of such truncated heads alerts us to the style of semi-extemporaneous speaking that he adopted for his works. Such notes and sparse outlines were the tips of proverbial icebergs, providing only the barest glimpses of the submerged wealth of specific information in the mind of the speaker. A single word or a truncated phrase could cue an expansive collection of scriptural references and proofs, illustrations, anecdotes, sequences of principles, related topics, and an assortment of applications and exhortations, all interrelated and clustered together in the preacher's mind and fortified by study, meditation, written or mental arrangement of ideas, repetition, private rehearsals, and prior performances.

In other words, short notes acted as memory cues that triggered *sermon routines*—formulaic units of instruction and material, templates of memorized sequences, specific doctrinal principles, and associated phraseology—that acted as a blueprint for any given performance and that could be invoked by little more than taking a quick glance at written short notes, or, if the preacher used no notes at all, by taking a short pause to reflect on the main sermon heads within a mental outline. Indeed, when dealing with generic commonplaces of gospel teachings (baptism, repentance, faith, etc.), the simple naming of a familiar topic—without any notes at all, written or mental—could potentially trigger hours-long discourses.

The short notes of Abraham Marshall (1748–1819), a Baptist semi-extemporaneous preacher, offer a typical example of the variety and styles of notes common among evangelical preachers. Like so many of his colleagues, Marshall preached according to the inspiration of the Holy Spirit, but he also came to the pulpit prepared. "His method of preaching," according to Marshall's grandson, "was extemporaneous. He, indeed, made copious skeletons, many of which were included in the biography which was written by his son [Jabez Marshall]."[52] In all, Marshall's biography, *Memoirs of the Late Rev. Abraham Marshall* (1824), contains a total of seventy-six examples of short notes, one set of long notes (the account of a dream written in a sermon format), and a full-length sermon. His short notes come in various lengths, reflecting how much or how little Marshall needed to prompt his memory.

For his sermon on 2 Kings 9:11, for instance ("Then Jehu came forth to the servants of his lord: and one said unto him, Is all well?"), Marshall's skeleton for the entire sermon consists of six spare divisions of a single concept: "2 Kings, ix. 11—*Is all well?* 1, with the minister; 2, deacons; 3, church; 4, Christians out of the church; 5, seekers; 6, sinners of all sorts."[53] At the other end of the spectrum, Marshall's sermon notes could be much more detailed, such as his skeleton for Matt. 22:21 ("Render therefore unto Cæsar the things which are Cæsar's; and unto God the things that are God's"), which, because of his descriptions of different forms of government institutions in the world (Monarchy, Aristocracy, Theocracy, and Democracy/Republic), extended to over 470 words.[54]

The majority of Marshall's notes, however, fall into a middle range between these extremes, such as the following outline for Num. 10:29 ("And Moses said unto Hobab, the son of Raguel the Midianite, Moses' father in law, We are journeying unto the place of which the Lord said, I will give it you: come thou with us, and we will do thee good"). Note how Marshall follows the common conventions of sermon culture by identifying his main heads with Roman numerals (I. II. III., etc.), and the subdivisions of each head with Arabic numerals (1, 2, 3, etc.), which organize a chronological narrative:

> Numbers x 29—*Come thou with us, &c.* I. Their leaving Egypt. II. Their journey. III. Where they were going—Canaan. IV. What good we will do you—[I.] 1, Israel in bondage and prison; 2, willing; 3, God sent Moses to call them; 4, hard to get them to go; 5, brought by the power of God; 6, left Egypt; 7, travelled three days in the wilderness; 8, crossed the sea. II. [1] They sang God's praise; 2, led by a cloud; 3, drank of the rock; 4, gathered manna; 5, had to fight. III. [1] They were going to a place of peace, 2, rest, 3, plenty, 4, happiness, 5, cities, houses, wells, in a word, every thing. IV. Do thee good—how? 1, shew the way; 2, encourage; 3, help up; 4, help fight the devil; 5, pray for you; 6, bear the cross; 7, shew kindnesses.[55]

Considering Smith's use of this same style in his introduction to the 1843 sermon on the Prodigal Son (in a shorter variation, of course), the issue of training and education becomes material.

Marshall's childhood education was purportedly "confined to about forty days instruction," leaving little time for him to learn the techniques of writing and composition in school.[56] Indeed, given this particular style of chief heads and subdivisions, Marshall undoubtedly learned this composition skill from his participation in sermon culture (his father, also named Abraham, was, in fact, a famous Baptist minister). Smith's demonstrable use of this particular style similarly suggests that he derived his method from exposure to the sermon cultures in his immediate environment (training as a Methodist exhorter; attending the services of Baptists, Congregationalists, Methodists, and Presbyterians; and exposure to texts on pulpit eloquence), as much as any possible exposure to composition exercises in a common school classroom.

Finally, among all the reasons ministers might use short notes, the ability to compose concise sermon skeletons in a short period of time, coupled with the ease and portability of these brief outlines, offered distinct on-the-job benefits. The brevity of short notes made them ideal for busy itinerants in preaching circuits, where travel from one service to another limited the amount of time for study and preparation. Rather than committing a substantial amount of attention to the composition of one or two fully written sermons during the week, the preacher could sketch out a sermon outline (on paper or in the mind) and thereby free up time for other duties.

With practice, such a method could greatly facilitate the preacher's work. If the preacher "acquired that ready command of thought and language, which will enable him to speak without written preparation," according to Ware, "the time and toil of writing are saved, to be devoted to a different mode of study. He may prepare his discourses at intervals of leisure, while walking or riding; and having once arranged the outlines of the subject, and ascertained its principle bearings and applications, the work of preparation is over. The language remains to be suggested at the moment."[57] From a more pragmatic perspective, short notes took up much less room in an itinerant's saddlebags than a prohibitive stack of fully composed sermons in manuscript form.

A single piece of paper, for example, could contain dozens of sermon skeletons, if not more, written in the truncated and often cryptic style of short notes. Evangelical preachers often carried a small collection of such notes while on their circuits, stored and organized in a variety of ways. Presbyterian James Turner (1759–1828), for instance, according to his son's testimony, apparently kept his sermon skeletons on individual sheets of paper. Turner "usually wrote, on a very small piece of paper, and in as few words as possible, the leading ideas [main heads] on which he was to dwell, including the divisions and subdivisions of his discourse. This paper, thus prepared, he placed between the leaves of a small pocket Bible, where it remained till it was needed for use."[58] Similarly, Presbyterian John Breckenridge (1797–1841) kept a "small packet" filled with sermon skeletons on separate letter-sized sheets of paper. Each page was folded into quarters and contained the main heads of his discourses with a number of "hints" (mnemonic cues), which Breckenridge pinned to pages of his Bible and referenced during his sermons. According to the Reverend John M. Krebs, the writing on Breckenridge's pages was brief and spare, so that the notes of a sermon "might easily have been read off in less than five minutes."[59] Understandably, sermon skeletons written on separate pieces of paper might tend to get lost during the shuffle of preparation, travel, study, and performance, prompting a number of preachers to find other ways to save their collected notes. One of the most prevalent ways they dealt with this problem involved the use of cheap blank books and commonplace books to keep their materials organized.

Whether the preachers purchased a readymade blank book from a local bookstore, or simply created a homemade version by folding sheets of paper and sewing them together with a simple binding, blank books became an inexpensive and lightweight solution for organizing sermons. Presbyterian William Stephens Potts (1802–52) offers a typical example of a minister who used blank books to compose the structure and outline of his orations. "His discourses were usually prepared with full analysis," recalled the Reverend Hiram P. Goodrich, "and written, as they were prepared, in a series of blank books of pocket size." Though he recorded his notes in these pocket-sized booklets, Potts rarely used them in the pulpit and usually reserved them for study and meditation. "He seldom wrote out a discourse," continued Goodrich, "and seldom, when he did write, read the manuscript, or committed it to memory, or carried the fragment of a note into the pulpit."[60] In such cases, the blank books filled with sermon skeletons acted as reference texts for study and preparation, rather than operating as mnemonic aids during delivery.

Presbyterian Stephen Bloomer Balch (1747–1833) offers another example of a semi-extemporaneous preacher who recorded his sermon skeletons in a blank book, without taking any notes into the pulpit during delivery. As his colleague the Reverend Elias Harrison recalled, Balch was "greatly in favour of preaching without a manuscript, and especially without writing at all; and he seemed, at that first interview, to take quite a fancy to me, because I had avowed my determination never to take even short notes into the pulpit."[61] When describing Balch's method, Harrison observed that Balch "generally formed a brief outline of his discourse in the early part of the week, and then occupied himself leisurely in filling it up before the Sabbath. These skeletons were written in *very small paper books*, made for the purpose, *each of which would perhaps hold a hundred or more*; but they were never taken with him into the pulpit."[62]

Dee Andrews notes a similar collection of sermons in a blank book by the Methodist preacher James Dempster (1740–1804), who, while "traveling in the Middle Atlantic, filled a small notebook with fifty-five sermon outlines while on shipboard and twenty-five more while stationed in New York and Philadelphia."[63] As these examples suggest, preachers writing their sermon skeletons with truncated language and memory cues for "short notes" could fit a vast amount of information into small and compact booklets or individual pieces of paper. The point is significant: an entire year's worth of sermons could easily fit onto a couple dozen pages within a very small blank book, and a larger

book filled with sermon skeletons could potentially keep a preacher well supplied with orations and lecture material for several years.

From Spiritual Autobiographies to Extended Narratives

While the technique of laying down heads served as a central method of sermon composition, preachers did not reserve the technique for religious discourses alone. Ministers also used this method, to one degree or another, when
composing texts or portions of texts in different genres, such as letters, journal entries, and (auto-)biographies. Such applications emerged as a natural ex-
tension of sermon preparation. Funeral sermons, biographical sermons, and
"commendatory discourses" about the lives and qualities of prominent people,
for instance, blended scriptural and doctrinal orations with historical narratives. And in the search for illustrations of gospel principles, many ministers
incorporated stories and personal anecdotes, all structured within the architectonics of sermon construction and the method of laying down heads.

In his lectures on pulpit eloquence, for example, George Campbell argued
that "a very powerful way" to teach religious principles was "to exhibit properly any known good character of a person now deceased, by giving a lively
narrative of his life, or of any signal period of his life, or an account of any particular virtue, as illustrated through the different periods of his life."[64] When
demonstrating how to fit such narratives within conventional sermon patterns,
Campbell further identified three different approaches. First, a "historical"
method, which divided the entire life of the subject into "certain distinct periods," with accompanying lessons. In other words, the "historical" method was
chronological. Because the structure followed the chronology of a person's life,
Campbell recommended that, "it will be better to follow the natural order [of
a person's life], without using the formality of proposing to the hearers, or dividing the discourse into separate heads."[65] Next, Campbell suggested a "logical" method, which focused on "the most eminent virtues displayed in the life
you propose to recommend to the admiration of your hearers." Thus, instead
of using chronology as the guiding structure, Campbell suggested using the
important qualities of the individual as the primary divisions of the address
(e.g., "virtues of humility, temperance and fortitude").[66]

For his last approach, Campbell proposed the "dramatical," which might focus on "two or three memorable events or actions," and treat them "as the
separate heads of discourse" in the organization of the sermon, with the purpose of illustrating "the virtues displayed in the person's conduct on these several occasions."[67] Thus, in this final category, the preacher would focus on a

limited number of experiences in the life of the deceased, amplifying each virtue and lesson to create a full discourse. Campbell was certainly not the only author on pulpit eloquence to describe the different structural approaches to historical sermons. "In *texts of history*," the Reverend Jean Claude declared, "divisions are easy." After a quick description of different ways to divide a historical sermon (circumstances, actions, occasions, etc.), Claude notes, "Sometimes it is not necessary to make any division at all: but the order of the history must be followed."[68] Thus, in terms of the oral and literary modes of composition in sermon culture, the differences between biographical sermons and biographical essays could be minimal. Both forms contained a substantial overlap of material, further sharing the same basic structural logic and moral focus.

For many lay preachers and exhorters, particularly those with limited opportunities for education, the fundamental techniques of sermon construction might be their only exposure to writing and composition. Thus, the oral and written narrative patterns for sermons within each denominational culture (not just sermons and exhortations, but also styles of conversion narratives, testimonies, relations of spiritual experiences, etc.) often became the default models of imitation for compositions of multiple varieties and genres. And for those aspiring preachers who received a nominal amount of school instruction, any compositional skills they learned in the classroom would only serve to enhance and reinforce the skills taught and demonstrated in sermon culture. After all, the similarities between school composition exercises and techniques of sermon construction were no coincidence. Many of the authors of schoolbooks on rhetoric and composition were also members of the clergy, who, whether for classroom instruction or pulpit oratory and training, drew on the same strategies and pedagogical methods to teach the basics of composition.

Such overlaps in training, education, and cultural practices therefore help to explain why the method of laying down heads appears in genres extending well beyond sermon construction. Moreover, the practice of laying down heads to compose nonsermon literature offers another opportunity to contextualize Smith's approach to composition. Given Smith's stated affinities for the Methodist faith—his one-time "desire to be united with them" and his participation in class meetings as a lay exhorter—a comparison of his writing style with Methodist compositions offers additional insights. Apart from their reputation as dramatic extemporaneous speakers, Methodist preachers were known for their personal spiritual autobiographies, along with the habit of keeping diaries of their experiences, or, as Andrews describes the practice, "that all-important itinerant avocation of journal writing."[69] John Wesley encouraged preachers to record their personal narratives, and he regularly solicited preachers for accounts of their lives, often with the intention of publishing the biographies as devotional and inspirational reading.[70]

One of the most prominent outlets for such narratives was Wesley's *Arminian Magazine* (later renamed the *Methodist Magazine*). As D. Bruce Hindmarsh indicates, Wesley initiated "a significant programme of periodical publication of religious autobiography from 1778 to 1811, as lives and portraits of lay Methodist itinerants appeared in successive issues."[71] Such spiritual narratives proved popular, with publications ranging from works devoted to the life of a single prominent preacher to collections of biographies and autobiographies.[72] American Methodists, for example, might read *The Experience of Several Eminent Methodist Preachers* (Philadelphia, 1791), later revised and re-titled *The Experience and Ministerial Labours of Several Methodist Preachers* (1812, with simultaneous publications in New York, Pennsylvania, and Vermont), which not only provided readers with contemporary stories of faithful ministers but also demonstrated and reinforced the narrative patterns for spiritual biographies and autobiographies.[73] A review of these narratives reveals that the technique of laying down heads to organize experiences and chronologies featured prominently in such works.

In general, the core narrative pattern of autobiographies among lay Methodist preachers, suggests Hindmarsh, "seems to be a conversion narrative followed by the curriculum vitae or itinerary of an evangelist."[74] Thus, conversion acted as a fulcrum point between the life leading up to conversion and the life that followed. "For the early Methodist preachers, often writing late in life or at least at some distance from their first spiritual awakening," Hindmarsh observes, "the whole of their lives had now become explicable in terms of conversion."[75] Hindmarsh continues by indicating how these ministers described "their own early formation, spiritual decline, awakening, and conversion," later followed by "their call to the ministry, their experience of perfection, and even their own deaths, as narrated by others."[76] In his 1832 history, Smith traces a similar pathway, echoing the two-part "before and after" convention of Methodist autobiographies. Thus, rather than confining his narrative to the events leading up to and including his First Vision, Smith continued his history by listing "all the mighty acts which he doeth in the name of Jesus Christ," including a promised "account of the rise of the Church of Christ in the eve of time," though, again, he did not complete the draft.[77]

Within this general pattern of autobiography, Methodist preachers often made use of laying down heads to describe personal experiences unrelated to the original sermonizing function of the method. Whereas laying down heads was a strategy for "dividing" a scriptural text or gospel subject into the main topics and subdivisions of a discourse, Methodist preachers often used the same technique to write about personal experiences, such as key events in their lives and times when they needed to make crucial decisions. A typical example appears in the autobiography of Methodist Robert Miller (1763–1829), who, when writing about a time when he had to choose between taking control of the family business or becoming a preacher, itemized his reasons to preach by laying down heads: "1, Because the gospel was not preached in Rugby [i.e., a town in Warwickshire where he felt inspired to go]. 2, I had no Christian friends to converse with. 3, I was but a young convert, consequently a novice in religion. 4, I was afraid that I should again be drawn away with wicked company. But the 5th and last reason was,—because I had an inward conviction that I was called to preach the gospel."[78] Miller was not alone in using the method of laying down heads to outline the reasons behind important decisions.

When offered a more stable and financially rewarding position outside the Methodist connection, Sampson Staniforth (1720–99) laid down explicit heads to enumerate his reasons to remain: "1. It was clear, God had blest me in this way [Methodism]: therefore I was afraid to go out of it: 2. I saw how much hurt had been done in the Society by these separations. And, thirdly, as to money or ease, my heart is not set on money, and I am not weary of my labour. So upon the coolest reflection, I can still say, and that with full purpose of heart, *This people shall be my people, and their God shall be my God.*"[79] Thomas Olivers (1725–99), the supervisor of the Methodist press from 1775 to 1789 and a one-time traveling companion of Wesley on preaching tours, made use of laying down heads to list the qualities that he hoped to find in a wife.[80] In fact, he not only made a list, he explicitly applied the sermon compositional technique of "arrangement" to list his criteria in their order of importance:

Here I fixed on the following properties, and ranged [arranged] them in the following order. The first was grace. . . . Secondly, she ought to have tolerable good common sense. . . . Thirdly, as I knew the natural warmth of my own temper, I concluded that a wise and gracious God would not choose a companion for me, who would throw oil, but rather water upon the fire. . . . Fourthly . . . as I was connected with a poor people . . . whoever I married should have a small competency [a small amount of personal wealth], to prevent her being chargeable to any.[81]

Olivers's use of laying down heads to organize portions of his autobiography was not limited to isolated events. He also used the method to outline his personal history.

In the final paragraph of his autobiography, Olivers revealed the relationship between laying down heads and the construction of his entire life story. Here, instead of announcing the skeletal outline to his readers in the opening of his narrative, Olivers reserved the sketch of main heads for a final climactic summary of his life (resulting in a blueprint of prior "concealed" heads, considering its final position in the story). This concise outline, combined with the normal practices of laying down heads in sermon construction and delivery, suggests that Olivers followed this premeditated sequence to compose his narrative, using it as a guide to organize his experiences. Note also the presence of resumptive repetition: Olivers frames the sequence of narrative heads with the repetition of "when I consider." This anchor forms an *inclusio* that borders the opening and closing of the summary of heads (i.e., "When I consider how the providence of God . . ." and "When I consider these things . . ."):

> When I consider how the providence of God provided for me in my infancy—Brought me up to the state of man—Preserved me from those evils which brought others to an untimely end—Directed my wandering steps to the means of my conversion—Cast my lot among his people—Called me to preach his word—Owned my preaching, to the conversion of others—Stood by me in many trials—Brought me back, so often, from the brink of the grave—Healed my manifold backslidings— Provided me a suitable companion—And put me in possession of all the necessaries of life. When I consider these things, I must say, Surely, goodness and mercy have followed me all the days of my life; and I hope to dwell in the house of the Lord forever.[82]

Olivers's strategy of composition—essentially a sermon skeleton adapted to an autobiography—was not exclusively a defining characteristic of Methodist autobiography. The technique reached far beyond these boundaries, offering aspiring writers from all backgrounds a structural template for the composition of complete books.

In his work *The Student and Pastor* (1755), John Mason (1706–63), an Independent minister and popular educator among dissenting sects, indicated how the method of laying down heads to create a sermon skeleton could also be used to create the outline for an entire book. "As every compleat Sermon resembles a little Book," Mason argued, "the Method of composing the former, may be the same with what *Ringelbergius* tells us he used in composing the latter."[83] Mason was referring to Joachimus Fortius Ringelbergius (aka Joachim Sterck van Ringelbergh, ca. 1499–ca. 1531 to 1536), an early sixteenth-century polymath and educator, who was best known for his treatise *De Ratione Studii* (1530), which outlined a systematic plan for students to develop proper study habits.

Mason's translation of Ringelbergius's method of composition reveals the process that Ringelbergius followed to write books, which started with a mental outline, forming "in my Mind, a perfect Plan of the Work before me [i.e., an outline for the entire work]." With this general overall shape in mind, he would then divide the central topic of the book into the main chapters, or "the several Heads" of the work, arranging and rearranging them "to see if they have their proper Place, Connexion and Coherence." Once complete, this step would result in the creation of a simple skeletal outline of the entire work, much like a table of contents. Next, under each individual chapter head, Ringelbergius would write "a brief Sketch [i.e., outline for each chapter] of what is proper to be said under each Head." When drafting these outlines for each chapter, he would write the various topics and issues on "a loose Piece of Paper," presumably to facilitate the process of arrangement and rearrangement until he achieved a final desired order.[84]

Once all of the topics were organized into a preferred sequence, he would then create a fair copy (a final clean draft) by including each chapter outline in a single master outline, which he called his "Plan." Once this overall skeletal blueprint was complete, Ringelbergius could view the overall structure of his entire work in a single glance: "By this means, I have the whole Subject and Method [organization] of the Work under my Eye at once."[85] Therefore, much like the semi-extemporaneous preachers who could carry a year's worth of sermons in a single notebook filled with short notes, Ringelbergius, and those who adopted his approach, could record the outline of an entire book on a dozen or so loose sheets of paper or in a common blank book. Mason's *The Student and Pastor* remained available to aspiring preachers in the early nineteenth century, both as a stand-alone publication and as part of collected essays on pulpit eloquence.[86] Given this context in sermon culture, the practice of creating and organizing skeletal outlines for (auto-)biographies and entire books becomes relevant when considering Smith's preparations for the Book of Mormon, especially how the master outline for an entire work could be organized on a few sheets of paper.

In addition, the technique of laying down heads also applied to storytelling—particularly stories delivered semi-extemporaneously. As a professional writer and storyteller in early nineteenth-century New England, Nathaniel Hawthorne (1804–64), the celebrated author of *The Scarlet Letter* (1850) and *The House of Seven Gables* (1851), provides what is perhaps the best description of this semi-extemporaneous technique through the voice of one of his fictional narrators, the self-described "wandering story teller." Here, the character not only depicts storytelling templates, "skeletons of tales," but also the semi-extemporaneous variations that can occur during each performance: "I manufactured a great variety of plots and skeletons of tales, and kept them ready for use, leaving the filling up to the inspiration of the moment; though I cannot remember ever to have told a tale, which did not vary considerably from my pre-conceived idea, and acquire a novelty of aspect as often as I repeated it. Oddly enough, my success was generally in proportion to the difference between the conception and accomplishment."[87] Hawthorne's vivid description of the oral storyteller's craft provides a window into semi-extemporaneous narrative production: the teller begins with a malleable story pattern in mind, and then improvises the words according to "the inspiration of the moment."

Hawthorne's storyteller thus made use of the same technique that semi-extemporaneous preachers followed when delivering sermons from short notes or memorized outlines, and the same technique that nineteenth-century schoolchildren used when writing themes, composing essays, and imitating the passages of notable authors. And like Hawthorne's storyteller, Smith also used the same method of laying down heads to create skeletal outlines for extemporaneous expansion. Indeed, this method emerges as Smith's central and most fundamental approach to composition. Whether he was composing his spiritual autobiography or delivering his sermons, Smith consistently followed this method to structure and articulate his religious experiences. And when reflecting upon Smith's historical context, we find schoolchildren, storytellers, writers, speakers, and preachers all using this same ubiquitous approach. Laying down heads to create skeletal outlines stood as one of the most common introductory and, indeed, advanced methods of composition in the early nineteenth century. As such, whether preparing a sermon skeleton for a single oration or combining together a collection of skeletal outlines to create the "plan" of a book or tale, authors and orators used the method of laying down heads to prepare, structure, compose, and guide their works.

The characteristics of Smith's oral compositions, however, point to more specific origins than a broad wash of cultural observations. While he likely encountered this form of basic introductory composition in his limited time in common school classrooms and/or self-improvement venues, Smith nevertheless expresses a form of composition and delivery that sits both comfortably and firmly within the traditions of sermon construction, the construction of spiritual autobiographies, and the performance techniques found among contemporary evangelical preachers, particularly those engaged in semi-extemporaneous sermonizing. Moreover, when turning to the Book of Mormon and analyzing its contents, we find that the text repeatedly reveals the same composition techniques at play, expressed in the same style that Smith adopted for his personal writings and sermons. Thus, while the nature of the Book of Mormon and the process of its construction may always remain contested, Smith's personal style of composition—profoundly influenced by contemporary sermon culture—nevertheless emerges time and again in the pages of the work.

CHAPTER FIVE

Sermon Culture in the Book of Mormon

Sermons and related orations in the Book of Mormon—prophecies, teachings, scripture quotations with commentaries, exhortations, and various hybrids of these and other closely related genres—constitute just over 40 percent of the entire work. Remove such passages and the Book of Mormon, composed of roughly 269,510 words, would decrease in length by more than 100,000 words.[1] The prominent and widespread presence throughout the text of such religious orations thus requires a closer examination of the ways in which Joseph Smith constructed and positioned them within his epic work. In the previous chapters we have contextualized Smith's personal style of preaching and oral composition within his vibrant contemporary sermon culture, and when we turn to the Book of Mormon we find that Smith incorporated the same strategies and techniques to construct his epic work, using methods that would have allowed him to dictate his oral compositions with minimal preparation and few, if any, notes. As such, the text of the Book of Mormon reveals how the pervasive sermon culture of Smith's world had firmly imprinted itself on his imagination, influencing the style, organization, and content of his prophetic voice.

In both composition and delivery, Smith's style was deeply entangled with contemporary sermon practices, and his methods stem directly from his religious background and context. As already observed, Smith's 1832 history openly displays the use of laying down heads to create a premeditated skeletal outline, which he amplified extemporaneously in the moment of dictation to his scribe. Likewise, the heads in the opening of his 1843 Prodigal Son sermon reveal his knowledge and awareness of laying down explicit enumerated heads, one of the most common techniques of sermon organization in his contemporary culture. Finally, his 1844 King Follett funeral sermon demonstrates the interplay between premeditated ideas and the extemporaneous amplification of a mental outline. Within all of these styles of composition and arrangement, Smith used extempore delivery and expression, which he had long practiced and advocated since at least the period when he was dictating the Book of Mormon.

Not all of these styles, however, appear directly, or at least overtly, in the Book of Mormon. The prophets in its pages do not lay down enumerated heads to outline the course of their sermons; neither do they begin their sermons in the same way that Smith began his 1832 history, by providing readers with a complete outline of explicit heads that announce the trajectory of entire sermons (though narratives, as we see in chapter 6, are another matter).[2] Rather, the primary methods that Smith adopted for sermons and sermonlike speeches in the Book of Mormon center on two interrelated techniques of delivery: the semi-extemporaneous expansion of premeditated but unspoken sermon skeletons (the common "concealed" method) and unpremeditated "extempore" passages, which, though labeled as "extempore," were nevertheless informed by a history of study, preparation, practice, and habit. Thus, Smith's chosen methods would heavily influence such factors as the speed of his oral composition; the amount of forethought and preparation required for the sermons and much of the didactic material in his epic, ranging from careful and measured premeditation to habituated delivery; and the varying lengths of passages, with notionally unlimited extempore and discursive potential.

For Smith, as well as contemporary preachers, the methods of semi-extemporaneous production and improvised delivery were not mutually exclusive, nor did they represent two completely distinct practices. Rather, both methods operated simultaneously, alternating back and forth during performance. Smith's approach to sermonizing thus reveals a core creative tension between planning and spontaneity, preparation and inspiration, premeditation and taking "no thought beforehand what ye shall speak" (Mark 13:11). Smith's decision to use these common, interrelated, and expansive techniques for the creation of religious speeches in the Book of Mormon yields important clues about his overall approach to composition and his deep indebtedness to contemporary sermon culture. Understanding how this method operates proves crucial when analyzing Smith's sermons in relationship to the overall text and oral production of the Book of Mormon.

To that end, this chapter focuses on three primary areas of Smith's style of oral composition: (1) the Book of Mormon's explicit references to sermon conventions for both premeditated and extemporaneous methods of composition, with a specific focus on the method of laying down heads (explicit and concealed), whether or not the text emerged from planning and preparation or from inspired digressions in the moment of performance; (2) the manner in which these sermon conventions package common religious topics and language, and what this reveals about Smith's background, training, and level of experience as a preacher; and (3) how these conventions, methods, and techniques, along with Smith's own training and preparations, ultimately facilitated Smith's rapid composition of the text.

Laying Down Heads in the Book of Mormon

While determining the precise origins of Smith's knowledge about contemporary techniques of written and oral composition may remain elusive, the fact that he repeatedly and skillfully used more than one variation of laying down heads to create skeletal outlines for semi-extemporaneous performances clearly demonstrates his facility with the method. Indeed, Smith likely absorbed these techniques from multiple avenues. The use of a skeletal outline to produce his 1832 history inclines toward classroom and self-improvement exercises, which regularly involved the imitation, construction, and expression of fables, myths, and short historical sketches. Smith's historical narrative details his personal life and background, specifically in the context of his divine calling as a modern-day prophet and his central role in the restoration of the primitive Christian church—a narrative that sits comfortably within the genres of biographical sermons, eulogies, and, perhaps with a morbid turn, funeral orations. Indeed, Smith's ability to move directly from a mental template to oral dictation, bypassing any apparent written component, evinces a reliance on contemporary sermon culture, rather than classroom exercises. Nonetheless, though scholars might choose to debate Smith's precise sources of influence or his level of exposure to these techniques, one thing remains certain: the prophet Nephi, whose autobiographical account opens the story of the Book of Mormon, certainly knew about these methods and the technique of laying down heads. So, too, did Nephi's younger brother, Jacob.

Toward the end of his account in the opening of the Book of Mormon, Nephi bequeaths the sacred records of their people to Jacob, together with a commandment that Jacob should document all the prophecies and revelations that their families would experience. Sometime later, Jacob recorded Nephi's instructions in the opening of his portion of the work, describing, in an explicit reference to modern composition techniques, how Nephi advised (Jacob 1:4, italics added), "if there were preaching which was sacred, or revelation which was great, or prophesying, that I [Jacob] should engraven *the heads of them* upon these plates, and *touch upon them* as much as it were possible."[3] Nephi's advice to lay down the main "heads" of revelations, prophecies, and sermons, along with the instruction to "touch upon them" when necessary, provides additional direct evidence of Smith's awareness of this ubiquitous sermon practice in early nineteenth-century America. Not only does he refer directly in this passage to the practice of laying down heads, Smith also provides an explicit and accurate description of this same method using contemporary terminology. Through Nephi, Smith also specifies the concept of amplification in the vernacular of Smith's day, when the phrase "touching upon heads," or any number of its common variations, was a familiar expression to describe the expansion of heads into lengthier oral or written passages.[4] Nineteenth-century readers would have immediately recognized Nephi's description as an everyday technique of contemporary composition, expansion, and declamation.

Extemporaneous Speaking in the Book of Mormon

Along with the method of laying down heads, Book of Mormon prophets delivered their teachings extempore, speaking words inspired by the Holy Ghost in the moment of performance. For example, Nephi, the opening writer in the Book of Mormon, often delivers what the text represents as unpremeditated exhortations to his wicked brothers, Laman and Lemuel. As Brian Jackson observes, Nephi's father, Lehi, attributed these "moments of inspiration" to the Spirit: "But behold, it was not him [Nephi], but it was the spirit of the Lord which was in him, which opened his mouth to utterance, that he could not shut it" (2 Nephi 1:27).[5] Jackson further describes how the prophet-brothers Nephi and Lehi, the sons of Helaman, named after their ancestors who originally journeyed to the Americas, "showed multivocality in their participant roles as preachers because they not only had 'power and authority given unto them that they might speak', but they also had '*what they should speak* given unto them' by the power of God."[6] A cursory review of additional prophets in the Book of Mormon offers similar descriptions.

Mosiah's sons—Ammon, Aaron, Omner, and Himni—converted thousands of Lamanites by preaching "according to the spirit of revelation and of prophecy, and the power of God, working miracles in them" (Alma 23:6).[7] When the preaching duo of Alma and Amulek began their circuit among the people, they were "filled with the Holy Ghost" and "began to preach and to prophesy unto the people, according to the spirit and power which the Lord had given them" (Alma 8:30, 32).[8] Samuel, the Lamanite prophet, preached and prophesied according to "the words of the Lord, which he doth put into my heart" (Helaman 13:5; see also 3–4).[9] Nephi, in a sweeping description of all the prophets who lived before his lifetime, claimed that this method of divine utterance produced both sermons and scriptural texts, depicting inspired holy writings as "the words which have been spoken by the mouth of all the holy prophets, which have been delivered unto them by the spirit and power of God" (1 Nephi 3:20).[10] Smith would mirror Nephi's claim in an early revelation in which the Lord, speaking through Smith, revealed how the prophets "spake as they were inspired by the gift of the Holy Ghost"—an assertion that further echoed the language of 2 Tim. 3:16, when Paul claimed, "All scripture is given by inspiration of God."[11] In terms of historical context, Smith's description of inspired preaching among the prophets and missionaries in the Book of Mormon thus reflected the same divinely inspired, semi-extemporaneous approach that he advocated among the members of his nascent faith.

In 1829, for example, when completing his dictation of the Book of Mormon, Smith offered a revelation to early leaders of the church that instructed them how to preach extempore: "Declare my gospel, according to the power of the Holy Ghost which is in you.... *These words are not of men nor of man, but of me.... For it is my voice which speaketh them unto you; for they are given by my Spirit unto you.*"[12] Later, in an 1833 revelation that typified Smith's philosophy, the Lord commanded both Smith and early church leader Sidney Rigdon to "lift up your voices unto this people; *speak the thoughts that I shall put into your hearts*, and you shall not be confounded before men; For *it shall be given you in the very hour, yea, in the very moment, what ye shall say.*"[13] As Jackson aptly observes, Smith's revelations and the narratives within the Book of Mormon "played a role in establishing the rhetorical culture of the early Latter-day Saints, both for what it was in itself and also what it revealed to them about divine communication."[14] Such grounding in popular semi-extemporaneous methods, often depicted as pure extempore speaking, thus offered a foundation by which early members of the faith could identify with a heritage of inspired practices and ancient prophets, while formulating an identifiable rhetorical culture within the emerging religion.

Within this dynamic oratorical period, however, it is important to recall that the full expression of Smith's philosophy of semi-extemporaneous preaching specifically involved study and preparation. "Seek not to declare my word, but *first seek to obtain my word,*" the Lord admonished Hyrum Smith in a May 1829 revelation, further adding, "*study my word* which hath gone forth among the children of men [the Bible], and also *study my word* which shall come forth among the children of men, or that which is now translating [the Book of Mormon].... Therefore, *treasure up in your heart* until the time which is in my wisdom that you shall go forth."[15] Smith would both embrace and advocate this preparative approach throughout his prophetic career. Indeed, Smith's method for the 1844 King Follett discourse hearkens back to the semi-extemporaneous approach that he taught and fostered when dictating the Book of Mormon. Smith's announcement that he would "offer you *my ideas* as far as I have ability and as far as I will be *inspired by the Holy Spirit,*" provided an explicit description of the way in which an individual "treasuring up" the word of God through study, meditation, and prayer could work hand-in-hand with the inspiration of the Holy Spirit when the time arrived to preach the gospel.[16]

Jacob's Sermons: Laying Down Heads and Extempore Expansion

In light of Nephi's explicit advice to Jacob to "engraven the heads" of sermons, revelations, and prophecies onto the plates and to "touch upon them as much as it were possible" (Jacob 1:4), questions may arise as to how well Jacob took Nephi's counsel, and as to what Jacob's style might tell us about Smith's own method of composition and delivery. A review of the sermons and writings that Smith produced for Jacob (a rather limited selection) reveals that Jacob's style of laying down heads leans heavily toward the "concealed" method, though not exclusively. In other words, Jacob does not provide his audience with full outlines in the opening of his sermons, with explicit and detailed heads that announce each major section of his orations. Rather, he offers only a few general and relatively vague heads, or simply does not announce them at all to his audience.

For example, Jacob's first sermon in the Book of Mormon (2 Nephi 6:2 through 2 Nephi 10:25) contains a total of three explicit primary heads. The first two, however, which appear in the introductory portion of the sermon, are general and lacking in detail. After a brief preamble (2 Nephi 6:2–3), Jacob lays down these opening heads of his outline at the same time that he announces the central text of the sermon: "And now, behold, I would speak unto you concerning [1] *things which are,* and [2] *which are to come; wherefore, I will read you the words of Isaiah* [the sermon text; Isa. 49:22–23]. And they are the words which my brother hath desired me that I should speak unto you" (2 Nephi 6:4).[17] Jacob then launches into his sermon (a two-part sermon series that he delivers over the course of two days), which ultimately centers on the role of Jesus Christ in relation to the theme of captivity and restoration, both physically (the restoration of the scattered tribes of Israel to the lands of their inheritance) and spiritually (the redemption of sinners through Christ's atonement).[18]

Apart from these opening heads, however, Smith does not alert his audience to the course of Jacob's oration beyond the broad strokes of "things which are" and things "which are to come." Yet, as vague as these heads might seem, Smith repeatedly uses variants of the phrase "things which are to come" with a special (but not exclusive) emphasis on the coming of Christ and his divine role in the salvation of mankind. The prophet Alma the Younger provides the clearest elaboration of this phrase when he declares, "For behold, I say unto you, *there be many things to come*; and behold, there is one thing which is of more importance than they all: for behold, the time is not far distant, that the Redeemer liveth and cometh among his people" (Alma 7:7).[19] Later in Jacob's sermon, when having Jacob address his audience and their desire to understand the prophecies regarding the restoration of Israel and the future state of their own souls, Smith reveals his continued adherence to his outline by repeating one of the initial opening heads: "For I know that thou hast searched much, many of you, *to know of things to come*; wherefore I know that ye know that our flesh must waste away and die; nevertheless, in our bodies, we shall see God" (2 Nephi 9:4).[20] Though he did not reveal the specific topics in the opening heads of Jacob's sermon, Smith nevertheless provides clear evidence that he is following a mental outline.

The only other head that Jacob explicitly announces to his audience occurs on the second day of his two-day sermon, when he introduces the continuation of his oration. At the end of the first day of the sermon, Jacob had referred to the descendants of his people in the Americas, saying that, "in future generations, they shall become *a righteous branch unto the House of Israel*" (2 Nephi 9:53).[21] In the opening of his discourse on the second day, Jacob reengages his sermon by laying down the central head of his ensuing discourse, announcing the previous day's topic again by stating, "And now I, Jacob, speak unto you again, my beloved brethren, *concerning this righteous branch of which I have spoken*" (2 Nephi 10:1).[22] Apart from these brief heads and references, however, Smith does not provide much explicit guidance to Jacob's audience regarding the trajectory of the sermon.

Nevertheless, Smith's construction of Jacob's sermon clearly situates the oration within nineteenth-century sermon practices. When expanding the view beyond Jacob's announcement of the text and the primary heads, we find that Jacob's sermon follows the common "doctrine and use" format typical of nineteenth-century preaching. Smith begins the sermon with an introduction (2 Nephi 6:2–3), followed by laying down the main heads of the sermon and announcing the text, Isa. 49:22–23 (2 Nephi 6:4–8). Smith further intersperses this opening with explicit applications to Jacob's audience, stating, "the words which I shall read, are they which Isaiah spake concerning all the House of Israel; wherefore, *they may be likened unto you: for ye are of the House of Israel*" (2 Nephi 6:5).[23] Smith then enters an explanatory section, interpreting Isaiah's prophecies in relation to the repeated scattering and gathering of Israel, along with a prophecy concerning the coming of Jesus Christ (2 Nephi 6:8-15). The sermon continues with lengthy quotations from Isaiah, including portions of chapters 49 and 52, along with the entire chapters of 50 and 51 (2 Nephi 6:16 through 2 Nephi 8:25), coupled with Jacob's commentary. The explanatory portion continues with interpretations of Isaiah's prophecies, the Lord's covenants with the Israelites, and Christ's central role in the plan of salvation (2 Nephi 9:1-26). Finally, the sermon switches into an application section, specifically in the form of exhortations (2 Nephi 9:27-54), after which Smith ends the first part of the sermon.

This constellation of sermon elements would have been deeply familiar to nineteenth-century audiences. The ubiquity of the "doctrine and use" pattern was all but second nature among religious communities in the early nineteenth century. From a narrative viewpoint that adopts Jacob's perspective, the sermon seems particularly aimed at nineteenth-century audiences, given the glaring anachronism of its contemporary and familiar sermon structure. The combination of an introduction, a scriptural text, the laying down of heads, the interpretation of scripture (an explanatory section), and a final section of exhortations (applications) creates a matrix of structural elements that constitutes a style of sermon that specifically developed out of the *sermo modernus* of late medieval scholasticism, more than a thousand years after Jacob's sermon purportedly took place in the ancient Americas of approximately 550 B.C.E.[24] Thus, nineteenth-century audiences would have been thoroughly acquainted with Jacob's sermon structure, providing them with a familiar format that would have allowed them to focus on the message of the sermon, rather than potentially distracting them with the differing structural and often enigmatic patterns and imagery of ancient Hebrew prophecy.

In addition, Jacob's use of only two main heads to summarize his entire sermon offers another clue about Smith's training and exposure to contemporary sermon culture. By reducing the opening outline of Jacob's sermon to two brief heads, which nevertheless offered enough information to trigger his memory and guide the speech, Smith provided himself with two succinct mnemonic cues that could encapsulate the entire oration. This strategy, as we have observed, was often used in a preacher's short notes and frequently recommended by writers on pulpit eloquence. John Quincy Adams, for example, argued that the main divisions of a sermon should be "short and complete and the heads few in number," and that the cues for such partitions should consist of "the smallest number of words possible to express your idea."[25] The Reverend Jean Claude was more specific about the number of heads (or divisions) that a good sermon should have. "Division, in general," stated Claude, "ought to be restrained to a small number of parts, they should never exceed four or five at the most: the most admired sermons have only two or three parts."[26] In his notes on Claude's text, Robert Robinson further argued, "Bad sermons have many divisions; good ones two or three: but the best none at all."[27] Whether he gleaned this information from books on pulpit oratory or learned of such techniques from active participation in exhortations and listening to sermons, Smith followed such suggestions when constructing and performing Jacob's discourse. Neither was this strategy reserved for Jacob. Throughout the Book of Mormon, Smith frequently summarizes the content of his prophets' sermons and orations with only two or three heads.[28]

In terms of preparation versus spontaneity, however, Jacob's "doctrine and use" pattern does not necessarily indicate that the sermon was fully composed and arranged in advance. Indeed, portions of the text point to a dynamic exchange between premeditated elements and extempore excursions, specifically manifesting themselves in Smith's style of resumptive repetition—the same style of repetition that Smith would later express in his King Follett funeral sermon. This effect emerges perhaps most clearly in the introduction of the two-day sermon, when Jacob announces the text and lays down the primary heads of his discourse. The passage reveals the following sequence: first, after a brief introduction, Jacob announces the main heads and the text from Isaiah, though he does not yet identify which Isaiah passage he will be using: "I will read you the words of Isaiah" (2 Nephi 6:4). Before revealing the specific text, Jacob then departs on a brief aside concerning his authority and good intentions, along with introductory applications or "uses," announcing that (1) Nephi asked him to preach on the topic, "they are the words which my brother hath desired me that I should speak unto you," and that (2) the audience should apply the lessons for their benefit, "I speak them unto you for your sakes, that ye may learn and glorify the name of your God" (2 Nephi 6:4).[29]

Following his tangential certifications and preliminary "uses," Jacob then returns to his announcement of the text. Even so, he still does not reveal the precise scripture he will be using from Isaiah, thereby keeping his audience in continued suspense and only offering hints about the passage: "And now, the words which I shall read, are they which Isaiah spake

concerning all the House of Israel" (2 Nephi 6:5). Yet again, instead of sharing the Isaiah passage he will use, Jacob departs on another excursion, informing the audience how they should apply Isaiah's passage to their own
lives (another early "application" segment in the overall sermon structure):
"Wherefore, they [the house of Israel] may be likened unto you: for ye are
of the House of Israel. And there are many things which have been spoken
by Isaiah, which may be likened unto you, because that ye are of the House
of Israel" (2 Nephi 6:5).[30]

Finally, after these two brief excursions, Jacob reveals the specific Isaiah passage: "And now, these are the words: Thus saith the Lord God . . . [Jacob
quotes Isa. 49:22–23]" (2 Nephi 6:6). After reading the prophecy, Jacob then
restates his intention to interpret the passage: "And now I, Jacob, would speak
somewhat concerning these words" (2 Nephi 6:8).[31] Smith's resumptive repetition appears more clearly when the text is reformatted:

[ANNOUNCING THE TEXT]: "And now, behold, I would speak
    unto you concerning [1] things which are, and [2] which are
    to come; wherefore, I will read you the words of Isaiah.
[TANGENT/"USES"]: And they are the words which my brother
    hath desired me that I should speak unto you.
    And I speak them unto you for your sakes,
    that ye may learn and glorify the name of your God.
[RESUMPTIVE REPETITION]: And now, the words which I shall
    read, are they which Isaiah spake concerning all the House of Israel;
[TANGENT/"USES"]: wherefore, they may be likened unto you:
    for ye are of the House of Israel. And there are many things
    which have been spoken by Isaiah, which may be likened
    unto you, because that ye are of the House of Israel.
[RESUMPTIVE REPETITION]: And now, these are the words:
[THE TEXT]: [Jacob reads Isa. 49:22–23]
[RESUMPTIVE REPETITION]: And now I, Jacob, would speak somewhat
    concerning these words."[32]

Such patterning suggests that Smith produced Jacob's sermon by means of a
semi-extemporaneous performance: the announcement of the text and
the repetitions of the first main head act as anchors for the opening of his
mental outline for the sermon, while the alteration between these anchors
and his assertions of authority, good intentions, and his counsel to the audience to apply Isaiah's prophecies to their own lives suggest impromptu di-

gressions (an approach, the careful reader might observe, that mirrors the classical rhetorical tradition of asserting the qualifications and good faith of the speaker).

By adopting this form of resumptive repetition, Smith does not make much of an effort to differentiate his own sermonizing voice from the voice of Jacob, and his choice to structure Jacob's sermon with a modern style would have appealed to nineteenth-century audiences. In terms of Smith's oral composition, the convenience of following an outline during a semi-extemporaneous performance would have certainly provided greater flexibility to pursue the spontaneous impulses of the moment. It bears mentioning, however, that this examination of the Book of Mormon does not attempt to divide Smith's texts into premeditated passages and extemporaneous expansions. Though the text offers an abundance of clues regarding Smith's dynamic and flexible process, we do not have direct access to Smith's intentions or possible notes. Thus, the purpose of analyzing these examples is to identify and observe Smith's techniques, along with exploring what his methods reveal about his familiarity with the range of contemporary sermon techniques, their conventions, and their inherently flexible applications.

Jacob's Concealed Heads

A brief look at another sermon by Jacob reveals further information about Smith's approach to oral composition and laying down heads (Jacob 2:2 through Jacob 3:12). Rather than announcing explicit and discrete heads for this sermon, Smith, like many of his contemporary semi-extemporaneous preachers, abandoned the preliminary announcement of each and every main topic in the sermon and substituted a general introduction instead. In terms of context, Jacob's sermon occurs at a time when Nephi has died and Jacob has become one of the "consecrated priests, and teachers" of the Nephite civilization (Jacob 1:18).[33] During his ministry, Jacob has watched two major problems of excess arise among the Nephites: First, the men have experimented with polygamy, seeking to have "many wives and concubines"; and next, the people have sought for "much gold and silver," which has resulted in the people being "lifted up somewhat in pride" (Jacob 1:15–16).[34] In the introduction to his sermon, however, Jacob does not declare polygamy, greed, and pride as special topics of his lecture. Rather, he announces a general summary, stating that he will "testify unto you [the Nephites] concerning the wickedness of your hearts," and that he "must do according to the strict commands of God, and tell you concerning your wickedness and abominations" (Jacob 2:6, 10; see also 9).[35]

Such a sermonizing approach reveals the speaker's general forethought and preparation of subject matter, without committing the speaker to a specific sequence of topics—a technique that offers greater flexibility than laying down a particular outline in the opening of a sermon. These prefatory statements, functioning as vague comprehensive heads, thus alert Jacob's audience to the general direction and content of his looming criticisms, but the specific topics nevertheless remain unspoken, or, in the terminology of sermon practices, "concealed." As he continues with the sermon, Jacob begins his rebukes by addressing the problem of pride, which has resulted from people seeking wealth and riches. He still does not announce to the audience his sermon outline with explicit heads, but he nevertheless reveals a conscious effort to follow an undisclosed outline when he switches from the topic of pride to the issue of polygamy.

In the transition between these two subjects, Jacob states, "And now my brethren, *I have spoken unto you concerning pride*" (Jacob 2:20), which, in another example of resumptive repetition, he repeats two verses later, "And now *I make an end of speaking unto you concerning this pride.* And were it not that *I must speak unto you concerning a grosser crime* [switching to the topic of multiple wives and concubines], my heart would rejoice exce[e]dingly, because of you" (Jacob 2:22):[36]

[OUTLINE ANCHOR: PRIDE]: "<u>And now my brethren, I have spoken unto you concerning pride</u>;

[TANGENT: REBUKE/EXHORTATION]: and those of you which have afflicted your neighbor, and persecuted him . . . . keep his commandments, and glorify him forever.

[RESUMPTIVE REPETITION]: <u>And now I make an end of speaking unto you concerning this pride.</u>

[TOPIC TRANSITION]: And were it not that I must speak unto you concerning a grosser crime, my heart would rejoice exce[e]dingly, because of you."[37]

For this brief moment, Smith's mental outline surfaces in the text, allowing the reader to see how Jacob consciously moves from one topic to another, only to have the outline submerge once again for the remainder of the sermon. Jacob's approach to sermon construction and delivery thus reveals the presence of "concealed heads," or a "concealed method," rather than an overt, explicit style. The text also demonstrates Smith's ability to depart from his prepared mental outlines to pursue extemporaneous tangents in the moment of performance.

Mormon's Explicit and Concealed Heads

As Jacob's sermons might suggest, Smith's use of both explicit and concealed heads in the oral construction of discourses fluctuates between these styles of extemporaneous delivery, often within the same sermon. Neither was this approach limited to Jacob's orations. For example, Smith's construction and performance of the prophet Mormon's sermon on faith, hope, and charity offers another explicit illustration of this dynamic. The prophet Mormon, after whom the Book of Mormon is named, is one of the last Nephite characters in the story. Indeed, Mormon's sermon appears in the text after he has already died. His son Moroni, the sole survivor of the Nephite nation and the keeper of the ancient records of their people, includes his father's sermon in the final pages of the work. By way of introducing the sermon, Moroni provides a brief summary announcing the subject (or the "text") of his father's oration: "And now I, Moroni, write a few of the words of my father Mormon, which he spake concerning faith, hope and charity" (Moroni 7:1).[38] The chapter then switches from Moroni's introduction to Mormon's first-person sermon.

After a lengthy introduction, in which he teaches his audience how to discern between good and evil, along with an admonition to "lay hold upon every good thing," Mormon finally lays down the first explicit head of his discourse: "And now I come to that faith, of which I said I would speak" (Moroni 7:21).[39] This statement might confuse the reader, given that this is the first time Mormon mentions faith in his sermon (Smith has introduced "faith" in *Moroni's* introduction of Mormon's sermon, but Mormon himself has not yet mentioned faith anywhere in his message prior to this point).[40] Nevertheless, after laying down this explicit head, Mormon proceeds to address the topic of faith. When finished with the topic, Mormon then lays down the second explicit head: "And again my beloved brethren, I would speak unto you concerning hope" (Moroni 7:40).[41] Accordingly, Mormon addresses the topic of hope. At this point in the sermon, Mormon's sequence has become entirely predictable: his sermon on faith, hope, and charity is following the same sequence in which these three virtues appear in Moroni's introduction, acting as a blueprint for each section. The sequence, moreover, derives directly from Paul's passage on charity, with a particular focus on the well-known formula, "And now abideth faith, hope, charity, these three; but the greatest of these is charity" (1 Cor. 13:13).[42]

Nonetheless, for the third segment of organization, addressing the topic of charity, Mormon switches from an explicit method to a somewhat concealed one, transitioning directly to the third topic, but *without* an explicit head to announce the shift. In other words, instead of stating an explicit head up front, such as "and now I would speak unto you concerning charity," Mormon, in a delayed fashion, quietly transitions from hope to charity, unobtrusively sliding from one topic to another within the regular course of the sermon: "And again: Behold I say unto you, That he cannot have faith and hope, save he shall be meek, and lowly of heart . . . and if a man be meek and lowly in heart, and confesses by the power of the Holy Ghost, that Jesus is the Christ, he must needs have charity: for if he have not charity, he is nothing; wherefore he must needs have charity" (Moroni 7:43–44).[43] Following this treatment of the three virtues, Mormon finishes his sermon with an exhortation to his audience to "cleave unto charity, which is the greatest of all," finishing the explanatory sermon in a common four-part "doctrine and use" pattern (Moroni 7:1–48):

> I. Text: "I, Moroni, write a few of the words of my father Mormon,
>   which he spake concerning faith, hope and charity" (7:1).
> II. Introduction with interpretations of gospel principles (7:2–20).
> III. The main heads of the discourse, treated progressively:
>   Faith, Hope, and Charity (7:21, 40, 42–44).
> IV. Applications/Exhortation (7:46–48).

As with Jacob's sermons, Smith's decision to follow a basic "doctrine and use" pattern would have facilitated the delivery and reception of his message among nineteenth-century readers by presenting them with a familiar and contemporary pattern of sermonizing.

Smith's composition of Mormon's sermon, moving sequentially through faith, hope, and charity, reflects the same progressive pattern that Smith used in Jacob's sermons, as well as the King Follett sermon. As previously noted, Mormon's son, Moroni, introduces his father's text with an announcement of the subject/text ("And now I, Moroni, write a few of the words of my father Mormon, which he spake concerning faith, hope and charity").[44] But this opening announcement of Paul's triad of virtues is not part of Mormon's actual sermon. Thus, within the sermon itself, Mormon moves progressively through the sermon from one topic to the next, keeping the outline concealed from the audience and developing each topic in succession.

This popular style of delivery—specifically, progressing through the topics of a written or mental outline, announcing them one at a time, *without* laying down all of the main heads in an explicit opening summary—was inevitably a more flexible variation of the technique of laying down heads, which, for the sake of clarity, might best be described as "progressive heads."[45] In effect, the style of laying down progressive heads provided an efficient compromise that took advantage of the flexibility of using concealed heads, which allowed speakers to follow their impromptu trains of thought during performance without upsetting a pre-announced outline, while simultaneously offering the clarity of explicit heads, which provided listeners with concrete statements describing the topic at hand.

As observed in the previous examples, Smith alternates between concealing and revealing his progression from one topic to the next in the sermons and discourses, which can obscure or, as the technique was meant to do, "conceal" the technique. At times, however, Smith provides overt examples of his method, where the consistent announcement of explicit heads in a progressive sequence demonstrates the process at work in a transparent manner. We can observe an example of this explicit arrangement in the Book of Alma, when the main character Alma (aka Alma the Younger), the high priest over the church and former chief judge over all the people of Nephi, instructs and reprimands one of his sons, the wayward Corianton.

Alma the Younger and Progressive Heads

In the overall narrative of the Book of Mormon, the time period for Alma the Younger's counsel to his sons occurs in approximately 74 B.C.E. Alma, along with two of his sons, Shiblon and Corianton, as well as a small group of religious colleagues, have all recently returned from a missionary tour among a group of idol-worshipping apostates known as the Zoramites (Alma 31–35). Upon his return to Zarahemla, Alma gathers his three sons together—Helaman, Shiblon, and Corianton—in order to "give unto them every one his charge, separately, concerning the things pertaining unto righteousness" (Alma 35:16).[46] Alma, as might be expected, begins with his eldest son, Helaman (Alma 36–37), followed by his middle son, Shiblon (Alma 38). When he turns to Corianton, Alma begins with a sharp reprimand, detailing his son's offenses with explicit heads that he will soon amplify: "Now this is what I have against thee: *Thou didst go on unto boasting in thy strength, and thy wisdom. And this is not all, my son. Thou didst do that which was grievous unto me; for thou didst forsake the ministry, and did go over into the land of Siron, among the borders of the Lamanites, after the harlot Isabel*" (Alma 39:2–3).[47] Once he finishes the scolding, Alma shifts into a lecture-sermon format.

With Corianton's sexual escapade fresh on his mind, Alma's thoughts turn to Jesus Christ and the plan of redemption. In an attempt to teach his son and help him reform his life, Alma expounds on Christ's role in salvation and the ramifications of the Lord's sacrifice. In doing so, Alma proceeds through his discourse, laying down explicit and formulaic heads for each main section, but *without* announcing all of the topics together in a single opening summary or a prefatory outline at the beginning of the lecture:

Alma's Progressive Heads

I. Alma 39:15: "And now, my son, I would say somewhat unto you concerning the coming of Christ."
(Alma speaks about Christ, 39:15–19)

II. Alma 40:1: "Now my son, here is somewhat more I would say unto thee; for I perceive that thy mind is worried concerning the resurrection of the dead."
(Alma speaks about the resurrection, 40:2–26)

III. Alma 41:1: "And now, my son, I have somewhat to say concerning the restoration of which has been spoken."
(Alma describes the restoration of all things, 41:1–15)

IV. Alma 42:1: "And now, my son, I perceive there is somewhat more which doth worry your mind, which ye cannot understand, which is concerning the justice of God in the punishment of the sinner."[48]
(Alma speaks about the justice of God, 42:1–31)

After his explanation of Christ's role in the salvation of mankind, Alma, following the conventions of typical nineteenth-century sermons, ends his lecture with an exhortation, urging Corianton to seek repentance and God's mercy (Alma 42:29–31). Nevertheless, it is Smith's use of progressive heads in the central body of the lecture that warrants our attention. The progression from one explicit head to the next exposes one of Smith's central approaches to oral composition and delivery, revealing his awareness of one of the most common variations of laying down heads within his contemporary sermon culture.

Progressive heads, however, should not automatically be associated with fully premeditated sermons. Progressive heads could appear in both premeditated and extemporaneous discourses. In the former, the preacher followed a prepared outline. In the latter, the preacher simply moved from one improvised topic to another, choosing successive topics according to the inspiration of the moment, while simultaneously adopting contemporary sermon conventions to announce an explicit head at the beginning of each new topic. As such, Alma's lecture-sermon to his son Corianton may have been a premeditated text in which Smith followed a mental skeletal outline of the lecture, or it may have been an extempore performance in which each new formulaic head tracked Smith's train of thought in the moment of oral composition. In fact, the speech may well have been a mixture of both.

Smith's Background and Training

While Smith's use of contemporary preaching techniques and sermon conventions in the Book of Mormon provides ample evidence of his familiarity with such practices, the content of his religious orations also offers clues about his background and level of preparation. Smith's training as a lay Methodist exhorter, along with his exposure to preaching styles in his cultural milieu, would have encouraged the conscious and focused study of fundamental gospel principles. As noted previously, aspiring preachers and exhorters, through institutional guidance and a wide variety of instructional manuals on pulpit oratory, were encouraged to study the scriptures and religious history in efficient and methodical ways—all with an aim toward performance. Such systematic preparations resulted in a storehouse of structured, well-organized, and well-practiced sermons and exhortations, which young preachers could deliver with little or no advance warning. Moreover, such programs stressed the mastery of core principles and doctrines of Christianity—usually a form of systematic theology often described as the "branches of divinity" or the "body of divinity"—in order to provide new preachers with a solid foundation on familiar gospel topics.

For young preachers embarking on such preparations, however, the countless religious topics, issues, and controversies in the branches of divinity could be vast and intimidating. Though many books and manuals were available on the subject and promised to give aspiring preachers a comprehensive view of doctrines and principles of the gospel, the texts were often dense multivolume works filled with list after list of detailed religious topics. Mastery of such manuals could take years. And, for young students like Smith, who participated as lay Methodist exhorters and aspiring preachers, Wesley's daunting fifty-volume *Christian Library* (1750) would have been the centerpiece for instruction, presenting the neophyte preacher with a seemingly overwhelming task. In the face of such challenges, mentors and authors on pulpit oratory often advised young preachers to begin their studies by

focusing on the core doctrines and teachings of Christianity before introducing additional and more extraneous topics into their repertoire of sermon and exhortation material.

In his *Lectures on Systematic Theology and Pulpit Eloquence* (1807), for instance, George Campbell identified the fundamental subjects that all new
preachers should master: "the doctrines of the unity, the spirituality, the natural and moral attributes of God, the creation, preservation and government of
the world by him; the principal events in the life of Jesus Christ, as well as his
crucifixion, resurrection and ascension, the doctrine of a future judgment,
heaven and hell, together with all those moral truths which exhibit the great
outlines of our duty to God, our neighbour and ourselves."[49] Campbell's work
typifies the advice found in manuals aimed at aspiring preachers in multiple
denominations. But the same recommendations, often functioning as supple-
ments to popular works on pulpit oratory, also appeared in works geared
toward specific religious traditions.

In *A Serious and Affectionate Address to the Junior Preachers in the Methodist Connection* (1798), John Pawson identified three core ideas as the "great
and important truths" for Methodist preachers: "1. Man is a fallen, guilty,
depraved, and helpless creature. 2. Jesus Christ has fully accomplished the
work of man's redemption. 3. The absolute necessity of Repentance, of
Faith in Christ, of the knowledge of salvation by the remission of sins, of
the new-birth, and of entire Sanctification of body, soul, and spirit."[50] Adam
Clarke, while advocating diligent study in science, literature, and philosophy, along with reading the Bible "at least once in the year" and taking notes
on topics suitable for discourses, urged new Methodist preachers to focus
their sermons on the basic, most essential message of the gospel: "As to the
matter of your preaching, I will only say, preach Jesus: preach his atonement—
preach his dying love—and through him proclaim a *free, full* and *present* salvation."[51] Such guidance for dedicated study and self-improvement sought
to instill in aspiring preachers a set of preplanned sermons addressing foundational Christian principles, which would facilitate the development of an
arsenal of premeditated modules on topics concerning doctrines, scriptures, theological propositions, religious controversies, and Christian commonplaces, all of which the Holy Spirit could draw upon in the moment of
performance.

Moreover, by arranging such topics in an orderly and logical manner, particularly in narrative sequences, the student could systematically study and
embed the subjects in the mind. When discussing what he termed the

branches of "sacred history" and the "christian system," for example, Campbell argued that Christianity was composed of "a most important narrative of a series of events, relating to the creation, the fall, the recovery, and the eternal state of man," which could be studied and memorized in relation to the historical periods in which sacred events occurred.[52] By arranging fundamental gospel topics into such a narrative and logical framework, the "theological student should have it in his power to contemplate them in their natural connection [i.e., their original historical context and relationship to other principles], and thus be enabled to perceive both the mutual dependence of the parts and the symmetry of the whole [i.e., the whole system of the gospel, as developed historically]."[53] Thus, rather than studying individual gospel topics in random, disconnected, and haphazard ways, the aspiring preacher could arrange several fundamental Christian topics into historically based narratives and thereby facilitate memorization and comprehension. Moreover, such sequences provided young preachers with easily memorized, ready-made patterns that they could put to immediate use in their exhortations and sermons.

When turning to the Book of Mormon, we find that Smith repeatedly incorporated this same type of basic narrative into his work. For instance, when Aaron, the missionary son of Mosiah, teaches the basics of the gospel to the king over all the Lamanites, Smith provides the reader with a core summary of fundamental Christian doctrines arranged into a commonplace pattern that outlines the plan of salvation, beginning with the creation of Adam and extending to Christ's atonement (Alma 22:12–14):

And it came to pass that when Aaron saw that the king would believe his words, he began from the creation of Adam, reading the Scriptures unto the king; how God created man after his own image, and that God gave him commandments, and that because of transgression, man had fallen. And Aaron did expound unto him the Scriptures, from the creation of Adam, laying the fall of man before him, and their carnal state, and also the plan of redemption, which was prepared from the foundation of the world, through Christ, for all whosoever would believe on his name. And since man had fallen, he could not merit any thing of himself; but the sufferings and death of Christ atoneth for their sins, through faith and repentance, &c.; and that he breaketh the bands of death, that the grave shall have no victory, and that the sting of death should be swallowed up in the hopes of glory.[54]

Earlier in the Book of Mormon, Ammon, Aaron's brother, presents a variation of this same outline to King Lamoni, the son of the king over all the Lamanites (Alma 18:36–39).

In fact, throughout the Book of Mormon, Smith presents the reader with multiple versions of this basic matrix in the writings and sermons of the prophets. When preaching to the people of Ammonihah, Alma and Amulek deliver another variation of this same narrative, progressing through Adam's fall, the effects on sin and death, the necessity of repentance, the resurrection of the dead, plan of redemption, and final judgment (Alma 12:22–27). And though the complete collection of fundamental gospel topics does not appear in every instance, and though the elements appear in a variety of sequences, Smith nevertheless adapts this same core matrix of doctrinal teachings to different narrative contexts.

Prophets who deliver similar doctrinal narrative passages include Lehi (2 Nephi 2:3–28); Nephi (2 Nephi 25:12–29 and 2 Nephi 31:1–21); Jacob (2 Nephi 9:4–26, Jacob 4:4–13, and Jacob 6:8–13); King Benjamin (Mosiah 3:5–19 and Mosiah 4:4–12); Abinadi (Mosiah 13:28 through Mosiah 16:15); Alma (Alma 7:7–25 and Alma 42:1–27); Ammon (Alma 18:36, 39); Amulek (Alma 34:2–16); Samuel the Lamanite (Helaman 14:11–20); Mormon (Moroni 8:22–26); and Moroni (Moroni 10:32–33). Smith's repetition of basic religious principles thus facilitates the rapid production (and reproduction) of passages. By returning repeatedly to these introductory core principles and their narrative arrangements, Smith significantly expanded the length of the Book of Mormon by producing variations of a single doctrinal matrix. Moreover, such arrangements of fundamental gospel elements would have been second nature, never requiring Smith to reference notes before dictation and only requiring little (if any) deliberate preparation.

At the same time, however, Smith did not simply rehash basic topics and modules. As the Book of Mormon repeatedly demonstrates, Smith was profoundly invested in a project to reinterpret traditional beliefs in an effort to construct a new Christian narrative. Accordingly, he also engaged in more advanced adaptations of biblical passages and creative reconfigurations of traditional concepts. As Philip L. Barlow observes, Smith "uses the Bible as revealed, if imperfect, truth, then proceeds to reuse parts of it, combined with nonbiblical elements, to express new revelation and to proclaim new or 're-stored' truth."[55] The tension between Smith's perfunctory repetition of commonplace doctrinal concepts and his creative innovation of new theological insights suggests that Smith was still in the process of developing his ideas and establishing his own prophetic voice when he was dictating the Book of Mormon to his scribes.

Gospel Controversies

Along with having an understanding of fundamental gospel principles, aspiring preachers were also encouraged to become familiar with theological controversies in order to defend the doctrines and scriptural interpretations of their given denominations. On the other hand, they were also often advised not to make such topics the focus of their sermons. As James Fordyce urged, the preacher should "avoid as much as possible, 'doubtful disputations,' or controversies concerning matters of mere speculation, and the subtil distinctions of parties [denominations]; such as lie at a distance from the vitals of religion."[56] Even so, as Campbell argued, many fundamental gospel topics were "made the subject of disputation," and therefore it was incumbent upon new preachers to study doctrinal controversies in order "to distinguish truth from error, and to defend the former against the most subtle attacks of its adversaries."[57] Knowledge of controversies, whether or not preachers actually defended their doctrines in public, was essential to proper training.

Nevertheless, because "a thorough knowledge of all the disputes that have ever arisen in the church" could result in a time-consuming project that "would be both endless and unprofitable," Campbell advised new preachers to begin their studies by focusing on the issues and controversies that existed within their own communities: "A more particular acquaintance therefore with the disputes and questions in theology of the age and country wherein we live, and with the distinguishing tenets of the different sects, with which we are surrounded, is necessary to the divine [minister], not only in point of decency, but even for self defence."[58] Such advice offers further insights regarding Smith's preparations and the composition of the Book of Mormon.

In 1831 Alexander Campbell (1788–1866; no relation to George Campbell), a prominent minister in the Restoration Movement and outspoken critic of Smith, published a detailed critique of the Book of Mormon. In light of studying local doctrinal controversies, Campbell's contemporary assessment offers compelling clues about Smith's background and preparation. When observing the presence of current nineteenth-century theological issues among the ancient Book of Mormon peoples, Campbell observed, "This prophet Smith, through his stone spectacles, wrote on the plates of Nephi, in his book of Mormon, every error and almost every truth discussed in New York for the last ten years. He decides all the great controversies;—infant baptism, ordination, the trinity, regeneration, repentance, justification, the fall of man, the atonement, transubstantiation, fasting, penance, church government, religious experience, the call to the ministry, the general resurrection, eternal punishment, who may baptize, and even the question of free masonary [*sic*], republican government, and the rights of man. All these topics are repeatedly alluded to."[59] Campbell's observations, though decidedly antagonistic, prove especially perceptive. According to Smith's personal account, the same ten-year period marked the time when he became intensely interested in reading the Bible and investigating the teachings and controversies among the various denominations in his world. Thus, rather than leaving historians to deduce his preparations indirectly from the text of the Book of Mormon, Smith provides direct evidence of his concentrated reading and preoccupations, which, according to his own account, began when he was only twelve years old and continued for several years.

"At about the age of twelve years," Smith recalled, "my mind become seriously imprest with regard to the all[-]important concerns for the well fare of my immortal Soul which led me to searching the scriptures believeing as I was taught, that they contained the word of God." After "applying myself to them," Smith compared what he had learned from the Bible with his "intimate acquaintance with those of differant denominations," and he determined that none of them practiced "a holy walk and Godly conversation agreeable to what I found contained in that sacred depository." Continuing with his precocious and concentrated studies "from the age of twelve years to fifteen," Smith pondered the various "contentions and divi[si]ons the wicke[d]ness and abominations and the darkness which pervaded the minds of mankind" and became convinced that all the denominations "did not come unto the Lord but that they had apostatised from the true and liveing faith and there was no society or denomination that built upon the gospel of Jesus Christ as recorded in the new testament."[60] Campbell's observation that Smith included in the Book of Mormon "every error and almost every truth discussed in New York for the last ten years" thus corresponded with Smith's own personal development, preparations, and religious concerns spanning the same period of time, in the same Western New York location where he lived.

Exhortations and the Language of Revivalism

Smith's attendance at the services of several denominations—his likely childhood attendance at Congregational services in New England with immediate and extended family, Sunday school in Palmyra at the Presbyterian church, Methodist class meetings, and joint revivals held by "the Baptists, Methodists and Presbyterians" in New York—no doubt informed his claim of having an "intimate acquaintance with those of differant denominations."[61] His awareness was not mere bookish knowledge or indirect hearsay but information derived from active attendance and participation. Within this performative milieu Smith would have witnessed countless sermons, complete with exhortations of several varieties—preachers' exhortations as part of their sermons, exhorters' admonitions following other preachers' sermons, and any number of personal exhortations among lay attendees at class meetings and similar venues.[62] His training as a lay Methodist exhorter would have further imprinted the patterns, language, and topics of exhortation, in which the speaker stressed the urgent need for listeners to seek a spiritual awakening. And while some exhortations could be specific to a particular sermon or lesson, others fell into generic patterns, often centering on calls to repentance and the necessity of embracing Christ.

When viewing Smith's use of exhortations in the Book of Mormon, we find a similar combination of spiritual appeals: ones that are tied to the specific teachings of sermons (or narrative events) as well as exhortations containing generic patterns of information that could appear in almost any narrative situation. In terms of understanding Smith's approach to oral composition, the latter exhortations, filled with generic language and patterns, offer tantalizing clues about his process. Just as young preachers developed perfunctory sermons and exhortations on fundamental gospel topics—that is, transposable preaching segments that could appear in virtually any sermon, regardless of topic—so, too, did they develop exhortation routines that they could produce on a moment's notice, with little or no preparation and without any need for notes. In order to view how such sections operate within sermons, we will turn our attention to one of the best-known sermons in the Book of Mormon: King Benjamin's final address to the Nephite nation.

In approximately 124 B.C.E., according to Book of Mormon chronology, King Benjamin, one of the last Nephite kings, "waxed old" and decided it was "expedient that he should confer the kingdom upon one of his sons" before he died (Mosiah 1:9).[63] He asked Mosiah, his son and heir to the throne, to gather the people together so that he could deliver a proclamation to them. In doing so, King Benjamin tells Mosiah what he wants to say, providing in advance two explicit topics that will guide his oration: (1) "I shall proclaim unto this my people, out of mine own mouth, that thou art a king, and a ruler over this people," and (2) "moreover, I shall give this people a name [i.e., the people of Christ], that thereby they may be distinguis[h]ed above all the people which the Lord God hath brought out of the land of Jerusalem" (Mosiah 1:10–11).[64] By announcing these topics before dictating the actual speech, Smith thus demonstrated his foreknowledge of the general sequence and contents of King Benjamin's proclamation.

As the story continues, and in a scene "that has been compared to the Jewish Feast of Tabernacles, to camp meetings in the nineteenth century, and to other forms," the people gather together and "pitched their tents round about the temple," with their doors facing toward the temple in order to "hear the words which king Benjamin should speak unto them" (Mosiah 2:6).[65] In the introduction to his proclamation, King Benjamin speaks about his experiences and responsibilities as the Nephite king, along with describing how his philosophies of service and righteous leadership have guided his treatment of the people. King Benjamin extends this background (with other minor digressions) into a lesson on the importance of serving God and serving one another, along with the importance of being obedient to God's commandments (Mosiah 2:9–28). Finally, after this discursive introduction, King Benjamin declares that the Lord God has commanded him to tell the people that his son Mosiah would become the new king and ruler over the Nephites (Mosiah 2:29–30).

With this announcement by King Benjamin, Smith arrives at the first of the two topics that he already announced in the previous chapter. Nevertheless, as he proceeds further into the proclamation (which transforms into a sermon), King Benjamin does not immediately move to the second preplanned topic to "give this people a name," or, rather, to identify them as followers of Christ. Instead, he admonishes the Nephite people to be obedient to the commandments of his son Mosiah (Mosiah 2:31). This admonition, whether by design or by inspiration, prompts Smith to take King Benjamin's speech onto a lengthy tangent, describing how those who obey the commandments receive God's protection and "prosper in the land," while those who disobey God's laws and follow "the evil spirit" risk losing their salvation (Mosiah 2:32–41).[66]

During this digression, King Benjamin's language transforms into a forceful style, reflecting the impassioned decrees of spontaneous exhortations. Mirroring the soul-shaking terror invoked by revivalist preachers in the Second Great Awakening, King Benjamin describes how those who have been taught the gospel of Jesus Christ and yet choose to rebel against God will suffer eternal damnation (Mosiah 2:38–40):

> If that man repenteth not, and remaineth and dieth an enemy to God, the demands of Divine Justice do awaken his immortal soul to a lively sense

of his own guilt, which doth cause him to shrink from the presence of the Lord, and doth fill his breast with guilt, and pain, and anguish, which is like an unquenchable fire, whose flames ascendeth up forever and ever. And now I say unto you, that mercy hath no claim on that man; therefore, his final doom is to endure a never ending torment.[67]

This passage, though ostensibly biblical in its archaic style and colorful expressions, is actually dominated by a patchwork of nonbiblical wording and nineteenth-century religious phraseology. While terms such as "unquenchable fire" and "enemy to/of God" appear in the scriptures (e.g., Matt. 3:12, Luke 3:17, and James 4:4), Smith fills King Benjamin's exhortation with the devotional vocabulary of contemporary revivalism.[68] The phrase "the demands of divine justice"; the description of an "immortal soul"; the act of "awakening" someone's "soul"; to have "a lively sense" of guilt or a spiritual experience; to "shrink" from divine beings, emotions, or spiritual experiences; to "fill the breast" with strong emotions, good or bad; to describe how "mercy" has "no claim" on the unrepentant; and the "final doom" of enduring "never-ending torment" are all nonbiblical terms from Smith's nineteenth-century religious milieu.[69]

Smith did not learn this language from reading, memorizing, or listening to passages from the Bible. Rather, the presence of such contemporary language, especially in the context of sermons and exhortations, provides direct evidence of Smith's exposure to the culture and venues of evangelical revivalism, supporting Smith's own claim that he had participated in such events in his personal spiritual journey to discover gospel truths. Moreover, Smith does not limit the language (or behaviors) of revivalism to the sermons and exhortations of prophets in the Book of Mormon. Audience responses also reflect the spontaneous, improvised language of conversion in dynamic call-and-response exchanges between the preacher and the audience.

Later in the sermon, King Benjamin warns the people to repent or face eternal damnation in "a state of misery and endless torment," which he describes in blistering (and repetitive) detail "as a lake of fire and brimstone, whose flames are unquenchable, and whose smoke ascendeth up forever and ever" (Mosiah 3:25, 27). After hearing these words, members of his audience replicate the "falling exercises" commonly practiced in nineteenth-century evangelical revivals and collapse on the ground, "for the fear of the Lord had come upon them" (Mosiah 4:1).[70] In this state of terrified self-reflection and spiritual awakening, "they all cried aloud with one voice" and provide the reader with an apposite refrain that draws on the language of evangelical conviction (Mosiah 4:1–2): "O have mercy, and apply the atoning blood of Christ, that we may receive forgiveness of our sins, and our hearts may be purified: for we believe in Jesus Christ, the Son of God, who created Heaven and earth, and all things; who shall come down among the children of men."[71] Such terrifying exhortations and fearful responses could be lifted—oftentimes verbatim—from the Book of Mormon and placed seamlessly back into nineteenth-century camp meetings.

Finally, it would be remiss not to mention additional aspects of King Benjamin's proclamation-sermon that reveal Smith's ability to compose lengthy passages without the need of a manuscript or notes. As discussed earlier, aspiring preachers and exhorters were encouraged to master the core doctrines and principles of Christianity for their sermons. Just as we observed this narrativized collection of principles in the teachings of Ammon, so too does King Benjamin invoke the same narrative package of gospel fundamentals in his sermon to the Nephite people. After announcing that his son Mosiah will become the new ruler in his initial exhortation (Mosiah 2:9–41), King Benjamin finally lays down the second main head of his sermon: "And again my brethren, I would call your attention, for I have somewhat more to speak unto you: for behold, I have things to tell you, *concerning that which is to come*" (Mosiah 3:1).[72] This head, we should recall, is a variant of the same head and/or phrase that other prophets evoke in the Book of Mormon to describe the coming of Christ and his role in the plan of salvation.[73] Given this announcement, it should come as no surprise that King Benjamin continues his sermon by preaching about the coming of Christ and salvation in his name through faith, repentance, baptism, and entering into a covenant to become his followers.

"I have things to tell you, concerning that which is to come," King Benjamin announces to his people, "and the things which I shall tell you, are made known unto me, by an Angel from God" (Mosiah 3:1–2). In recounting the angelic message, King Benjamin provides the reader with another example of a basic collection of fundamental Christian doctrines, packaged into a logical sequence and memorable narrative: that Christ will come to earth and dwell in a mortal body (Mosiah 3:5); that he will perform many miracles, such as healing the sick and casting out devils (3:5–6); that he will suffer from temptations and bleed from every pore (3:7); that his name will be "Jesus Christ" and his mother will be called "Mary" (3:8); that he will bring salvation to mankind (3:9); that he will be scourged and crucified (3:9); that he will rise from the dead after three days (3:10); that his life and death will bring about a "righteous judgment" (3:10); that his sacrifice will atone "for the sins of those who have fallen by the transgression of Adam" (3:11); that salvation only comes through repentance and faith in Christ (3:12); and that those who will believe in Christ "might receive remission of their sins, and rejoice with exceeding great joy" (3:13).[74]

Neither does King Benjamin's list of topics end with the previous narrative arrangement. He continues this passage by addressing several additional issues related to Christ's teachings and his divine mission, such as the Law of Moses (Mosiah 3:14–15); the innocence of children (a stance in the contemporary controversies over infant baptism, 3:16, 18, 21); Adam's fall and original sin (3:16, 19); salvation through Christ and his atonement (3:17–19); and the final damnation of the unrighteous (3:24–27). When viewing these passages as a whole, we find that King Benjamin's sermon topics consist of generic, fundamental Christian doctrines and controversies—lessons that could arguably appear at any time, in any place, and under any circumstances in the course of the Book of Mormon. Moreover, these fundamental principles could also appear, with little modification, in any revival or camp meeting in early nineteenth-century Western New York, especially when delivered by young and aspiring preachers.

Preaching the Book of Mormon

In a review of the sermons, prophecies, exhortations, teachings, commentaries, and related oral performances in the Book of Mormon, we find that the text systematically reveals the structures and conventions of the semi-extemporaneous preaching that saturated Smith's nineteenth-century environment. The abundance of such evidence in the text, combined with Smith's awareness and explicit use of the same techniques in his 1832 history and the sermons he performed throughout his career, provide important insights. Significantly, as the text repeatedly demonstrates, Smith avoided the explicit announcement of comprehensive sermon outlines in the introductions to his orations, opting to limit any preliminary notifications to brief and often generalized heads. This approach, however, should not be confused with purely extempore performances. Smith's overt references to impending subjects and changes in topic, particularly when he lays down explicit and progressive heads to do so, demonstrate his use of the common "concealed" method of preaching, along with revealing a history of premeditation concerning the structure, sequence, and direction of his orations. In turn, this considered approach suggests some of the choices Smith made in preparation for his project.

By removing the constraints imposed by explicitly stated preliminary sermon outlines, Smith allowed himself the freedom to address any subject that sprang to mind, in any order and for any duration, without unsettling his reader by diverging too far from any explicitly stated heads in the opening of orations. In other words, the evidence suggests that Smith adopted the same method for Book of Mormon sermons that he would later use for the King Follett discourse, following practices shared by countless revivalist preachers in his contemporary milieu: He approached sermons and other religious orations with a premeditated but largely concealed outline in mind, leaving the actual wording and duration to the moment of performance. He also avoided providing too much detail in any preliminary outline in order to allow himself the freedom to follow the inspiration of the moment and to expand his sermons with improvised digressions. By this means, Smith's method of composition of sermons and related orations in the Book of Mormon was highly productive, requiring minimal specific preparation on the one hand, while, on the other, allowing for maximum flexibility and unbounded expansion during performance.

Thus, whenever a sermon required information specific to the development of the narrative, Smith could prepare such main points beforehand, meditate on the key issues and information that he wanted to address, and then follow (however loosely) his mental outline in performance—all the while allowing for extemporaneous diversions and expansions along the way. By contrast, however, whenever a sermon or a section within a sermon did *not* require such specific narrative or chronologic information, such as topics expounding commonplaces of Christian doctrines—the creation and fall, the coming of Christ, the atonement, the resurrection, the plan of redemption, and salvation—Smith could deliver unpremeditated and virtually "extempore" sermons and exhortations, with little or no specific preparation beyond what he had previously "treasured up" in his heart and mind over the course of a young lifetime. With such a foundational storehouse of commonplaces, all of which carried their own traditions of implicit order and structure, Smith could therefore "extemporize" passages of varying lengths and seeming diversity by drawing on little more than tradition, experience, memory, and habit.

Smith's approach to oral composition thereby reveals how he was able to produce lengthy passages in rapid and highly effective ways. For better appreciation of what this means for the composition and very nature of the Book of Mormon itself, a comparison of the length and number of sermons, exhortations, and religious orations with the overall text of the Book of Mormon proves insightful. As indicated in the opening of this chapter, Smith's religious discourses in the Book of Mormon take up more than 100,000 words of the entire text of approximately 269,510 words. These discourses include lengthy quotations of biblical passages (e.g., Isaiah, Malachi, Matthew), coupled with didactic and interpretive commentaries by Book of Mormon prophets; premeditated and extemporized sermons and exhortations; divine messages from God, Christ, and angels; curses and warnings; the fraught language and exclamations of revivalism; the teachings and writings of prophets; conversion narratives and faith-promoting stories; and prayers of different types and varieties, from set forms to extempore expressions.

The following list offers a brief overview of the central religious discourses that Smith produced for his text. This catalog begins with the names of internal books, coupled with a *conservative* estimate of the word count for the religious discourses they contain, followed by a brief note about the narrative content and specific scriptural references.[75]

1 Nephi (approx. 7,345 words devoted to religious discourse): Lehi praises God (1:14); Lehi exhorts (2:9–10); the Lord exhorts, prophesies (2:19–24); Nephi exhorts (4:1–3); the Spirit exhorts (4:11–14); Nephi exhorts Zoram (4:34); Nephi paraphrases Lehi's prophecy (5:18–19); Nephi exhorts (7:8–15); revival-style prayer (7:17); Nephi exhorts, paraphrases Lehi's teachings (8:37–38); Lehi prophesies, exhorts, narrates (10:6, 8); Nephi exhorts (10:18–22); an angel prophesies, exhorts (14:1–7); Nephi exhorts (15:10–18); Nephi interprets, exhorts (15:32–36); dialogue turns into exhortation (16:2–4); Nephi exhorts (17:3); Nephi exhorts (17:15, 23–47, 50–51); Nephi teaches (19:9–21, 24); Nephi interprets scripture, prophesies (20:1–22:31).

2 Nephi (approx. 26,760 words): Lehi blesses, teaches, exhorts (1:4–4:11); Nephi's lament (4:16–35); Jacob's sermon (6:2–10:25); Nephi prophesies, exhorts, quotes and interprets multiple Isaiah chapters (12:1–30:18); Nephi's doctrine of Christ (31:2–21); Nephi instructs (32:1–6, 8–9); Nephi glories in Christ, exhorts (33:6–15).

Jacob (approx. 6,691 words): Jacob sermonizes, exhorts (2:2–3:12); Jacob teaches, exhorts, prophesies (4:8–18); Jacob quotes Zenos's allegorical sermon "that Zenos spake" (5:2–77); Jacob comments on Zenos, prophesies (6:1–13).

Omni (approx. 65 words): Amaleki exhorts (1:26).

Mosiah (approx. 9,916 words): King Benjamin exhorts (1:3–7); King Benjamin's proclamation-sermon, not including narrative (2:9–5:15); Abinadi's defense, prophecies, teachings, not including narrative and some dialogue (11:20–16:15); Abinadi's prophetic curse (17:15–19); Alma the Elder's sermon, baptismal prayer (18:8–10, 13); God speaks to Alma the Elder (26:15–32); an angel exhorts Alma the Younger (27:13–16); Alma the Younger's conversion narrative (27:24–31).

Alma (approx. 24,032 words): Alma the Younger preaches in Zarahemla (5:3–62); Alma's sermon in Gideon (7:1–27); Alma preaches in Ammonihah (9:8–30); Amulek preaches (10:2–11); Alma rebukes, exhorts (10:17–23, 25–27); Amulek's doctrinal exposition, preaching (11:39–45); Alma exhorts (12:3–6); Alma teaches, exhorts (12:9–18 and 12:22–13:30); Ammon's teachings (18:24–39); conversion exclamations of King Lamoni and his wife the queen (18:41, 19:12–13, and 19:29); Aaron's teachings, the Lamanite king's conversion language (22:5–18); Ammon's praise and thanksgiving (26:1–9, 11–37); story moral, apparently by Mormon (28:13–14); Alma's praise and thanksgiving (29:1–17); Zoramite prayer, Alma's commentary (31:15–18, 28–35); Alma's sermon on faith (32:8–43 and 33:2–23); Amulek's sermon on faith and Christ (34:2–41); Alma's conversion narrative, teachings to his son Helaman (36:1–30 and 37:13, 15–17, 20, 33–37); Alma conversion narrative, exhortations to son Shiblon (38:1-15); Alma's exhortations, teachings to son Corianton (39:1–42:31); Alma prophesies (45:10–14, 16); Mormon's story moral (50:19–22).

Helaman (approx. 7,601 words): Helaman exhorts (5:6–12); revival language, "What shall we do?" (5:26, 29, 32, 40–41, 47); Nephi on the garden wall, prays, preaches, prophesies of a murder (7:13-29; 8:11–28; and 9:21–36); Lord speaks to Nephi (10:4–11); Nephi prays (11:4, 10–16); Mormon's commentary (12:1–26); Samuel the Lamanite preaches, prophesies, exhorts (13:5–15:17).

3 Nephi (approx. 13,507 words): the Lord's voice (1:13–14); Mormon's testimony (5:20–26); voice of Christ to disaster survivors (9:2–22 and 10:4–7); Mormon exhorts reader (10:14–19); Christ's first visit: a divine voice, Christ visits and speaks, people praise, Christ's baptismal and sacramental prayers, Christ teaches doctrine, Sermon on the Mount, New Testament Matthew 5–7 incorporated (11: 7, 10–11, 14, 17, 21, 22–41; 12:1–16:20; and 18:5–7, 10–16, 18–35); Christ's second visit: teaches people, Isaiah and Malachi quoted (20:8,10–25:6); Christ's third visit: names the church, expounds doctrine (27:4–33); Mormon exhorts, prophesies (28:33–35; 29:1–30:2).

Mormon (approx. 4,304 words): the Lord's voice, Mormon exhorts (3:2, 17–22); Mormon's historical account becomes exhortation (5:10–24); Mormon's exhortative lament, "O ye fair ones" (6:17–22); Mormon addresses Lamanite readers (7:2–10); Moroni's historical account shifts to sermon, prophecy, exhortation (8:13–41); Moroni exhorts nonbelievers (9:1–37).

Ether (approx. 3,352 words): Moroni on the Promised Land (2:9–12); Christ speaks (3:13–16); Moroni shares Christ's words (4:7–19); Moroni's moral, land of inheritance (8:22–26); Ether exhorts (12:3–4); Moroni exhorts, recounts stories of faith (12:6–41); Moroni paraphrases Ether's prophecies (13:2–12).

Moroni (ca. 4,461 words): Christ's words to disciples (2:2); Moroni's ordination prayer (3:3); Moroni's sacrament prayer for bread (4:3); Moroni's sacrament prayer for wine (5:2); Mormon's sermon: faith, hope, charity (7:2–48); Mormon on infant baptism (8:2–30); Mormon's warnings, exhortations (9:15, 25–26); Moroni's final exhortation to readers (10:1–34).

Totaling approximately 108,099 words, these religious discourses—many of which contain variations on the same fundamental Christian principles that require little or no preparation—compose just over 40 percent of the entire text of the Book of Mormon. Given the prominence of such passages, it would not be inaccurate to say that Smith *preached* the Book of Mormon as much as he composed it.

By situating Smith's performance of these religious discourses within his contemporary sermon culture, we discover further important insights. For instance, both in length and thematic content, Smith's oral performance of the sermons and exhortations in the Book of Mormon was not unlike the common "sermon series" discourses—that is, "an extensive sequence of thematically related sermons"—that had played an important role in the sermon culture of America ever since the colonial period.[76] Thomas Hooker (1586–1647), one of the best-known Puritan preachers in colonial New England, offers a relevant example for comparison. As Phyllis M. Jones and Nicholas R. Jones observe, Hooker's sermon series titled *The Soul's Vocation* (1638) contained an impressive 200,000 words.[77] In fact, the "reasons and uses" section of this extended discourse alone was "over 100,000 words in length," which approximates the same amount of material as Smith's religious discourses found scattered throughout the entire Book of Mormon.[78] In such contexts, the amount of material Smith produced was not unusual. Rather, it was the way he packaged it within the narrative framework of an ancient Native American epic that provided a relatively uncommon vehicle for expression.

Preaching the Word

Smith's personal style of composition and delivery in his 1832 history, the introduction to his 1843 Prodigal Son sermon, and his 1844 King Follett discourse reveals his familiarity with a variety of common and interrelated sermon conventions, including but not limited to his arrangement of sermons and exhortations into modern preaching formats (variations of the common "doctrine and use" pattern); the use of preliminary skeletal outlines to structure and guide the performance of subsequent discourses; the technique of laying down heads (progressive and enumerated); and the use of mental outlines. In combination with these strategies, Smith's explicit descriptions of "treasuring up" the word of God and speaking extemporaneously according to the inspiration of the Holy Ghost further reveal the scope of his preaching techniques, while simultaneously positioning his method directly within the sermon culture of contemporary revivalism.

When turning to the pages of Book of Mormon, we find that the same performance techniques that underpin Smith's individual sermons and narrative productions undergird the sermons, exhortations, and prophecies found in his epic work. From the opening narrative of Lehi's journey to the prophet Moroni's final exhortation, the text reveals the influence of an author who had become proficient in the basic techniques of nineteenth-century evangelical preaching. If Smith played no role in the creation and articulation of the Book of Mormon, then the real author(s)—mortal or divine, via covert manuscripts or luminous words appearing on the surface of a seer stone—managed to predict and imitate Smith's techniques so well that the results are indistinguishable from the young prophet's documented style and methods of later years.

Along with these conventions and techniques, the topics of Smith's religious orations in the Book of Mormon also contribute to the understanding of Smith's background and training. Throughout the work, Smith's religious discourses inevitably gravitate toward the same set of core fundamental Christian topics, arranged into memorable narrative sequences, that young evangelical preachers studied and memorized when they first prepared to become exhorters and ministers. Such introductory lessons, ingrained through repeated study and practice, served as spontaneous sermon routines that required little forethought or preparation to perform. By repeatedly infusing the Book of Mormon with these familiar and preplanned topics, Smith provided himself with a method through which he could effectively expand any given passage at will, amplifying what otherwise might be short sermons and brief exhortations into lengthy semi-improvised discourses. Indeed, the extent of the amplification and expansion of such topics was limited only by the speaker's imagination, endurance, and ambition.

This dynamic provides crucial information regarding Smith's ability to dictate texts in a rapid manner. For a substantial number of passages in the Book of Mormon, Smith would have required little or no advance preparation to produce lengthy theological discourses, whether performing them as standalone sermons or as sections within larger discourses. Considering that more than 40 percent of the Book of Mormon consists of a variety of religious orations, the amount of preparation for this material would have been minimal, perhaps only limited to those portions of text tied to immediate narrative concerns, chronologically sensitive narrative material, or sections delving deeper into theological issues than a fundamental overview of Christian concepts might otherwise address. These strategies and methods help to explain Smith's ability to peer into a seer stone and produce a torrent of sermons and exhortations, all packaged within the well-worn conventions and popular rhetorical patterns of his day.

Finally, Smith did not confine his application of these performance skills and sermon techniques to religious discourses in the Book of Mormon. Using the same approach that he adopted for his 1832 history, Smith also used narrative skeletons as guides to create the historical progression of his stories. This application, of course, was not original. The very nature of moving progressively from one topic to the next lent itself to the development of narrative plotlines, which moved from one illustrative story event to another. As noted in chapter 4, this observation explains why authors like John Mason, the popular Independent minister and author of *The Student and Pastor* (1755), recommended the method of laying down heads to outline the narrative structure of entire books as a way of organizing and preparing one's thoughts prior to composition.[79] This natural ordering also explains why Methodist preachers with little or no formal education likewise extended the same techniques of sermon construction to the composition of biographical funeral sermons and spiritual autobiographies. Given such awareness of the applications of laying down heads in Smith's contemporary sermon culture, the appearance of such techniques in the historical narratives of the Book of Mormon should come as no surprise.

CHAPTER SIX

Constructing Book of Mormon Historical Narratives

Even though Smith's semi-extemporaneous production of the sermons, prophecies, and exhortations within the Book of Mormon would have required minimal preparation, the historical chronology of the narrative, spanning a thousand-year period (with varying degrees of specificity), would have required much more detailed and conscious preparation. A speaker can ramble and take any number of excursions over the course of an oration without interrupting the plot of the story in which the oration is embedded. By contrast, the sequential framework of a historical narrative does not offer the same flexibility. Leaving the construction of a detailed chronology to a succession of purely extempore or even semi-extemporaneous performances certainly increases the chance of making uncomfortable mistakes. Thus, the careful preparation of a story outline—the management of the sequence of events, the dates and locations where they occur, and the characters involved—would have been a critical and central anchor for the entire Book of Mormon. Such constraints help to explain why Smith's method of laying down heads for his historical narratives emerges as the most prominent and visible compositional feature of the Book of Mormon. Indeed, Smith puts his explicit method of laying down heads on open display throughout the text, beginning with the opening chapter of the work.

While Nephi's admonition to Jacob to "engraven the heads" of his spiritual writings on the plates and to "touch upon them as much as it were possible" provides an explicit and unambiguous description of laying down heads in the context of sermon culture, Nephi goes beyond his advice to Jacob by actually demonstrating the centrality of this technique in his own work. Far from being reserved exclusively for sermons and spiritual texts, the method of laying down heads to form narrative outlines operates as the fundamental method of composition for Nephi's entire historical record. At the beginning of the Book of Mormon, prior to the well-known opening line, "I, Nephi, having been born of goodly parents," the prophet Nephi provides the reader with a skeletal outline that structures and arranges the majority of his ensuing record, "The First Book of Nephi." In order to map the stepwise progression of the narrative outline, the following diagram lists the sequence of heads (1 Nephi 1, heading):

An account of Lehi and his wife Sariah, and his four Sons,
  being called, (beginning at the eldest,) Laman, Lemuel, Sam, and Nephi.
  The Lord warns Lehi to depart out of the land of Jerusalem,
  because he prophesieth unto the people concerning their iniquity;
  and they seek to destroy his life.
  He taketh three days' journey into the wilderness with his family.
Nephi taketh his brethren
  and returns to the land of Jerusalem after the record of the Jews.
  The account of their sufferings.
They take the daughters of Ishmael to wife.
They take their families and depart into the wilderness.
  Their sufferings and afflictions in the wilderness.
  The course of their travels.
  They come to the large waters.
Nephi's brethren rebelleth against him.
  He confoundeth them, and buildeth a Ship.
  They call the place Bountiful.
They cross the large waters into the promised land, &c.
This is according to the account of Nephi;
  or, in other words, I Nephi wrote this record.[1]

As the final head indicates ("I Nephi wrote this record"), Smith attributes this authorial outline to the character Nephi. This skeletal framework thereby forms an integral component of the narrative itself, revealing Smith's approach to the composition of Nephi's religious history and spiritual autobiography.

Nephi also appears to be addressing a nineteenth-century audience, given that he uses a contemporary composition technique to frame his narrative. This is the same method that Smith used to create his 1832 history, suggesting that Smith, consciously or otherwise, was not trying to separate his voice entirely from the voice of Nephi. For comparison, observe the text of Smith's 1832 history, reformatted to highlight the catalog of events in his narrative:

A History of the life of Joseph Smith Jr.
an account of his marvilous experience and of all the mighty acts
  which he doeth in the name of Jesus Ch[r]ist[,]
  the son of the living God of whom he beareth record
and also an account of the rise of the church of Christ in the eve
    of time[,]
  according as the Lord brought forth and established by his hand
<firstly> he receiving the testamony from on high

secondly[,] the ministering of Angels.

thirdly[,] the reception of the holy Priesthood by the ministring
of Aangels
to administer the letter of the ~~Law~~ <Gospel—>
<—the Law and commandments[,]
as they were given unto him—>, and ~~in~~ <the> ordinencs [ordinance],

fo[u]rthly[,] a confirmation and reception of the high Priesthood[,]
after the holy order of the son of the living God[,]
power and ordinence from on high to preach the Gospel
in the administration and demonstration of the spirit
the Kees [keys] of the Kingdom of God confer[r]red upon him
and the continuation of the blessings of God to him &c—[2]

At first glance, Smith's inclusion of a skeletal outline attributed to Nephi in the opening narrative of the Book of Mormon seems curious. The insertion of such a prominent anachronism seems counterintuitive to the project of producing the translation of an ancient work.

A comparison with contemporary Bibles, however, suggests that Smith was attempting to imitate the textual and editorial apparatus found in many Bibles of the early nineteenth century. As Seth Perry has argued, Smith "drew on the full character of his era's print-Bible culture: not just the diction of the Authorized Version, but the formats, paratextual apparatus (textual features such as cross-references, indices, and prefaces that mediate between text and reader), and translational variety of early-national bibles."[3] Consider the following summary for Genesis 12 from Adam Clarke's Commentary (1810–25), which, as previously noted, may have been a text that Smith consulted during the period when he produced the Book of Mormon (Clarke's heads are also reformatted here for comparison; the numbers at the end of each head refer to the specific verses):

God calls Abram to leave Haran, and go into Canaan, 1;
promises to bless him, and through him all the families of the earth, 2, 3.
Abram, Sarai, Lot, and all their hous[e]hold, depart for Canaan, 4, 5.
Abram passes through Sichem, 6.
God appears to him, and renews the promise, 7.
His journey described, 8, 9.
On account of a famine in the land, he is obliged to go into Egypt, 10.
Through fear lest, on account of the beauty of his wife, the Egyptians
should kill him, he desires her not to acknowledge that she
was his wife, but only his sister, 11,—13.
Sarai, because of her beauty, is taken into the palace of Pharoah,

> king of Egypt, who is very liberal to Abram on her account, 14–16.
> God afflicts Pharoah and his household with grievous plagues
>   on account of Sarai, 17.
> Pharoah, on finding that Sarai was Abram's wife, restores her honourably,
>   and dismisses the Patriarch with his family and their property, 18–20.[4]

Clarke was certainly not the only commentator adding such opening summaries to chapters in the Bible, and Smith could easily have adopted this practice from observing any number of other nineteenth-century Bibles and commentaries.[5] Smith's potential exposure to Clarke's popular commentary, however, might have offered both a model for imitation as well as one of several possible explanations for adopting such an apparatus.

For Clarke, providing summaries was a conscious effort to facilitate scripture study. "The *Summaries* to each Chapter are entirely written for the purpose," Clarke apprised his readers, "and formed from a careful examination of the Chapter, verse by verse, so as to make them a faithful Table of Contents, constantly referring to the verses themselves. By this means, all the subjects of each Chapter may be immediately seen, so, as in many cases, to preclude the necessity of consulting a Concordance."[6] Whatever his specific model, Smith mimics this contemporary form of biblical apparatus in an apparent attempt to duplicate the same pedagogical effect and further to lend authoritative weight to the text of the Book of Mormon.

In spite of these clear parallels between Smith's opening summaries and contemporary print culture, some Mormon scholars have nevertheless claimed that these outlines come from an entirely different source, arguing that the opening summaries represent translations of ancient colophons engraved on the gold plates. In 1967 Hugh Nibley argued that the opening summary for the First Book of Nephi, among other prefatory headings within the work, represented ancient colophons.[7] Yet, contrary to this speculation, the summarizing headers that appear in the Book of Mormon represent a fundamentally different textual apparatus.[8] Colophons in ancient texts are *scribal* notations (not authorial summaries), usually at the end of copied texts (not original compositions), which provide largely technical information about the accompanying work, such as the name of the scribe, the date the copy was made, and the location of the work.[9] They are not, however, tables of contents, indices, story outlines embedded within narratives, or narrative summaries like Nephi's first-person preliminary outline.

At this stage, I want to alert readers to the fact that the attempt to conflate Smith's outlines with ancient colophons is not a doctrinal claim of any denomination in the Latter Day Saint movement. Rather, this theory arises from a good faith effort on the part of some believing scholars to identify ancient textual features in the Book of Mormon, and thereby locate evidentiary support for the sacred authenticity of the work. As such, we are dealing with speculative theories of individual scholars regarding the unofficial and non-doctrinal "barnacles of faith," which I described in the preface of this work—that is, the nondoctrinal propositions to explain various textual phenomena in the Book of Mormon and/or to reconcile textual evidence with historical claims. Nonetheless, framing Smith's preliminary outlines as ancient colophons proves problematic.

The specific summarizing prefaces in the Book of Mormon, particularly the phrase-by-phrase outlines of forthcoming narratives (whether written by an author or an editor), do not have verifiable or unambiguous antecedents in either biblical or ancient Mesopotamian texts. Classifying Smith's summaries as ancient colophons therefore introduces a peculiar expansion and redefinition of the traditional term and the apparatus it describes, rendering the many substantial distinctions between third-person scribal notations and first-person authorial or editorial summaries essentially meaningless. Aware of this challenge, John A. Tvedtnes, who further addressed the theory of colophons in the Book of Mormon, observed that using the term "colophon" as a technical descriptor for these summaries results in an awkward fit: "For lack of a better word, I call them colophons, though technically colophons are notes or guidelines after a text."[10] In spite of Tvedtnes's reservations, however, some scholars have continued to embrace the theory and use it to further the argument for the ancient origins of the Book of Mormon.[11]

But the speculative leap from the structures of ancient colophons to the summaries in the Book of Mormon strains for evidentiary support. The transformation requires a scenario in which ancient Nephite authors adapted and modified colophons (and, perhaps, superscripts) to create the prefatory outlines that appear in the Book of Mormon—in other words, a scenario in which they created an entirely new and innovative textual apparatus that no longer constituted or functioned as a traditional colophon but emerged as an entirely different paratextual feature for ancient texts. Such a theory does not provide any evidence to explain this abrupt and historically idiosyncratic transformation (e.g., how *scribal* conventions for *copied* texts transformed into *authorial* notations in *original* compositions), nor does it offer explanations as to why the character Nephi, born and raised in Jerusalem and purportedly "the only Book of Mormon author to receive a classical Hebrew/Egyptian education," immediately dropped the conventions of his scribal culture to create such radical transformations.[12]

Moreover, as we will observe, Smith's narrative outlines are not limited to the paratextual features of book summaries and chapter headings. Smith also embeds these outlines in the middle of narratives, incorporating them into the development of the stories themselves—a feature that emphatically negates the assertion that Smith's outlines represent ancient colophons, given that such paratextual features never appear within the main body of such texts as part of the authorial voice and as an integral component of the main narration. Though supporters of the colophon hypothesis will no doubt supply additional theories to explain such anomalies, the inescapable observation remains that the morphology of these anticipatory passages in the Book of Mormon precisely mirrors ubiquitous practices in Smith's own time: the paratextual features of nineteenth-century print and Bible cultures, the pedagogical strategies aimed at teaching students the basics of introductory composition, and the method of laying down heads to form skeletal outlines for the composition and delivery of sermons. Indeed, these summaries mirror the same specific style and format of Smith's prefatory outline for his 1832 history.

Competing theories aside, the desire to create a biblical-style text was not the only reason Smith appears to have included these prefatory summaries in the Book of Mormon. Evidence from the original manuscript suggests that these outlines were key features that facilitated Smith's oral composition. By way of comparison, Smith's dictation of his 1832 history becomes germane. Recall that Smith's method of composition for his 1832 text followed a simple and common method: first, he dictated a prefatory outline by laying down the heads of a narrative skeleton, and next, he orally composed the history by using the outline as a guide, extemporaneously amplifying each of the main heads into an expanded section of narrative.[13] The same procedure applies as well to the Book of Mormon, where, for example, Nephi's opening outline reveals the same process at work: a preliminary summary of the narrative of the First Book of Nephi appears at the beginning of the story, prior to Smith's dictation of the extended story itself.

Yet, observing how this sequence of composition occurred during dictation requires a different example than Nephi's outline, because the original manuscript page containing this summary no longer exists (indeed, only 28 percent of the original scribal manuscript remains).[14] Instead, we can look at the opening summary for the Book of Helaman, which offers an opportunity to observe

Smith's characteristic sequence of narrative production in the original scribal manuscript. By way of narrative context, the summary for the Book of Helaman encapsulates the central stories that take place in the tumultuous period before Christ's visit to the ancient Nephite civilization in the Americas (the following outline takes inspiration from Royal Skousen's "sense-lines" of Smith's dictation, though I have altered the formatting):[15]

> *The Book of Helaman*
>
> CHAPTER I.
>
> *An account of the Nephites.*
> > *Their wars and contentions, and their dissension.*
> > *And also the prophecies of many Holy Prophets,*
> > > *before the coming of Christ,*
> > *according to the record of Helaman,*
> > *which was the son of Helaman,*
> > *and also according to the records of his sons,*
> > *even down to the coming of Christ.*
> *And also many of the Lamanites are converted.*
> > *An account of their conversion.*
> *An account of the righteousness of the Lamanites,*
> > *and the wickedness and abominations of the Nephites,*
> > *according to the record of Helaman and his sons,*
> > *even down to the coming of Christ,*
> > *which is called the Book of Helaman, &c.*[16]

In the original scribal manuscript, this preliminary summary occurs in the middle of a sheet of foolscap paper, taking up a total of eleven lines (including solid lines drawn above and below this preface, in order to offset it from the surrounding text).[17] Immediately before this summary, Smith dictated the last portion of the Book of Alma (the previous book in the overall structure of the Book of Mormon). And immediately following this summary, Smith dictated the opening narrative of the Book of Helaman. The ink flow of the transcription further indicates that Oliver Cowdery recorded Smith's dictation in the same sequence as it appears on the page.[18]

In other words, the dictation of the opening summary for the Book of Helaman occurred during the regular course of Smith's oral composition, rather than being a later addition—more specifically, Smith dictated the outline first, before expanding the outline into a fully developed story. Smith's ability to compose the outline of the Book of Helaman before he actually dictated the narrative therefore provides direct evidence that Smith was aware of the contents of the Book of Helaman before he started to compose the main body of the story.

In addition, Smith's sequence of dictating a summary before dictating its corresponding narrative is not limited to the prefaces of the Book of Helaman or the First Book of Nephi. Evidence from the original scribal manuscript suggests that Smith dictated *all* of his prefatory outlines first, before proceeding directly to the dictation of the extended narratives.[19] In *The Book of Mormon: The Earliest Text*, his edition of what he believes to be the original text of the Book of Mormon, Skousen affirms that these summaries were part of Smith's process. When addressing "the prefaces (or summaries) that appear at the beginning of most of the books in the Book of Mormon (as well as at the beginning of some sections in the middle of books)," Skousen indicates that, "these prefaces, along with the division into books and sections, were part of Joseph Smith's dictation and hence are also included in *The Earliest Text*."[20]

Grant Hardy concurs with Skousen's observation, indicating, "These editorial guideposts occur regularly in the Book of Mormon, and they were part of the original dictation rather than later additions to the text."[21] In the context of Smith's practice of dictating the outlines of forthcoming narratives, the original scribal manuscript of the Book of Mormon thus offers strong evidence that Smith did not produce the stories in sudden bursts of improvised, extempore performances. Rather, the manuscript indicates that Smith worked from premeditated outlines, which he then expanded into full-length narratives during dictation. In other words, like the sermonizing of preachers all around him throughout his life, Smith prepared and laid down the main heads of skeletal outlines before creating his extended sermons and narrative passages.

Alternative Views

At this stage, it is important to acknowledge that some (though not all) Mormon scholars take a different view concerning these summaries. Royal Skousen, for example, believes that Smith did not actually "translate" the Book of Mormon (in the traditional sense of the term) but rather "transcribed" the text by reading it directly from a divinely prepared, English-language translation that appeared supernaturally via the seer stone.[22] His argument therefore implies that Smith never actually saw the opening narrative summaries until the moment he produced the work. In the paragraphs that follow, I challenge some of Skousen's theories in order to demonstrate how the textual evidence he enlists to support his views actually has multiple viable interpretations, and that these alternative interpretations offer equally compelling evidence of Smith's participation (as author or translator) in the construction of the Book of Mormon. For the sake of clarity, I also want to point out that this discussion addresses topics that fall into the area of the "barnacles of faith"—that is, the speculative theories surrounding Smith's work—but not the LDS belief system itself. Moreover, though I will be providing alternatives to Skousen's interpretations, I wish to acknowledge that his monumental, decades-long efforts on the manuscripts of the Book of Mormon stand as priceless contributions to Mormon scholarship, and my own conclusions are frequently indebted to his dedicated and perceptive work.

Turning to the text, the first theory to address is Skousen's assertion that Smith did not know the contents of the Book of Mormon until he actually dictated the work. Citing textual modifications in the original manuscript, Skousen concludes that, "Joseph himself did not know in advance the contents or structure of the text."[23] Moreover, Skousen argues, the evidence in the original manuscript "does not support theories that Joseph Smith composed the text himself or that he took the text from some other source. Instead, it indicates that the Lord exercised what I [Skousen] refer to as 'tight control' over the word-by-word translation of the Book of Mormon [i.e., that Smith did not actually translate the text, but 'saw specific words written out in English and read them off to the scribe']."[24] Thus, according to this theory, Smith had no prior knowledge of the overall structure or the individual sections of the Book of Mormon; instead, he only learned of each successive story as the work unfolded during translation.

To support his interpretation, Skousen seeks for evidence in the manner in which Smith assigned chapter breaks and chapter numbers to the text. Specifically, Skousen focuses on three areas: (1) Smith identified chapter breaks during his dictation of the text, but he (or his scribe) did not provide chapter numbers until a later time; (2) Smith assigned chapters to books that contained only one section; and (3) in one instance, Smith started a new chapter at the end of the First Book of Nephi (which would have been "Chapter VIII" in the original format), only to delete this chapter assignment by changing the narrative break into the opening of a new book ("The Second Book of Nephi").[25] A review of Skousen's theory and the evidence he enlists, along with alternative interpretations, can thus prove instructive to understanding, and also to uncovering, what I would argue to be Smith's far more engaged process of composition.

To begin, the original manuscript, as Skousen has observed, reveals that Smith indicated where chapter breaks should occur, though he did not stop to assign chapter numbers during his dictation.[26] Sometime later, the scribe (apparently Cowdery) went back and wrote in the chapter numbers, presumably under Smith's direction (though it remains unclear who was responsible for assigning the actual numbers). For Skousen, this textual feature offers evidence that Smith was unaware of the overall structural framework and narrative content of the Book of Mormon.[27] Skousen's theory thus seems to operate on the unspoken assumption that if Smith were in fact aware of the overall structure, then he would have included chapter numbers during the initial dictation. Yet, the fact that Smith did not assign chapter numbers during the course of his initial performance does not inevitably reveal Smith's ignorance of the overall content or structure of the Book of Mormon. The evidence simply demonstrates that Smith did not assign chapter numbers before he dictated the text, and that is the limit of the direct proof. All else is supposition. Smith's reasons for not assigning chapter numbers in advance can be attributed to any number of equally viable explanations.

For example, the structural framework of the Book of Mormon does not center on chapter divisions. Rather, the controlling logic of the text anchors on narrative episodes embedded within chronological and geographically grounded sequences (for example, the succession of leaders and/or the locations where events occur).[28] As such, the *content* of the stories—the variety and differing lengths of narratives—stands as the determining factor that dictates the location of chapter divisions in the text, as opposed to predetermined chapter breaks that force the text into prefabricated literary frames. As Skousen himself observes, "The original chapters are generally longer [than in modern editions] and tend to end whenever there is a natural break in the narrative."[29] Moreover, if Smith had in fact attempted to assign chapter numbers during the course of dictation, while simultaneously developing a date-specific chronological succession of narratives, then he would have unnecessarily complicated the oral composition process by trying to mediate between two concurrent and competing structural/numerical systems. The Book of Alma, for instance, offers a good example of the unnecessary difficulties that Smith would have imposed upon himself by simultaneously following two structural systems with different sequences of numbering to organize the text.

According to the original chapters of the Book of Mormon (1830), chapter 1 of Alma contains year one of "the reign of the Judges" (a one-hundred-year chronology leading up to the birth of Christ). But the correspondence between the two numerical systems immediately falls apart as the narrative progresses, because chapter 1 also includes years two, three, four, and five.[30] Chapter 2 then begins with year six, but also includes years seven, eight, and part of nine.[31] Chapter 3 continues with year nine, and year nine continues through chapters 4 and 5.[32] Chapter 6 finally ends year nine and then begins year ten.[33] Chapters 7, 8, 9, and 10 all continue year ten, and so on.[34] Keeping mental track of these two competing and nonsynchronous numbering systems, particularly without the apparent use of notes during the act of dictation or without constantly consulting a prewritten manuscript draft during the actual oral performance, would have been a recipe for disaster. Instead of venturing into such a confusing numerical morass, Smith, as also suggested by the same evidence that Skousen enlists for his theory, followed a much simpler approach: he dictated the Book of Mormon according to the narrative events and the internal chronological logic of the story boundaries, and then he (or his scribe) went back and assigned chapter numbers after he completed the work.

Next, Skousen argues that Smith could not have known the contents of the Book of Mormon prior to dictation because Smith assigned chapters to books containing only one section. Skousen's argument thus hinges on the underlying assumption that if Smith had known that the books only contained one passage, then he would not have assigned "Chapter I" to the opening of the book. "These books contain only one section," Skousen observes, "but at the beginning of each of these short books, Joseph Smith apparently had no knowledge that this was the case."[35] If this assumption were true, however, then the evidence would likewise indicate that Smith was an irredeemably slow learner. In the Book of Mormon, the short books containing only one chapter all appear in immediate succession: the Book of Enos, the Book of Jarom, the Book of Omni, and the Words of Mormon. As such, when he commenced dictating this sequence of books, Smith would have started with the Book of Enos by assigning "Chapter I" to the text, only to discover a few minutes later that the book contained only one section and therefore did not need the chapter numbering designation.

In spite of this discovery, however, Smith proceeded to dictate the next book, the Book of Jarom, by immediately making the same "mistake" and, once again, assigning "Chapter I" to the opening of the book, only to discover a short time later that this book also contained only one chapter. Undaunted by these clerical mishaps, and only fifteen verses later, Smith made the same "mistake" for the third time in a row, assigning "Chapter I" to the opening of the Book of Omni, only to discover once again that the book contained just one chapter. If baseball's three-strike rule applied to composition, Smith would be back in the dugout. Yet, in spite of his quick succession of "blunders," Smith ran afoul yet again by launching the very next book, the Words of Mormon, committing the same mistake once more and assigning "Chapter 1" to the opening of the passage, only to discover that this book, like the three before it, contained only one section. In the end, rather than providing evidence of Smith's purported ignorance of the structure and contents of the Book of Mormon, Smith's use of "Chapter I" emerges as a formulaic structural pattern that he used throughout the Book of Mormon to initiate internal books, regardless of their length or number.

Along with providing a perfunctory formula to initiate internal books, Smith's use of "Chapter I" for his one-passage books provides an opportunity to pay closer attention to one of the key dynamics of Smith's method of oral composition: semi-extemporaneous preachers did not know the actual wording or length of their semi-extemporaneous narratives until *the moment of performance*. Speakers using this semi-extemporaneous style of composition would know only the narrative outline in advance—the framework for the beginning, the sequence of events and topics, and the resolutions—but would not know beforehand precisely how long it would take to articulate the story, or how many words and/or divisions would be required to recite it. Not until the actual performance does the speaker unfold the actual length of narratives.

Whether the skeletal summary of a text will become a one-chapter passage or a ten-chapter narrative depends upon the speaker's immediate strategies, plans, desires, interests, level of energy, whims, and audience responses at the very moment when he or she speaks the actual words of the narrative. Thus, the actual amount of text produced in a semi-extemporaneous performance does not need to be, and indeed probably cannot be, precalculated. Smith's use of "Chapter I" at the opening of one-section passages does not therefore inevitably reveal his ignorance of the content of the subsequent narratives, and it certainly does not offer compelling evidence to support the broader claim, as Hardy has proposed, "that Smith had not planned out the macrostructure of the text beforehand."[36] Rather, the evidence simply suggests that Smith knew the central topics and the sequence of narrative events in advance, but he did not know beforehand precisely how long the resulting text would become.[37]

Skousen's third example centers on the narrative boundary located between the First Book of Nephi and the Second Book of Nephi in the scribal manuscript. In the original format of the 1830 Book of Mormon, the First Book of Nephi contained only seven chapters. At the end of the seventh chapter, however, Smith dictated the word "Chapter" to his scribe, in anticipation of starting a new chapter. Later, however, Smith changed this "Chapter" into the beginning of a new book, The Second Book of Nephi. "At this point," Skousen remarks, "Joseph Smith had no indication that a new book was beginning. All he could see [supernaturally via the seer stone] was the end of

Chapter VII."[38] Thus, Skousen believes that if Smith had known in advance the chapter breakdown and the length of books, then he should have known that the next passage started a new book, not a new chapter. Therefore, according to Skousen's theory, Smith was ignorant of the content, direction, and structure of the entire work.

While Skousen draws attention to an important textual clue that offers potential insights into Smith's process, it is again critical to recognize that there are alternative and equally viable interpretations. Recall, for example, that Smith's method of oral composition begins with a premeditated skeletal outline of a narrative unit, which he amplifies with the actual words during the moment of dictation. This process, combined with the emendation occurring between the first and second books of Nephi, suggests that Smith composed the Book of Mormon by focusing his attention on a specific number of skeletal outlines in preparation for each session of oral composition. In other words, Smith would begin a dictation session by first meditating on the outline of the immediate story that he was about to produce (or the outlines of multiple stories, depending on how many he prepared to dictate during a given session), after which he would later produce the amplified narratives during dictation, using these mental templates as guides. Once the given passages were complete, Smith could then move to the next outline or set of outlines, meditate on them, and then likewise perform them.

Smith's dictation of "Chapter" at the end of the First Book of Nephi therefore suggests that during his composition of the last chapter of the First Book of Nephi, Smith may have initially assumed that the next outline in his story plan would become another chapter. Yet, when he returned to the overall plan of his work between dictation sessions (either by reviewing private notes that he did not consult during the actual dictation, or by simply meditating on his mental plan for the work), Smith realized that the next outline started a new book. Therefore, he simply proceeded with his dictation of the Second Book of Nephi, while having his scribe eventually emend the manuscript accordingly. As such, the alteration in the text would not provide evidence of Smith's lack of advance knowledge about the structure or content of the Book of Mormon. Rather the evidence would reveal that Smith was focusing his attention on the immediate outlines in queue for each of his oral performances, without necessarily looking ahead to the sketch outlines of all the narratives that would follow.

The matter is further complicated by the historical context. For this section of the manuscript, Smith was redoing the original opening portion of the Book of Mormon. Martin Harris, one of Smith's associates and financial backers, lost the original 116 pages of the manuscript, which, at the very least, contained the Book of Lehi.[39] Instead of redoing this lost portion, however, Smith retold the story from the point of view of Lehi's son, Nephi. As such, Smith revised the original lost text (the Book of Lehi followed by the [First] Book of Nephi) into the current text (the First Book of Nephi followed by the Second Book of Nephi). Thus, rather than progressing from the writings of Lehi to the writings of Nephi, with a clear demarcation between the two authors, the revised narrative moved from one book of Nephi to yet another book of Nephi, requiring Smith to insert a new and prominent narrative boundary between the two books by the same "author" or persona. This emendation at the break between Nephi's books therefore potentially reveals both the location and the process by which Smith chose to end the First Book of Nephi and to initiate the Second Book of Nephi (again, the location where the original, lost "Book of Lehi" had ended and the original "First Book of Nephi" had begun). In such a scenario, the evidence would indicate that Smith initially intended to continue the First Book of Nephi with a new chapter, only to change his mind and use the same location to carve out the Second Book of Nephi.[40] In the final analysis, all of these manuscript alterations provide strong evidence of Smith's approach to structural revisions. Indeed, I argue that such revisions provide as much, if not more, support for Smith's active involvement in the construction of the text than they support Skousen's theory that Smith did not know the contents of the Book of Mormon before starting his dictation of the work.

Short Historical Outlines

While the opening summaries for the First Book of Nephi and the Book of Helaman are relatively detailed and lengthy, most of the other original prefatory headings in the Book of Mormon are quite short. Nevertheless, even with these brief outlines, Smith's approach to oral composition and the characteristics of his performative style continue to emerge. The eponymous Second Book of Nephi, which contains only four brief summarizing heads, stands in contrast to Nephi's first book and offers an appropriate example (note, in particular, Smith's use of ampersands, which indicate his awareness of additional narrative events that he did not state in the outline):

1. An account of the death of Lehi.
2. Nephi's brethren rebelleth against him.
3. The Lord warns Nephi to depart into the wilderness, &c.
4. His journeyings in the wilderness, &c.[41]

Within the overall story of the Book of Mormon, this opening summary appears after Lehi's extended family has completed their journey from ancient Israel to the Americas. The elderly Lehi, sensing his imminent death, gathers his family and friends to offer his final words. "At the end of his life, following the pattern of the biblical patriarch Jacob," Hardy observes, "Lehi gathered his kin around him to give counsel and blessings."[42] The scene, in turn, sets up the sequence of events that follows, and the preliminary summary in the opening of the book functions as a blueprint for the subsequent stories. Nonetheless, this brief preliminary outline does not provide a comprehensive listing of every significant event that occurs in the corresponding amplified story. This lack of complete coverage in the summary therefore offers an opportunity to observe Smith's semi-extemporaneous style, particularly concerning his use of resumptive repetition and extemporaneous excursions from his original outline.

To begin, the opening phrase of the outline, "[1] an account of the death of Lehi," summarizes the entire scene portraying Lehi's final blessings and exhortations before he dies. In the main body of the text, this scene stretches from 2 Nephi 1:1 through 2 Nephi 4:12, ending with Lehi's death: "And it came to pass that after Lehi had spake unto all his household . . . he waxed old. And it came to pass that he died, and was buried."[43] In the very next verse after Lehi's death, Smith moves to the second head of the opening outline, "[2] Nephi's brethren rebelleth against him," and expands the phrase in the main body of his narrative: "And it came to pass that not many days after his [Lehi's] death, *Laman and Lemuel, and the sons of Ishmael, were angry with me* [Nephi]" (2 Nephi 4:13).[44]

At this dramatic point in the story, however, Smith takes a detour from the preliminary outline at the opening of the book. Instead of proceeding to the third main head in the summary ("[3] The Lord warns Nephi to depart into the wilderness, &c."), Smith diverges into a lengthy and unannounced digression concerning Nephi's personal spiritual challenges and his frustrations with his unrighteous brothers and wicked in-laws (2 Nephi 4:15–35). The passage, often described as "Nephi's Psalm," being composed in the spirit of David's Psalms in the Old Testament, stands as one of the more poetic passages in the Book of Mormon.[45]

When he finally finishes this digression, Smith immediately returns to his narrative outline and resumes where he left off by reconnecting with the second main head in the story skeleton, "[2] Nephi's brethren rebelleth against him." The corresponding text reads, "I, Nephi, did cry much unto the Lord my God, *because of the anger of my brethren. But behold, their anger did increase against me*" (2 Nephi 5:1-2).⁴⁶ As a result, Smith provides yet another example of his resumptive repetition: Nephi's brothers are angry with him (outline anchor), Nephi departs into his Psalm (digression), and then Nephi returns to the anger of his brothers (resumptive repetition, outline anchor).⁴⁷ Thus, Smith uses the head "Nephi's brethren rebelleth against him" in two ways: (1) to amplify the phrase itself into a fully developed passage in the main body of the narrative, and (2) to provide a guiding anchor point that allows him to depart on extemporaneous tangents, without fear of wandering too far from his original outline.

After returning to his outline following this section, Smith continued to use the opening summary as a guide for the sequence of narrative events in the main body of his text. Moving to the third phrase in the summary, we find "[3] The Lord warns Nephi to depart into the wilderness, &c." When turning to the corresponding text, we find that Smith expanded this head in the main body of the story, following the same sequence: "And it came to pass that *the Lord did warn me, that I, Nephi, should depart from them, and flee into the wilderness*" (2 Nephi 5:5).⁴⁸ Immediately after this expansion, Smith then amplified the fourth summarizing head, "[4] His journeyings in the wilderness, &c.," to tell the origin story of the Nephite nation in the main body of text: "I, Nephi, did take my family [and many other families]. . . . and *did journey in the wilderness* for the space of many days. And *after that we had journied* for the space of many days, we did pitch our tents. And my people would that we should call the name of the place Nephi; wherefore, we did call it Nephi. And all they which were with me, did take it upon them to call themselves the people of Nephi" (2 Nephi 5:6–9).⁴⁹

The juxtaposition of Smith's brief opening summary with the corresponding passages in the main body of the text reveals that Smith composed the story by following the same sequence established in the prefatory outline, using each of the opening phrases as a narrative guidepost to anchor his semi-extemporaneous performance of the storyline. This relationship between the prefatory outline and the main body of the text also provides important information about the characteristics of Smith's oral style and the composition of the Book of Mormon. For instance, the *absence* of Nephi's Psalm in the opening summary of 2 Nephi reveals the dynamics that can occur between premeditated and improvised story elements. As illustrated above, the phrase "Nephi's brethren rebelleth against him" in the opening summary corresponds with the text that appears both *before* and *after* Nephi's Psalm, revealing Smith's awareness of the phrase as a narrative anchor, as well as his conscious effort to reconnect with the original outline after his excursion. Thus, the sequence and the textual evidence suggest that Smith did not prepare Nephi's Psalm in advance but rather improvised the lament during the actual performance of the Book of Mormon.

Moreover, when we step back from this specific example to observe the techniques involved in Smith's approach to oral performance, we find that Nephi's summary and its correlated expanded text make use of the same techniques and express the same characteristics, including resumptive repetition, that Smith adopted for his King Follett sermon. If we enlarge the scope of observation even further, we find that this method of oral performance—following a skeletal outline, while retaining the flexibility to depart and return from extended improvised digressions—demonstrates the same approach that countless semi-extemporaneous preachers brought to the pulpit in the nineteenth century.

Headings as Mnemonic Cues

Smith's opening summary for the Second Book of Nephi provides additional evidence about his skills in narrative amplification and the role that memory plays in the construction of stories. For a closer examination of this process, we return to the first main head in the summary, "[1] An account of the death of Lehi." This single phrase represents more than one isolated action within a larger narrative. These seven words encapsulate the *entire episode* of Lehi's final blessings to his immediate and extended family. The phrase invokes a *scene* that presents the reader with a story both simple in imagery and yet somewhat complex in content. As Hardy has observed, Lehi offers a diverse assortment of blessings and admonitions to "Laman, Lemuel, Sam, and the sons of Ishmael (2 Ne. 1:28-29), Zoram (2 Ne. 1:30-32), Jacob (2 Ne. 2:1-13), Joseph (2 Ne. 3:1-25), the children of Laman (2 Ne. 4:3-7), the children of Lemuel (2 Ne. 4:8-9), and again the sons of Ishmael (2 Ne. 4:10), and Sam (2 Ne. 4:11)."[50] At the same time, however, the imagery for this entire account remains quite simple, merely consisting of a single mental snapshot: Lehi giving advice and offering blessings to different individuals among his immediate family, friends, and posterity.

When comparing the primary head "[1] An account of the death of Lehi" with its corresponding text in the main body of the narrative, we find that Smith expanded this seven-word phrase into a quite lengthy passage. In the 1830 Book of Mormon, this scene stretches over ten pages (59 to 69), which corresponds with the content contained in the first four chapters of the modern edition (2 Nephi 1:1 through 2 Nephi 4:12). As such, Smith's seven-word phrase acts as a *mnemonic cue* for the entire scene, and the scene itself contains a total of 4,655 words.[51] Smith's ability to amplify such a short cue into a 4,655-word narrative not only reveals his ability to expand the heads of skeletal outlines into lengthy texts—a skill common enough among revivalist preachers and, indeed, students in common school classrooms—it also provides clues concerning Smith's preparations before his dictation.

One of the reasons Smith could encapsulate an entire scene with a seven-word phrase pertains to the nature of the narrative circumstances. Rather than encompassing a complex sequence of actions, the scene contains a single trope: a variant of the deathbed scene, in which relatives and friends gather to hear the last words of a prominent dying family member. Given the ubiquity of this conventional trope and the array of narrative elements associated with it, Smith could have easily expanded the phrase "an account of the death of Lehi" into an extended passage by simply envisioning the circle of friends and relatives around Lehi, and then offering semi-extemporaneous exhortations and blessings to each of the recipients. As such, the amplification of the seven-word phrase into a lengthy text would not be remarkable, nor would the dictation of such a moment require elaborate premeditation.

Nevertheless, the content of Lehi's addresses suggests that Smith's preparations were more extensive than deferring the entire story to the impulses of performance. Rather than displaying a series of generic blessings (though some elements are, in fact, generic and repetitive), Lehi's counsel includes messages tailored to the recipients, along with material that facilitates the development of the wider story structure of the entire Book of Mormon. For example, Lehi warns his rebellious sons and in-laws that if they harden their hearts and refuse to keep the commandments they might be "cursed with a sore cursing" (2 Nephi 1:17–22). This warning foreshadows upcoming events in the story of the Book of Mormon, when the rebellious relatives do, in fact, get cursed. Thus, the warning was likely the result of preplanning on Smith's part, acting as a necessary and integral event in the story of the Nephites and Lamanites, rather than information that arose spontaneously during Smith's dictation.

Predictably, Lehi's rebellious children do not reform (the dramatic tension sustaining the Book of Mormon would otherwise collapse), and four chapters later, in a racially charged plot point that remains controversial today, the Lord "caused the cursing to come upon them, yea, even a sore cursing, because of their iniquity . . . wherefore, as they were white, and exceeding fair and delightsome, that they might not be enticing unto my people, therefore the Lord God did cause a skin of blackness to come upon them" (2 Nephi 5:21).[52] The curse of dark skin creates a racial barrier between Lehi's righteous (white-skinned) and unrighteous (dark-skinned) descendants, and thereby becomes a key marker of identification that undergirds the conflicts between the two primary civilizations that emerge in the narrative.[53]

Other blessings and prophecies that reach beyond the immediate deathbed scene include Lehi's blessings for the descendants of Laman, Lemuel, and Joseph, revealing that they would not be completely destroyed (2 Nephi 3:3, 23; and 2 Nephi 4:7, 9)—blessings that provide the reader with proleptic information related to the end of the book, thereby revealing Smith's own advance knowledge of the overall narrative. And in a prophecy that reaches beyond the temporal boundaries of the Book of Mormon into Smith's own nineteenth-century world, Lehi also predicts the coming of Joseph Smith Jr. and his translation of the Book of Mormon (2 Nephi 3:5–21). Thus, the ways in which the blessings are tailored to each of the recipients, along with their consistency within the overall narrative structure of the Book of Mormon (and beyond), suggest that Smith's composition of these blessings and orations involved more preparation than mere extempore performances. Rather, the text suggests that Smith had a clear idea of the topics (or at least many of the topics) that he wanted to cover in advance, even though his prefatory outline for the Second Book of Nephi does not itself provide specific information regarding the contents or the recipients of Lehi's exhortations and blessings. The succinct head "an account of the death of Lehi" therefore acted as a *mnemonic cue*—a single cognitively potent phrase that invoked a network of narrative elements related to the scene, far beyond the ostensible information contained in the phrase alone.

Mnemonic Cues: Alma's Counsel to his Sons

Smith's use of mnemonic cues to invoke narrative segments occurs throughout the Book of Mormon, organizing the overall shape of the narrative with simple but condensed phrases. The story of Alma and his advice to his three sons, mentioned in chapter 5, provides a similar example. Like Lehi's deathbed scene, Alma's scene with his three sons, Helaman, Shiblon, and Corianton, provides readers with a story simple in imagery, though more complex in content: the patriarch goes around the circle, offering counsel, instructions, and exhortations, yet the scene itself consists of merely another single mental snapshot—Alma speaking in turn to each of his sons. Nevertheless, unlike Lehi's deathbed scene, in which Smith initiates the story with a heading that stands outside the narrative (the paratextual phrase "an account of the death of Lehi"), Smith embeds the opening summary within the main body of the story: "[Alma] caused that his sons should be gathered together, that he might give unto them every one his charge, separately, concerning the things pertaining unto righteousness. And we have *an account of his commandments, which he gave unto them* according to his own record" (Alma 35:16).[54] The last phrase, "an account of [Alma's] commandments, which he gave unto [his sons]," thus functions as the mnemonic cue that launched Smith's performance into the ensuing narrative.

Moreover, the announcement that Alma would give each son "his charge, separately," alerts the audience to Smith's division of the primary head into three subheads, or one lecture for each son. Such partitioning creates three additional mnemonic cues that divide the general description of Alma's counsel into three formulaic subcues, which Smith then amplified into expanded passages. For the subhead *"The Commandments of Alma, to his son Helaman"* (the heading for Alma 36), Smith produced a passage of 3,255 words. For *"The Commandments of Alma, to his son Shiblon"* (Alma 38), Smith produced a passage of 649 words. And for *"The Commandments of Alma, to his son Corianton"* (Alma 39), Smith produced 3,875 words.[55] Smith's ten-word mnemonic cue that prompted all of these passages—"an account of his [Alma's] commandments, which he gave unto them [his sons]"—thus invokes the entire scene, which, including the subheadings, contains a total of 7,811 words.

Mnemonic Cues Up Close

In chapter 4, we touched on the potency of mnemonic cues to evoke complex matrices of narrative segments, scriptural references, parallel topics, illustrations, anecdotes, exhortations, applications, and any number of related ideas. Because mnemonic cues feature prominently in Smith's opening summaries and embedded outlines, a closer look at how they function in semi-extemporaneous compositions and what they reveal about Smith's preparation for his work provides critical insights into his process. In terms of function, mnemonic cues and prefatory outlines have the capacity to invoke larger narrative patterns, yet mnemonic cues do not require a complete outline of a story to be effective. In fact, a short phrase or even a single word can evoke complex narratives.

To borrow an example from the work of cognitive scientists Gilles Fauconnier and Mark Turner, consider the phrase "Jesus on the Cross," which we might also shorten to the single word "Crucifixion."[56] For people who are familiar with the beliefs and practices of Christianity, "crucifixion" evokes more information than a dictionary-like description of an archaic and brutal form of execution. This single word also has the potential to catalyze a mental bombardment of related associations, such as specific individuals within the narrative and their traits (Jesus Christ; Mary, the Mother of Jesus; Mary Magdalene; Roman soldiers), words and phrases ("To day shalt thou be with me in paradise," "Woman, behold thy son," "My God, my God, why hast thou forsaken me"), empathetic embodied sensations (imagining the taste of vinegar, the sting of thorns, gaping physical wounds, rolling thunder), and the visualization of traditional mental imagery (three crosses, Golgotha, dark clouds, lightning flashes). Such mental imagery, triggered by the single word "crucifixion," thus activates neural networks of related information, story elements, and ideas that effortlessly evoke the complex and multifaceted narrative of Christ's death.

According to their model, Fauconnier and Turner refer to the phrase "Jesus on the Cross" as a "frame," consisting of "entrenched mental spaces that we can activate all at once."[57] Put another way, our minds contain a vast number of conceptual building blocks (mental spaces) that combine together to form basic narrative segments (frames). And, when certain combinations of conceptual events repeatedly occur, the patterns can become entrenched in the mind, whether they are specific traditional narratives ("Jesus on the Cross") or generic actions and behaviors (going to the grocery store).[58] Because these frames assist the ability to process information quickly, the mind constantly associates our experiences against these entrenched patterns in order to interpret information. As such, tiny clues, in the form of single words and short phrases, can evoke complex and expansive narrative associations.

Moreover, as Fauconnier and Turner argue, the activation of a single mental space can further evoke the memory of related mental spaces, allowing single words and short phrases to call forth a *series of narratives* within the extended world of a story: "Jesus on the Cross evokes the frame of Roman crucifixion, of Jesus the baby, of Jesus the son of God, of Mary and the Holy women at the foot of the Cross, of styles of painting the crucifixion, of moments of the liturgy that refer to it, and many more."[59] Thus, the phrase "Jesus on the Cross" has the potential to ripple out from the immediate narrative of Christ's crucifixion to activate additional narrative segments, such as "Jesus the baby"—a narrative that further evokes such additional episodes as Joseph and Mary searching for a room at an inn, taking shelter in a manger, the appearance of a new star, the journey of the three wise men, and the visitation of angels to the shepherds in the fields. As such, words, phrases, objects, and ideas carry clusters of narrative baggage.

Thus, key words and phrases can evoke mental worlds and activate complex matrices of information and "mental spaces," which fill the barest references and mnemonic cues with rich and multifaceted information. Along with facilitating rapid comprehension and communication, such mental processes play an indispensable role in the production and delivery of narratives, because these same networks of related ideas and their encyclopedic inferences have direct influence on the way we create and tell stories. As such, the use of such truncated cues—consciously or otherwise—suggests additional information about Smith's preparations.

The brevity of many mnemonic cues in the Book of Mormon indicates that Smith was familiar with the stories that his cues evoked. That such bare-minimum phrases could cue Smith's memory suggests that he spent a long time with his stories—meditating on them, generating and developing ideas, choosing topics to address, establishing sequences of events, choosing names and places, and making any possible revisions along the way—until he became sufficiently familiar with them for the stories to become entrenched in his mind. In doing so, such preparations and mental rehearsals would enhance his memory of the narratives. A single summarizing phrase for such premeditated and familiar tales would be all that Smith needed to evoke the content and structure of his creations.

Mnemonic Cues in the Book of Mormon

In the course of dictating the Book of Mormon, Smith regularly inserted succinct and memorable summaries of narratives before dictating the stories themselves. The opening headings for some of the missionary labors of the prophet Alma, for instance, provide brief but ample overviews, which suggest both the content of the stories and the scenarios in which they occur: *"The words which Alma, the High Priest, according to the holy order of God, delivered to the people in their cities and villages throughout the land"* (Alma 5, heading); and *"The words of Alma which he delivered to the people in Gideon, according to his own record"* (Alma 7, heading).[60] These phrases thereby cue entire narrative events. Similar previews, appearing as both headings and as summaries embedded in the text, include, "THE PROPHECY OF SAMUEL, THE LAMANITE, TO THE NEPHITES" (Helaman 13); "The words of Christ, which he spake unto his disciples, the twelve whom he had chosen, as he laid his hands upon them" (Moroni 2:1); "The manner which the disciples, which were called the Elders of the church, ordained priests and teachers" (Moroni 3:1); "The manner of their elders and priests administering the flesh and blood of Christ unto the church" (Moroni 4:1); "An epistle of my father Mormon, written to me, Moroni; and it was written unto me soon after my calling to the ministry" (Moroni

8:1); and *"The second epistle of Mormon to his son Moroni"* (Moroni 9).[61] Such brief headings, which Smith dictated before the expanded texts themselves, repeatedly reveal Smith's advance knowledge of the content of the material that he had yet to compose semi-extemporaneously into his fully fleshed-out passages.

In addition to these headings and outlines, Smith also provides cues that alert the reader to stories that would appear sometime later in the text. When Nephi begins to describe the different metal plates that he created, on which to inscribe the history and teachings of his people, Smith announces to the reader the existence of a narrative that will occur later in the Book of Mormon: "And an account of my [Nephi's] making these plates shall be given hereafter" (1 Nephi 19:5).[62] Similar cues appear throughout the text: "They [the people of Limhi] were desirous to be baptized . . . and an account of their baptism shall be given hereafter" (Mosiah 21:35); "And this account [the Book of Ether] shall be written hereafter: for behold, it is expedient that all people should know the things which are written in this account" (Mosiah 28:19); "thus commenced a war betwixt the Lamanites and the Nephites, in the eighteenth year of the reign of the Judges; and an account shall be given of their wars hereafter" (Alma 35:13); "there was one Gadianton, who was exceeding expert in many words, and also in his craft, to carry on the secret work of murder and of robbery . . . . And more of this Gadianton shall be spoken hereafter" (Helaman 2:4,12); "he [Christ] did truly manifest himself unto them . . . and an account of his ministry shall be given hereafter" (3 Nephi 10:18–19); and "the disciples bear record that he [Christ] gave them power to give the Holy Ghost. And I will shew unto you hereafter that this record is true" (3 Nephi 18:37).[63]

While such cues do not provide an immediate outline or full introduction to the narratives they describe, they nevertheless reveal that Smith had specific narratives in mind that he was delaying for later times in the story. These cues therefore act as notices that not only alert the reader to upcoming narratives but also reveal Smith's advance awareness of their placement within the overall macrostructure of the entire work. The textual evidence thus strongly suggests that Smith worked from a master plan for the entire Book of Mormon. Moreover, as a literary device, these cues endow the narrator (usually, but not always, the character Mormon) with a quality of godlike mastery and omniscience about Nephite history.

Throughout the Book of Mormon, mnemonic cues of varying lengths and narrative scopes riddle the text in the form of chapter and book headings (specifically, produced in the course of the original dictation), prophecies, admonitions, historical sketches embedded within the narrative, and editorial comments. Hardy has touched on several of these internal previews, describing them in terms of "*Prophecy and Fulfillment*," or including them within a broader rubric of "editorial interruptions," further sorting them into such categories as "Editorial promises," "Summaries," and "Narrative foreshadowing."[64] However useful such classifications might be, these prefatory summaries and anticipatory statements nevertheless function primarily as mnemonic cues for oral performance that anticipate Smith's overall structure for the work and his production of fully developed narrative episodes later in the text.

Along with succinct mnemonic cues, Smith also provided more elaborate previews that reflected his method of laying down heads for oral composition—again, revealing his advance awareness of narrative sequences. Consider, for instance, the following list of selected headings and embedded summaries, taken from the 1830 edition of the Book of Mormon. Recall also that Smith dictated these outlines before dictating the actual narratives, providing evidence of his foreknowledge of the content. All italics in the following summaries are in the original 1830 Book of Mormon, and the summaries have been reformatted to highlight the sequence of narrative events:

THE BOOK OF JACOB, THE BROTHER OF NEPHI [JACOB 1, HEADING].

The words of his preaching unto his brethren.
He confoundeth a man [Sherem]
 who seeketh to overthrow the doctrine of Christ.
A few words concerning the history of the people of Nephi.

THE BOOK OF MOSIAH, [MOSIAH 23, HEADING].

An account of Alma and the people of the Lord,
 which was driven into the wilderness by the people of king Noah.

THE BOOK OF ALMA, THE SON OF ALMA [ALMA 1, HEADING]

The account of Alma, who was the son of Alma
 the First, and Chief Judge over the people of Nephi,
 and also the High Priest over the Church.
An account of the reign of the Judges,
 and the wars and contentions among the people.
And also an account of a war between the Nephites and the Lamanites,
 according to the record of Alma the First, and Chief Judge.

THE BOOK OF ALMA [ALMA 9, HEADING]

The words of Alma, and also the words of Amulek,
   which was declared unto the people
   which was in the land of Ammonihah.
And also they are cast into prison,
and delivered by the miraculous power of God which was in them,
   according to the record of Alma.

THE BOOK OF ALMA [ALMA 45, HEADING]

The account of the people of Nephi,
   and their wars and dissentions, in the days of Helaman,
   according to the record of Helaman, which he kept in his days.

THE BOOK OF HELAMAN [HELAMAN 7, HEADING]
   [which includes]
THE PROPHECY OF NEPHI, THE SON OF HELAMAN.

God threatens the people of Nephi,
   that he will visit them in his anger, to their utter destruction
   except they repent of their wickedness.
God smiteth the people of Nephi with pestilence;
   they repent and turn unto him.
Samuel, a Lamanite, prophesies unto the Nephites.

THE BOOK OF NEPHI [3 NEPHI 11, HEADING]

Jesus Christ sheweth himself unto the people of Nephi,
   as the multitude were gathered together in the land Bountiful,
   and did minister unto them;
   and on this wise did he shew himself unto them.

BOOK OF ETHER [ETHER 1:1, 5; EMBEDDED]

And now I, Moroni, proceed to give an account of those ancient
      inhabitants
   which were destroyed by the hand of the Lord
   upon the face of this north country . . . .
But behold, I give not the full account, but a part of the account I give,
   from the tower [of Babel] down until they were destroyed.[65]

Because Smith dictated these summaries prior to composing the stories, they
reveal the same process of composition (in both shorter and lengthier forms)

that he would use to compose his 1832 history: he dictated the skeletal frame-work of these narratives first, followed by a detailed expansion of the same. Thus, Smith's mnemonic cues and skeletal outlines, consisting of keywords, brief phrases, and sketch summaries, easily and effectively encapsulated the overall shape of narratives and evoked the production of fully expanded stories. Furthermore, the regular appearance of such prefatory summaries throughout the work, marking the succession of narratives from one stage in the work to another, reveals Smith's detailed preparations and strategic place-ment of narratives within his overall story plan.

Finally, even when headings do not reveal a meticulous outline of a forth-coming narrative, they can nevertheless reveal information about Smith's knowledge and awareness of the overall story structure of the Book of Mormon. Consider the heading for the Third Book of Nephi:

THE [THIRD] BOOK OF NEPHI,

THE SON OF NEPHI, WHICH WAS THE SON OF HELAMAN.

CHAPTER I.

And Helaman was the son of Helaman, which was the son of Alma,
which was the son of Alma, being a descendant of Nephi,
which was the son of Lehi, which came out of Jerusalem
in the first year of the reign of Zedekiah, the king of Judah.[66]

While this heading ostensibly appears as a simple biblical-style genealog-ical listing, Smith's semi-extemporaneous composition of this text reveals his awareness of the sequence of these primary characters in the history of the Nephites and his ability to trace their lineage back to Lehi and the origin narrative of his family's departure from Jerusalem. Because each name in the list can operate as a mnemonic cue for the stories in which they appear, Smith's short retrospective genealogy simultaneously oper-ates as a summary of the narrative episodes attached to these names, along with the chronological sequence in which they appeared within the over-all plan of the Book of Mormon. This genealogy-based structure for Smith's project has not gone unnoticed. As Hardy has aptly observed, "The story of the Book of Mormon is told, to a large extent, as a series of interlocking biographies. First one and then another individual comes to the fore-front of the national narrative to carry the plot forward."[67] Smith's semi-extemporaneous composition of the heading for the Third Book of Nephi thus provides evidence of his awareness of the sequence and contents of the narratives in the overall construction of the Book of Mormon, particularly in the way that the historical narratives attach to the biographies of prominent characters.

Mnemonic Cues and Embedded Outlines: The Record of Zeniff

While mnemonic cues have the capacity to invoke complex networks of related story elements, the actual amount of narrative information that a speaker summons with such a device will always depend upon that individual's preparation, the effectiveness of the cues involved, the degree of familiarity with each given story, the circumstances surrounding the production of the narrative, and any number of related variables. Such conditions therefore leave us with questions regarding Smith's use of mnemonic cues and what they had the potential to evoke in his mind. We do not, of course, have access to Smith's thoughts, nor would we have the ability to measure such cognitive networks and associations if we did. Nevertheless, the text of the Book of Mormon provides important clues about the amount of story information that Smith could have in mind at any given moment when he dictated his prefatory headings, summaries, and mnemonic cues. One way to observe this dynamic involves analyzing all the story information that Smith dictated prior to composing the fully developed stories themselves. For an example of this relationship, we will turn to the narrative known as the "Record of Zeniff." But first, we need to situate Zeniff and his story within the overall work.

Near the beginning of the Book of Mormon, in the Second Book of Nephi, the prophet Lehi dies. And Nephi, one of his righteous sons, decides to take his family and friends and flee into the wilderness in order to escape from his wicked brothers and their warmongering family members. After journeying several days in the wilderness, Nephi's company settles in a new land, which they called the Land of Nephi (2 Nephi 5:5–8). The people, who now refer to themselves as Nephites, establish a new city and live in the Land of Nephi for several centuries. Generations pass. Then one day the Lord warns the Nephites to flee again from the descendants of Laman and Lemuel, now known by the appellation "Lamanites." So, once again, the Nephites pack their belongings and flee into the wilderness, eventually arriving at a city called Zarahemla. This city is already populated by another group of ancient Israelites called "Mulekites," who, like Lehi and his family, fled Jerusalem and came to the Americas prior to the Babylonian exile (Omni 1:12–16). At this point, the Nephites and the people of Zarahemla join together to form a single nation, and they collectively call themselves Nephites.

Yet, not all of the Nephites are happy about relocating to Zarahemla. Some of them, in fact, want to return to the Land of Nephi in hopes of negotiating a peace treaty with the Lamanites to reclaim the lands of their inheritance (Omni 1:27–30). At this point, the character Zeniff makes his entrance: Zeniff is the leader of the homesick group that returns to the Land of Nephi, where they negotiate a peace treaty with the Lamanites. They resettle the land, but wars break out between the two groups. Time passes, Zeniff grows old, and then he confers the kingship on his son, Noah. But Noah, infamous for his wickedness, rules badly. In time, the Lamanites defeat the Nephites, King Noah and his inner circle of followers flee the city, and the remaining Nephites are taken into bondage and oppressed with burdens and heavy taxes. With Noah gone, one of his sons, Limhi, becomes the king. Meanwhile, back in Zarahemla, King Mosiah has sent out a search party, led by a warrior named Ammon (a different Ammon than the missionary mentioned in the previous chapter), to find out what happened to the people of Zeniff. After wandering through the wilderness, Ammon and his party eventually discover King Limhi and his beleaguered people, and together they form a plan to escape from the clutches of the Lamanites. Their plan proves successful, and all the people eventually return to the Land of Zarahemla.

For first-time readers of the Book of Mormon, all of the specific details about the story of Zeniff and his group of settlers appear in the "Record of Zeniff," which is nestled within the Book of Mosiah, specifically in chapters 9 through 22. Nevertheless, this is not the first time that readers learn about the story of this group of long-suffering people. Before readers arrive at the official Record of Zeniff in Mosiah 9–22, Smith had already provided two separate summaries of this story. The most obvious one, appearing at the beginning of the record, is the concise prefatory heading that provides a broad overview of Zeniff's history (Mosiah 9):

THE RECORD OF ZENIFF.

An account of his people,
    from the time they left the land of Zarahemla,
        until the time that they were delivered out of the hands of the Lamanites.[68]

This summary, spare as it may be, operates as a mnemonic cue that provides the overall shape of the story: Zeniff and his people leave Zarahemla, they implicitly fall into bondage to the Lamanites, and then they are finally delivered.

First-time readers of the Book of Mormon might be disappointed with this opening summary in Mosiah 9, because it spoils the ending of the story. The account of Zeniff's escape does not occur until much later in the book, in Mosiah 22. Thus, the opening summary at the beginning of the Record of Zeniff reveals how the story will end before it actually begins. In like manner, this summary also demonstrates that Smith knew how the story would play out before he started dictating the narrative to his scribe.

But a question remains: how detailed was Smith's knowledge of this story before he dictated the prefatory heading and the narrative itself? The Record of Zeniff covers roughly three generations of people in the Land of Nephi, so the brief opening summary omits a great deal of information for the reader. So how much information did this cue evoke for Smith? When turning to the text of the Book of Mormon, we find that Smith was actually quite familiar with the story, enough to provide a detailed outline of the narrative long before he dictated either the prefatory summary or the fully developed story itself. Two chapters before the Record of Zeniff begins, Smith had already presented the reader with a detailed sketch of the entire narrative, providing a complete outline of forthcoming events.

Back in Mosiah 7, Ammon and his search party from Zarahemla discover the lost people of Zeniff. King Limhi, the current leader over the people, is overjoyed at the prospect of receiving help from Ammon and the Nephites in Zarahemla: "Our brethren will deliver us out of our bondage, or out of the hands of the Lamanites" (Mosiah 7:15).[69] By way of introducing Ammon and his search party to his people, as well as offering his followers a message of hope, King Limhi gathers all his subjects together and rehearses their sad and troublesome history (Mosiah 7:17–33). In doing so, King Limhi provides an embedded sketch outline of all the major events that occurred to their people from the time they left Zarahemla until the day when Ammon and his search party discovered them.

All of the events in King Limhi's rehearsal of his peoples' history, however, have *not yet occurred* in the Book of Mormon narrative. Thus, Smith, through Limhi's speech in Mosiah 7, delivers a detailed preview of the entire Record of Zeniff, before the record actually appears in the text and before the prefatory summary that will appear in Mosiah 9 at the beginning of Zeniff's record. Thus, by default, King Limhi's historical sketch demonstrates Smith's detailed and intimate familiarity with the contents of the Record of Zeniff, well before he started to dictate the fully developed story two chapters later in the work. The following illustration shows the sequence of events that Smith dictated, prior to dictating the actual story (Mosiah 7:20–33):

King Limhi's Embedded Outline:

1. Zeniff's people are in bondage because of iniquity and abominations (7:20).
2. Zeniff was deceived by King Laman and entered into a bad treaty (7:21).
3. King Laman created the treaty for the purpose of bringing Zeniff and his people into bondage and forcing them to pay burdensome tributes (7:22).
4. The peoples' afflictions derive from transgressions and ignoring the Lord (7:23–25).
5. Contentions arise among the people, resulting in bloodshed (7:25).
6. The people slay a prophet of the Lord (Abinadi), (7:26–28).
7. The people do many more wicked things that incur God's wrath (7:28).
8. Therefore, the people of Zeniff are in bondage and suffer sore afflictions (7:28–32).
9. [Foreshadowing] But if the people repent, they will be delivered (7:33).[70]

When we take into account that Smith would later condense this story outline into a brief summary of twenty-eight words (the heading for the "Record of Zeniff"), we find direct textual evidence that demonstrates how Smith's short summaries and brief mnemonic cues could compress and conceal a wealth of narrative information already swirling in Smith's mind and imagination.

Varieties of Cues: The Sons of Mosiah

Throughout the process of composing the Book of Mormon, Smith used a variety of structural devices to guide the performance of the text. Skeletal outlines composed of primary heads, mnemonic cues, and narrative references all operated as interrelated compositional techniques that provided Smith with a framework for structured, semi-extemporaneous oral performances. Such evidences further reveal Smith's advance awareness of the narrative structure of his stories, their placement within the overall plan of his epic work, and his deep familiarity with their content. This awareness becomes even more apparent when Smith provides the reader with multiple cues within and surrounding a particular story, revealing the shaping processes at work in the development and resolution of narratives. The narrative about the missionary labors of the sons of Mosiah, which we discussed in chapter 5, provides a variety of cues that reveal the dynamics of Smith's composition process. These cues fall into three main categories: first, an anticipatory cue, which, appearing several chapters before the actual narrative, alerts the reader to the account of the sons of Mosiah; second, headers and embedded references within the story that reveal Smith's awareness of discrete narrative units within the overall account; and third, a skeletal outline of heads that summarizes their journey.

By way of background, recall that King Mosiah, the son of King Benjamin, had four sons—Ammon, Aaron, Omner, and Himni (again, this Ammon is a different character than the Ammon who discovered the people of Zeniff). After behaving badly in their youth and rebelling against their church, these four sons repent of their sins and eventually decide that they want to preach the gospel to the dangerous and unrighteous Lamanites (Mosiah 28:1–9). At this point in the story, however, Smith does not launch immediately into their journey into Lamanite territory. Rather, Smith continues the narrative with events happening within the Nephite civilization, saving the story of the sons of Mosiah for a later time. Smith nevertheless alerts the reader to the existence of these forthcoming missionary stories by embedding a place-holder in the text: "They [the sons of Mosiah] took their journey into the wilderness, to go up to preach the word among the Lamanites: and *I shall give an account of their proceedings hereafter*" (Mosiah 28:9).[71] The actual narrative of this missionary effort will not appear for several more chapters, covering Alma 17 through 27. Thus, from a compositional viewpoint, this announcement reveals Smith's foreknowledge of these missionary accounts, along with his conscious placement of them within the overall plot of the Book of Mormon.

The second announcement about the sons of Mosiah appears as a mnemonic cue, which opens the account of their missionary labors with a general description of their experiences:

THE BOOK OF ALMA [Alma 17, heading]
An account of the sons of Mosiah,
    which rejected their rights to the kingdom, for the word of God,
    and went up to the land of Nephi, to preach to the Lamanites.—
    Their sufferings and deliverance, according to the record of Alma.[72]

This opening summary, though following a basic chronology of subsequent events (traveling to the Lamanites, facing persecution, and then being delivered), does not provide the reader with much detail, nor with a specific skeletal outline of the narratives that will follow. It does, however, provide a general story arc—a beginning, middle, and end—that reveals Smith's advance awareness of the overall structure of the yet unspoken story.

In terms of the narrative context, the sons of Mosiah, along with a few of their friends, journey to the borders of the Lamanite lands, where they decide to split up and go to different cities to preach the gospel (Alma 17:13,17). Two parallel stories thus emerge. The first story focuses on the efforts of Ammon, and then eventually shifts to the missionary labors of Aaron. Smith marks the shift from Ammon to Aaron with two additional references. The first appears as the chapter heading for Alma 21: "*An account of the preaching of Aaron and Muloki, and their brethren, to the Lamanites.*"[73] In the course of telling this story, however, Smith wanders back to the story of Ammon, necessitating another overt cue to shift the narrative once again from Ammon's story back to Aaron's account. This cue appears in the opening of the next chapter (Alma 22:1): "Now as Ammon was thus teaching the people of Lamoni continually, *we will return to the account of Aaron and his brethren.*"[74] Apart from guiding the development of the text, these two references reveal Smith's awareness of these two stories as discrete narrative units.

Next, as Smith continues with Aaron's story, the readers discover how Aaron, in a missionary triumph, converts the king over all the Lamanites. The king's conversion then leads to a mass conversion of his Lamanite followers, and he sends a proclamation throughout the land, commanding his people to listen to the sons of Mosiah and not to obstruct their preaching. At this stage, however, Smith wanders off onto a long tangent concerning Lamanite and Nephite territories within the overall geography of the Book of Mormon (Alma 22:27–34). At the end of this distracted and apparently improvised excursion, Smith makes an abrupt shift back to his central story with another narrative cue: "And now I . . . return again to the account of Ammon, and Aaron, Omner and Himni, and their brethren" (Alma 22:35).[75] Thus, once again, Smith reveals his awareness of discrete narrative units. The narrative continues with a mass migration of converted Lamanites from the Land of Nephi to the Land of Zarahemla. An army of wicked Lamanites pursues the migrants into the Nephite territories, and a great battle ensues between the Lamanite army and the armies of the Nephite nation. Yet, the Nephites eventually triumph.

As he moves toward the end of this story, Smith presents the reader with a final summary of all the events that occurred by laying down a series of explicit sequential heads in an embedded outline. In addition, note how Smith frames the narrative events with resumptive repetition, creating an *inclusio* that marks the boundaries of the sequence (Alma 28:7–9, verses reformatted, underlining mine):

> and <u>thus ended the fifteenth year of the reign of the Judges</u> over
> the people of Nephi;
>> and this is the account of Ammon and his brethren,
>> their journeyings in the land of Nephi, their sufferings in the land,
>> their sorrows, and their afflictions, and their incomprehensible joy,
>> and the reception and safety of the brethren in the land of Jershon.
>> And now may the Lord, the Redeemer of all men, bless their souls
>>> forever.
>> And this is the account of the wars and contentions among
>>> the Nephites,
>> and also the wars between the Nephites and the Lamanites;
> and <u>the fifteenth year of the reign of the Judges is ended</u>.[76]

This structural framework, we should recall, mirrors the same approach that some of Smith's nineteenth-century contemporaries used to summarize narrative events in a concise and orderly fashion. As noted in chapter 4, Methodist preacher Thomas Olivers concludes his autobiography in the same manner, using resumptive repetition to form an *inclusio* that framed a series of heads for the major events of his life:

> <u>When I consider how the providence of God</u>
> provided for me in my infancy—
>> Brought me up to the state of man—
>> Preserved me from those evils which brought others
>>> to an untimely end—
>> Directed my wandering steps to the means of my conversion—
>> Cast my lot among his people—Called me to preach his word—
>> Owned my preaching, to the conversion of others—
>> Stood by me in many trials—
>> Brought me back, so often, from the brink of the grave—
>> Healed my manifold backslidings—
>> Provided me a suitable companion—
>> And put me in possession of all the necessaries of life.
> <u>When I consider these things</u>, I must say, Surely, goodness and mercy
> have followed me all the days of my life; and I hope to dwell
> in the house of the Lord forever.[77]

By laying down heads to recapitulate the story of the sons of Mosiah, Smith reveals his awareness of the ways in which many of his nineteenth-century contemporaries used the same method as a structuring and summational device.

Outlining the Entire Book of Mormon

Of all of Smith's narrative summaries, the embedded outlines in one of Nephi's visions (1 Nephi 12) and one of Nephi's prophecies (2 Nephi 26) are two of the most comprehensive, providing the reader with a synopsis of the entire story of the rise and fall of the Nephite nation. These two examples, however, present an interesting complication. Even though these summaries appear in the beginning of the Book of Mormon, Smith did not actually dictate them until the end of his project. The reason for the inverted order of composition lies in the history of the production of the original scribal manuscript. Recall that Martin Harris, Smith's associate and financial backer for the project, borrowed and subsequently lost the first 116 pages of the work. Rather than immediately going back and redoing that lost portion, Smith continued forward with the project, starting with the Book of Mosiah and continuing to the end of the work. Once he reached the end of the book, Smith then returned to the opening of the Book of Mormon and dictated a replacement text for the missing portion, extending from 1 Nephi through the Words of Mormon. This explanation is known as the "Mosiah Priority" or "Mosian Priority."[78]

Given this sequence of the production of the text, Smith's composition of the embedded outlines for Nephi's vision and prophecy occurred *after* he had already dictated the fully developed stories. Thus, Nephi's summaries were likely influenced by Smith's prior completion of the stories associated with them. And while it is possible that Smith dictated Nephi's vision and prophecy in his first attempt (the lost 116 pages), we do not know if these narrative outlines appeared in the original pages or if they were later additions or versions. In any event, whether the outlines are reproductions of lost material or new (or modified) additions, they offer important insights into Smith's ability to articulate extemporaneously the entire narrative outline of the Book of Mormon, evidently without the use of notes or a manuscript.

By way of story background for Nephi's far-reaching prophecies, the first of these embedded outlines occurs when Lehi and his family are still traveling in the Middle East, before they reach the Americas. During their journey, Lehi receives a vision popularly known as "Lehi's Vision" or "Lehi's Vision of the Tree of Life" (1 Nephi 8:2–35). In the dream, Lehi sees throngs of people searching for the Tree of Life (symbolic of salvation and eternal life). After listening to Lehi's story, Nephi, anxious "to behold the things which my father saw" (1 Nephi 11:3), is also caught up in a vision that reveals the same events that Lehi witnessed, along with additional scenes and information about the future. Among these scenes, Nephi receives a panoramic vision that traces out the entire narrative of the Nephite people. As he looks into the future, he sees all the generations of his descendants, as well as the descendants of his rebellious brothers. He witnesses the rise and development of the Nephites, their wars with the Lamanites, the events surrounding the visitation of Christ in the Americas, and then the final destruction of the Nephite civilization.

In relaying this visionary account, Smith provides the reader with an embedded outline that covers the overall trajectory of the central narrative of the Book of Mormon. The following list details the sequence of events (1 Nephi 12:1–23), and the reader is encouraged to compare the list with the text of the Book of Mormon:

Nephi's Vision of the Rise and Fall of the Nephite Civilization
1. Nephi sees his descendants and those of his brothers (12:1).
2. Their descendants wage war for many generations (12:2–3).
3. Their descendants build countless cities (12:3).
4. Nephi observes a "mist of darkness" and natural disasters (12:4).
5. Many cities are sunk, burned, or tumbled to the ground (12:4).
6. The vapor of darkness goes away, revealing the survivors (12:5).
7. Christ appears and descends out of heaven (12:6).
8. Christ chooses twelve men to minister to the church (12:7–10).
9. Three generations live in righteousness (12:11).
10. Many of the fourth generation also live in righteousness (12:12).
11. But the Lamanites and Nephites start warring again (12:13–15).
12. Pride and sin will destroy the Nephite nation (12:19–20).
13. The Lamanites populate the land and war among themselves (12:20–21).
14. The Lamanites forget their religious and cultural heritage (12:22–23).[79]

This detailed outline of the entire Nephite history provides the reader with a preview of all the major events that occur in the rise and fall of the nation. Moreover, in the next book, 2 Nephi, Smith provides yet another overarching narrative plan that outlines the history of the Nephite nation, covering much of the same material (2 Nephi 26:3–10).

Smith's ability to produce these comprehensive embedded narrative outlines—dictated without the aid of notes in the moment of performance and therefore produced from memory—reveals his deep familiarity with the over-all storyline, along with his ability to condense and summarize the events. In terms of Smith's preparations, however, these outlines still raise the intriguing question of his foreknowledge: when he started his dictation project, did Smith already have these overarching summaries in his mind, or do Nephi's summaries merely represent convenient synopses produced after the fact? Fortunately for the reader, Smith peppers the text with prophecies about the future, particularly in relation to the coming of Christ, and these contain all or part of the same information found in Nephi's prophetic outlines. Such brief but informative references constantly remind the reader of future events in the narrative, but in terms of Smith's composition process they also reveal Smith's advance awareness of his plan for the work. Even so, not all of these references are brief.

Further into the main narrative, a lengthy prophecy emerges that contains much of the same information found in Nephi's embedded outlines. Approximately five years before Christ's birth, a Lamanite prophet named Samuel chastises the Nephite people for their wickedness and sins (Helaman 13–15). In the course of his prophecy, Samuel foretells the destruction of the Nephite people, along with signs and events that will accompany the birth, death, and resurrection of Christ. When comparing Samuel's prophecy with Nephi's summarizing outlines, we find that many of the events foretold in Nephi's accounts also appear in Samuel's prediction. Yet, unlike Nephi's summaries (dictated *after* Smith had already completed the corresponding narrative), Smith provided Samuel's prophecy *before* he dictated the corresponding expanded text (Helaman 13–15):

Samuel the Lamanite's Prophecy

1. The Nephites face destruction in four hundred years (13:5–6, 9–10).
2. Signs for Christ's birth, death, and resurrection (14:3–6, 20).
3. Natural disasters will occur at Christ's death (14:21–23).
4. Many cities will be destroyed (14:24).
5. A dark mist will cover the earth (14:27).
6. If they do not repent, the Nephites will be destroyed (15:17).[80]

Thus, Samuel's prophecy provides direct evidence of Smith's advance awareness of the contents and trajectory of several key events in the central structure of the Book of Mormon, extending from the signs of Christ's birth to the eventual destruction of the Nephite nation.

Framing the Book of Mormon

When reviewing the entire text of the Book of Mormon, we find repeated evidence of Smith's forethought and preparations, which militate against the theory that Smith produced the work in spontaneous, unpremeditated outbursts of creativity. The repeated preliminary outlines, which frame the story arcs of forthcoming narratives, do not suggest a process of pure improvisation or exclusive acts of extempore storytelling. In other words, Smith did not formulate the plot or create the content of his narrative in the course of performance, not knowing from one day to the next where the story would lead. Rather, the stories were carefully planned, with preliminary summaries and embedded outlines that revealed the shape of individual episodes, along with how those episodes fit within the larger scheme of the entire work. Neither does the evidence support the theory that Smith extemporized the Book of Mormon from a single, general narrative outline. Rather, Smith reveals a complex matrix of skeletal summaries and mnemonic cues that operate as interlocking structural blueprints for his semi-extemporaneous expansions. The number and specificity of the preliminary outlines thus indicate that Smith was deeply familiar with his stories and that he had worked out the shapes of his narratives in great detail prior to performance. The work was clearly premeditated and the preparation was extensive.

Moreover, the nature of Smith's outlines and mnemonic cues provides further important insights. As we have observed, Smith was able to extrapolate lengthy narratives from very short outlines and extremely brief cues. When observing the actual outlines and cues that Smith provided in the Book of Mormon and comparing those key words and phrases with the actual texts that he subsequently produced, we find that Smith regularly expanded a relatively small collection of succinct narrative skeletons and key phrases into very lengthy and extensive passages. These small kernels of potent narrative seeds thus swelled into full-grown towering stories, revealing Smith's intimate knowledge of the narratives that he expressed. Whatever the extent of the notes that he may (or may not) have used during the period of meditation and dictation, Smith would not have needed much space to sketch out a comprehensive plan of his work, whether tracing out the narrative lineage of his Nephite kings or framing the hundred-year span of the "reign of the judges over the people of Nephi."[81] If the opening summaries, headings, embedded outlines, and mnemonic cues that appear throughout the text offer any indication of what appeared in his notes and/or mental preparations, then Smith could have easily written the entire plan of the Book of Mormon on roughly a dozen sheets of paper.

Moving Forward

When Nephi commanded his brother Jacob to "engraven the heads" of sermons, revelations, and prophecies onto the gold plates and to "touch upon them as much as it were possible" (Jacob 1:4), both Nephi and Jacob, and many of the author-prophets who followed, did not limit the technique of laying down heads to oratorical performances.[82] They also used the technique to organize their historical narratives, providing the structural architectonics for the entire Book of Mormon. Crucial to understanding Smith's process of narrative production, however, is the recognition that these methods and techniques emerged in a different place and time than the period in which the stories of the Book of Mormon occurred, signaling the authoritative presence of a modern hand—whether as translator or author—in the construction of the work. The Book of Mormon reveals systemic evidence of laying down heads in the creation of oral performances and historical narratives, mirroring the same processes and techniques of oral and written composition that nineteenth-century children learned at home and in school, as well as the same strategies of composition that semi-extemporaneous preachers used to compose and perform their sermons, exhortations, and spiritual autobiographies. To that end, having explored the techniques of oral composition and rhetorical performance in Smith's cultural setting, along with the extensive textual evidence of these practices within his body of work, we begin to arrive at a place where it is possible to propose an informed and evidence-based theory of Smith's method of oral composition of the Book of Mormon.

CHAPTER SEVEN

A Theory of Translation

Whatever position the reader might take on the origins of the Book of Mormon, a careful review of historical claims favors the idea that Joseph Smith himself sincerely believed, to one degree or another, that his epic work contained an authentic historical account of ancient American civilizations. The theory proposed in this chapter therefore operates on the assumption that Smith believed that his process of constructing the text did, in fact, involve divine inspiration and guidance. While "defenders of the faith" and "critics of the church" will no doubt continue to debate the historical authenticity of the text, I believe that the academic study of the Book of Mormon finds a much more productive focus when shifting to a position that seeks to understand what Smith himself thought about his project and how his personal beliefs and practices informed the production of the work. In this respect I am following Ann Taves's lead in analyzing the evidence and various theories about Smith's process of translation "to highlight what they suggest regarding Smith's subjective experience."[1] With that aim in mind, this chapter proposes an explanation of Smith's translation that offers a framework for both believers and nonbelievers to account for the production of the Book of Mormon, while also accommodating and carefully reflecting on the textual and historical evidence.

Filling the Historical Gaps

As every good historian knows, the project of reconstructing the past is tantamount to the task of assembling a complex jigsaw puzzle with the majority of pieces permanently missing. No recapitulation of the past, however detailed the original documentation or how careful the scholarship, can fully recapture a historical event or past experience. As historian David Henige observes, "All evidence is vestigial. The sources in which it is embedded cannot possibly replicate the events that, wittingly or unwittingly, they testify to. They can never be treated as *representing* a larger reality, but only as hinting at it."[2] The attempt to reconstruct the period leading up to Smith's creation and publication of the Book of Mormon remains particularly problematic. Smith first mentioned the gold plates to his family in late September of 1823 and then possibly started some of the translation (perhaps the opening of the lost 116 pages) as early as December of 1827.[3] Yet, as Larry E. Morris observes, "a host of crucial Book-of-Mormon events took place between September of 1823 and the end of 1827, but not a single document—no letter, diary entry, legal record, newspaper article, or anything else—mentioning the Book of Mormon has survived."[4] As such, all the historical accounts about this crucial period are retrospective, all contingent and deeply informed by subsequent events, and all responsive to controversial issues in Joseph Smith's life and the rise of the Latter Day Saint movement.

With such gaps in the external historical evidence, the internal textual evidence—evidence within the Book of Mormon itself—becomes all the more significant. Whatever competing claims might be made about the origins of the work, the text of the Book of Mormon nonetheless provides extensive collections of interrelated structural components, which, in turn, reveal the techniques involved in its creation. When gathered together and viewed as a whole, these techniques uncover a systematic process at play that remains consistent throughout the entire work. And in terms of the evidence in the text and Smith's documented methods and techniques of semi-extemporaneous production, there are four interrelated points to be made about this careful preparation.

First, the narratives frequently begin with an advance summary of an ensuing story, appearing in the form of detailed opening headings, outlines embedded within the main body of the narrative, or mnemonic cues. These anticipatory summaries and phrases either trace the narrative development of story episodes or they encapsulate narrative scenarios with succinct key phrases. Second, the number and detail of the outlines and summaries, the nature of the mnemonic cues, and the consistent appearance of these textual elements throughout the work reveal a process of careful preparation and familiarity with the stories, made in advance of their actual production. In other words, the Book of Mormon was neither an improvised text, nor was it merely the result of an extempore expansion of a broad, generalized mental template. Rather, the dictated text reveals a preliminary process of careful preparation and narrative structuring for all the stories it contains. Moreover, the preparatory work was extensive; the process involved time, meditation, careful attention, and a good memory.

Third, the mnemonic cues and the narrative outlines, or "skeletons," consist of the distinctive style of phraseology and organizational schematics that derive from the contemporary compositional method of laying down heads, ubiquitously practiced in Smith's time and place. Fourth, and finally, the actual composition of the stories generally involved the expansion and amplification of summarizing outlines and mnemonic cues by means of semi-extemporaneous oral production, as evinced by the eyewitness accounts of Smith's process of dictation, the direct references in the text itself describing the process of speaking according to the inspiration of the Holy Spirit, and the systemic appearance of orally related characteristics in the text (such as resumptive repetition).

Taking all of these techniques and structural features together, the text of the Book of Mormon repeatedly and systematically puts on open display the central compositional methods involved in its production. Whether theorists attribute the authorship to God, ancient prophets, angels, mystical translation devices, or Smith himself, the technique of laying down heads to formulate narrative skeletal outlines and to create potent mnemonic cues represents the compositional bedrock that coordinates the entire structure of the Book of Mormon and provides the guiding framework for its oral performance. These features and characteristics thereby alert us to the genealogy of the technical components of the text. Specifically, the method and techniques involved in the production of the work derive from the most common and widespread practices of introductory composition in early nineteenth-century America, thereby situating the entire narrative structure of the Book of Mormon within a contemporary and therefore anachronistic framework. Whoever was ultimately responsible for the text, the method that undergirds the work tells us that the author(s) of the Book of Mormon adopted a specific compositional approach that would have resonated deeply and specifically with nineteenth-century audiences.

Theories of Construction

The structural characteristics within the Book of Mormon open themselves to multiple interpretations, both for those who believe the text represents an authentic history and those who attribute the work to Smith's own creative efforts. For example, the argument can be made that Smith actively participated as an actual translator in the production of the Book of Mormon. In this scenario, the anachronistic structures within the text would indicate that Smith articulated the historical content of the plates within the constraints of his own vocabulary, limited education and training, and habituated structural patterns. As such, one would expect to see nineteenth-century compositional techniques and the structural features of contemporary sermonizing in the Book of Mormon as a natural outgrowth of Smith's own knowledge and development.

Alternatively, for those who believe that Smith merely dictated a preexisting translation, which either appeared on the surface of the seer stone or within a supernatural vision of the text, then the argument can also be made—as, in many respects, it already has—that the anachronisms derive from God or his angels, who modified the original writings of the ancient prophets in order to assist nineteenth-century audiences in comprehending the work by providing them with familiar patterns and vocabulary.[5] For those who adhere to this view, however, the theory requires an update. The nineteenth-century elements in the Book of Mormon do not merely present an abstract nineteenth-century style. Rather, the ubiquitous presence of the language of revivalism, the use of laying down heads to structure the narratives, the tendency of doctrinal passages to gravitate toward basic fundamental doctrinal principles, and the litany of contemporary religious controversies all reflect the specific style and focus of an early career evangelical preacher in nineteenth-century America. If Smith did not participate in the construction of the text, then God and the angels created a text that gave the appearance of being composed by Smith or someone with his same background, training, and level of experience.

Apart from these theories, however, I believe that the evidence points to a different but related history of the production of the Book of Mormon. The ubiquitous presence of nineteenth-century compositional techniques, the pervasive residue of contemporary sermonizing strategies, and the saturation of the work with nineteenth-century concepts, phraseology, and vocabulary all point directly and specifically to Joseph Smith as the source and assembler of these narrative components. Moreover, the evidence reveals that behind the project lay a systematic approach of careful planning and preparation, which, in turn, suggests that Smith spent a significant amount of time in the creation of the work. In addition, the content of the stories also suggests a process of elaborate preparatory construction. Grant Hardy, for example, records a litany of textual features that reveal such a process, including, among many others, the presence of flashbacks, parallel narratives, a hundred-year chronicle of Nephite leaders and judges, as well as several genealogies and successions of rulers.[6]

When combined together, all of these factors suggest that Smith began his work on the Book of Mormon long before he actually started to dictate the text. Taking into consideration the textual evidence and the array of historical accounts surrounding the production of the work, the best explanation of Smith's process involves a scenario in which he announced the existence of the gold plates containing the narrative of the Book of Mormon in September 1823, after which he spent several years constructing and revising preliminary outlines (*not* fully written manuscripts) that framed the work before dictating the current text in 1829. These outlines would have included the organization of such story elements as the many chronologies within the work (e.g., the hundred-year reign of the Nephite judges and the various genealogies of leaders); the dramatic shape of the successive and parallel narrative episodes; the names and general descriptions of the main characters; and perhaps the basic content of some sermons. At the same time, the evidence also suggests that Smith's flexible semi-extemporaneous method left much of the actual language of the work—along with the amplification of narratives, sermons, tangential topics, and story elements—to improvisations in the moment of performance.

In addition, given his multiyear preparation (more on this below), Smith would also have had an extensive amount of time to rehearse and familiarize himself with the characters and narratives, thus only requiring, as the text often demonstrates, the promptings of brief sketch outlines, individual mnemonic cues, or nothing more than his memory to recall story episodes. In fact, the large number of brief outlines and mnemonic cues in the Book of Mormon suggests that Smith was deeply and extensively familiar with the narratives, long before expanding them in the moment of performance. Moreover, given his exposure to contemporary evangelical sermon culture and the evidence of semi-extemporaneous composition techniques in the construction of lengthy and moderately complex narratives, Smith may well have developed a small collection of private notes for personal use and reflection. Yet, considering the four-to-five-year period of preparation, one could also argue that Smith may not have needed any notes at all by the time he dictated the narratives. Nonetheless, if the narrative skeletons and mnemonic cues in the text of the Book of Mormon offer any indication, Smith could have outlined the entire work on a small handful of papers, whether as loose individual sheets or as bound sheets in the back of a common "blank book" (store-bought or homemade). Whenever he needed to refresh his memory, Smith could simply take his private notes to a secluded location for review. When the time finally arrived for his oral performances, however, Smith, as eyewitness accounts suggest, would not have needed these notes during the actual dictation sessions.

Whatever the mental or written preparations involved, it is critical to view Smith's process in a way that takes his own perspective and beliefs into account. Though he did not leave a record regarding the specifics of his method, the contemporaneous historical evidence—fragmentary and limited as it may be—suggests that Smith's preparations involved what he believed to be a revelatory translation process guided by the Holy Spirit. In other words, attributing his years-long process of preparation to deceptive motives and clandestine practices does not adequately account for the full array of historical evidence, nor does it recognize the complexity of Smith's thought or reveal the paradigms of his belief. As stated at the outset of this chapter, I imagine that Smith sincerely believed, to one extent or another, that the Book of Mormon represented an authentic history of ancient civilizations in the Americas. And using the ways and means available to his understanding and ambition, Smith engaged in a years-long project to bring that history to light.

Yet, the idea that Smith engaged in preparatory work on the Book of Mormon generates as many questions as it answers, and several issues need to be addressed. For example, Emma Smith and David Whitmer, both firsthand witnesses of the creative process, insisted that Joseph never consulted written materials during dictation.[7] Their statements ostensibly appear to preclude the use of notes—or even a Bible, for that matter—during Smith's oral performance of the text. Yet, a close examination of their descriptions reveals problems that resist the uncritical acceptance of their claims. In order to respond to this issue, along with other related matters, the following sections address three central topics: first, the timing of Smith's initial preparations and an exploration of the evidence that suggests his early development of story content; second, a closer examination of Smith's approach to revelatory translation; and third, an analysis of the historical contexts in which the statements of Emma Smith and David Whitmer occurred.

Timing and Content

According to Smith's testimony, the angel Moroni, the last prophet of the Nephite people, appeared to him on the night of 21 September 1823 and told him about the gold plates and how they contained the historical record of ancient people in the Americas.[8] Even so, Smith would not start the actual dictation of the project until late 1827 or early 1828.[9] Thus, from the first announcement of the text to the actual dictation of the work, Smith had at least four years of preparation time. Moreover, given that Martin Harris lost the original 116 pages of the first manuscript, delaying the start of the translation of the present-day version of the Book of Mormon until April of 1829, Smith would have had a total of five and a half years from Moroni's first visit to Smith's renewed attempt at dictation, providing additional time to organize and refine the work. Consequently, in terms of the moderate complexity of the Book of Mormon narrative, the period of time would have been more than sufficient for Smith, using his process of revelatory translation, to anticipate most of the structural and technical challenges of the work and to orchestrate the intricacies of the overall narrative.

In terms of story content, several reminiscences also suggest that Smith already had in mind some basic story elements and a general outline of the Book of Mormon when he announced the existence of the plates in September of 1823. The day after the angel Moroni's visit, Joseph told his family about the encounter. In an 1845 manuscript (revised and published in 1853), Lucy Smith, Joseph's mother, recorded how Joseph began telling stories to his family about the "ancient inhabitants of this continent" during their evening fireside gatherings, with "all seated in a circle, father, mother, sons, and daughters ["listening in breathless anxiety," (1845 manuscript)], and giving the most profound attention to a boy, eighteen years of age, who had never read the Bible through in his life."[10] William Smith, one of Joseph's younger brothers, recalled these evening storytelling sessions. In an 1883 booklet, William claimed that Joseph told the family how the angel Moroni had given "a short account of the inhabitants who formerly resided upon this continent, a full history of whom he said was engraved on some plates which were hidden."[11] If William's account is correct, then in 1823 Joseph also provided a brief initial historical sketch of the Book of Mormon civilizations. Even so, William's reminiscence, though a firsthand eyewitness account, was given sixty years after the fact, raising questions about his memory and accuracy.

Nevertheless, in an account much closer to the historical events in question, Oliver Cowdery made a similar claim. In 1835 he wrote a series of letters published in the *Latter Day Saints' Messenger and Advocate*, stating that the angel Moroni gave Joseph "a history of the aborigines of this country, and said they were literal descendants of Abraham. He represented them as once being an enlightened and intelligent people, possessing a correct knowledge of the gospel, and the plan of restoration and redemption."[12] Cowdery's claim therefore asserts that Joseph had received a basic history of the Nephites that included their origins and their Christian teachings. Yet, Cowdery, of course, was not an eyewitness to Joseph's discussions with the angel Moroni. Even so, Joseph appears to have approved of Cowdery's depiction. According to the editors of the Joseph Smith Papers, "Although there is no evidence that Joseph Smith assigned Cowdery to write the letters, he [Joseph] offered his assistance to ensure that the 'narrative may be correct,'" indicating that Joseph may well have reviewed Cowdery's narrative and approved of the content before publication.[13]

If Smith saw and approved of Cowdery's account, it would not be surprising. Cowdery's description was little more than a reflection of Smith's own firsthand narratives. According to Smith, the angel Moroni told him that "there was a book deposited, written upon gold plates, giving an account of the former inhabitants of this continent, and the source from whence they sprang. He also said that the fullness of the everlasting Gospel was contained in it, as delivered by the Savior to the ancient inhabitants."[14] But this was not Smith's only such description. In a March 1842 letter to newspaper editor John Wentworth, Smith offered further details, stating, "I was also informed [by Moroni] concerning the aboriginal inhabitants of this country, and shown who they were, and from whence they came; a brief sketch of their origin, progress, civilization, laws, governments, of their righteousness and iniquity, and the blessings of God being finally withdrawn from them as a people."[15] If these accounts are accurate, then Moroni, from the very beginning of the project in September of 1823, provided Smith with a detailed description of the contents and narrative development of the Book of Mormon.

Moreover, according to the account of Smith's mother, Lucy, the young prophet also appears to have had additional story elements already in mind. When describing Smith's evening fireside stories about "the ancient inhabitants" of the Book of Mormon, Lucy indicated that Joseph's stories were part of an ongoing process of discovery and development. "From this time forth [September 1823]," Lucy recalled, "Joseph *continued to receive instructions from the Lord*, and we continued to get the children together every evening, for the purpose of listening while he gave us a relation of the same."[16] Thus, rather than a one-time event, Smith related a series of narratives over a period of time. In addition, Lucy's description suggests the type of information that Joseph shared. During these "most amusing recitals," Lucy recalled Joseph describing "the ancient inhabitants of this continent, their dress, mode of travelling, and the animals upon which they rode; their cities, their buildings, with every particular; their mode of warfare; and also their religious worship. This he would do with as much ease, seemingly, as if he had spent his whole life with them."[17] Lucy's account provides intriguing information that offers clues concerning the early stages of the creation of the Book of Mormon.

When comparing Lucy's description of Joseph's stories to the narrative of the Book of Mormon, the careful reader will notice that all of these elements appear in the pages of the work. The Book of Mormon describes the dress of ancient American characters (e.g., Alma 3:5; Alma 43:19–21; Alma 49:6; Enos 1:20; Ether 10:24), their mode of travel and the animals they rode on (e.g., Alma 18:9–10, 12; Alma 20:6; Enos 1:21; 3 Nephi 3:22), and their cities and buildings (e.g., 2 Nephi 5:16; Mosiah 11:8–13; Helaman 3:9–14; Alma 16:13). This list of topics is of particular interest, given that Lucy first recorded it in her 1845 manuscript, fifteen years after the publication of the Book of Mormon. One might have expected Lucy's description to contain anachronistic interjections from the main narratives in the completed Book of Mormon. Yet, she only includes minor, basic, and preliminary story elements, without situating them within any of the Book of Mormon narratives. If Lucy's reminiscence is accurate, then this collection of raw story materials suggests that young Joseph was in the earliest stages of his preparation during those evening storytelling adventures around the family hearth. Her account further indicates that Smith was delivering his ideas in an oral medium—an act of rehearsal that would enhance his memory of the story elements and also facilitate his eventual dictation process.

Dynamics of Revelatory Translation

The problem of defining Smith's conception of the word "translation" has received a great deal of attention, ranging from the notion that Smith translated works using his own vocabulary and phraseology to the idea that Smith merely transcribed a preexisting text that some divine entity or mystical object had already translated for him.[18] Yet Smith himself never recorded precisely how he translated the Book of Mormon.[19] Nevertheless, when going back to contemporaneous accounts, we find that Smith's descriptions of the act of "translation" involved, at the very least, some measure of contributions from the "translators" in the traditional sense of the word, rather than as a simple conveyance of preexisting language.

For example, in the course of Smith's production of the Book of Mormon, Cowdery, Smith's primary scribe on the project, asked if he could participate as a translator of the work. In an April 1829 revelation, Cowdery was told how the gift of translation operated and how the Lord would provide correct translations through revelatory inspiration: "Yea, behold, I [the Lord] will tell you in your mind and in your heart, by the Holy Ghost, which shall come upon you and which shall dwell in your heart. Now, behold, this is the spirit of revelation."[20] Even so, when Cowdery attempted to translate, nothing happened. Smith then dictated another revelation from the Lord, informing them of what went wrong:

> Behold, you have not understood; you have supposed that I would give it [the translation] unto you, when you took no thought save it was to ask me [i.e., no effort on the part of the translator; passive reception]. But, behold, I say unto you, that *you must study it out in your mind; then you must*

ask me if it be right [i.e., active forethought and engagement], *and if it is right I will cause that your bosom shall burn within you; therefore, you shall feel that it is right.* But if it be not right you shall have no such feelings, but you shall have a stupor of thought that shall cause you to forget the thing which is wrong; therefore, you cannot write that which is sacred *save it be given you from me.* Now, if you had known this you could have translated.[21]

These revelations to Cowdery offer the most direct and suggestive explanations of the translation process, as articulated by Smith himself. As Taves notes, the description of the process, "coming to us directly from the Lord via Smith (or from the recesses of Smith's mind) at the time when Smith and Cowdery were in the midst of producing the Book of Mormon, is the closest thing we have to a real-time subjective report."[22] Even so, as some have argued, this revelation to Cowdery does not necessarily reveal Smith's own precise process.

Because this revelation was directed at Cowdery (who usually used a divining rod) and not Smith (who preferred the seer stone), some scholars have questioned whether or not this revelation provides an accurate description of Smith's own revelatory translation process during the production of the Book of Mormon.[23] Nonetheless, as Taves observes, "the description of the role of the Holy Ghost in D&C 8 appears to be a general statement about the subjective experience of receiving revelation, which is specified as knowledge of the engravings on the ancient records."[24] Moreover, these revelations indicate, with explicit language, that the process of divine translations—whether by a seer stone, divining rod, or inspiration alone—involve a *dialectical* process, rather than a unidirectional endowment of words: a process in which "translators" engaged their minds in the creation of possible renderings, and then consulted their affective spiritual sensations for evidence of confirmation from the Holy Ghost.[25]

Indeed, in a 6 September 1842 letter, Smith made an indirect but telling comment about his understanding of the process of "translation," including the translator's ability to choose among alternative renderings. When expounding on Malachi 4:5–6 of the Old Testament, Smith used the word "translation" to describe his revelatory revisions of the King James Bible, indicating that, "I might have rendered a plainer translation to this [scripture], but it is sufficiently plain to suit my purpose as it stands [as it is written]."[26] Though he was not, of course, specifically describing his process of translating the Book of Mormon, Smith nevertheless reveals that his personal definition and conceptualization of the process of "translation" included an explicit dynamic in which the translator could choose among alternative renderings of a passage, rather than being limited to a predetermined set of fixed phrases revealed from a divine source. In Smith's developing cosmology, speaking and exhorting according to the impulses of the Holy Spirit thus involved a process in which the inspired mortal contributed to the articulation and shaping of God's words. Instead of being a passive instrument in the hands of heaven, the divinely inspired speaker appropriated an active measure of mortal agency to participate as a co-author and co-translator of divine utterances.

When we consider how Smith's conception of translation involved a process of meditation and study, as well as the trial-and-error testing of possible alternatives measured against spiritual confirmations from the Holy Spirit, we also begin to understand Smith's larger spiritual worldview. The process described in such personal revelations reflects, in fact, the common hermeneutical approach known as *sola scriptura*, or "the Bible alone," a belief that readers of the Bible could arrive at the correct interpretation of scriptural passages through personal research and spiritual affirmations.[27] The idea was not new, having evolved, at least in part, from the ideological movement known as the "Priesthood of Believers," in which "each believer has immediate access to God through the one mediator, Jesus Christ."[28] The concept and practices were common in the early national period in America. As Seth Perry observes, "Many religious leaders of the era declared that each of their listeners could read and interpret the Bible for him- or herself, discovering through his or her own reading how it answered the various questions to which they sought authoritative answers."[29]

This process of spiritual verification specifically involved both instruction and confirmation from the Holy Spirit. "The Apostles themselves did not understand the meaning of the Gospel," argued the Reverend Edward Bickersteth (1786–1850) in his guide for Bible readers, "till they were taught by the Holy Ghost. Whenever, therefore, you open your Bible, never forget to pray that the Holy Ghost may open your understanding."[30] Such divine impressions and personal instruction not only taught the truth about doctrines and principles but also confirmed the reality of miracles and historical events. Thus, the Spirit could confirm that Adam and Eve truly existed; the Fall actually happened; Abraham really did almost sacrifice Isaac; Noah actually built an ark to survive a global deluge; Christ the Son of God was truly born of Mary; and Jesus turned water into wine, healed the sick, and arose from the tomb. Within this personalized paradigm of belief, doctrinal truths and historical realities required no further evidence for validation than the whisperings of the Holy Spirit.

Smith's conception of truth seeking through divine inspiration and confirmation also appears to have extended beyond the verification of scriptural interpretations to encompass all sources of truth. When preaching the King Follett funeral sermon, for example, Smith ridiculed the "learned doctors [of religion] who are preaching salvation" for having an incomplete understanding of the historical circumstances involved in the creation of the world. He countered traditional beliefs with his own historical perspective, supporting his views by couching his claims in the assertion that he knew "more than all the world put together—*the Holy Ghost does, anyhow*. If the Holy Ghost in me comprehends more than all the world, I will associate *myself* with it."[31] Smith's declaration that the Holy Ghost could inspire him to know the truth of all doctrines, principles, and historical occurrences better than "all the world put together" thereby implies that the Holy Ghost confirms truth in all its forms and manifestations, ranging from correct doctrinal understandings to the reality of historical events.

Thus, truth—any truth, in any area of knowledge—could be discovered and verified through spiritual confirmation. In a move that did not require much of a logical lift, Smith adapted this common method of determining scriptural truths into a method of confirming scriptural translations. In other words, if he could study, meditate, and pray regarding the doctrines and historical events in the Bible, then it stood to reason that he could likewise study, meditate, and pray regarding the doctrines and historical events of ancient civilizations in the Americas. Through such a mind-set and its attendant process of spiritual confirmation, Smith formed the basis of his translation work, enabling himself to discover the history, origins, personalities, narratives, and teachings of ancient cultures that no longer existed. Once he laid the groundwork with this preparation, Smith could then follow his story plotlines as prefabricated mental maps. In turn, this preparation would allow Smith to switch from the careful and deliberate process of creating and verifying narrative outlines to the rapid and semi-extemporaneous expansion of the same outlines into full-blown stories during the moment of oral performance.[32]

Furthermore, within his conception of revelatory translation, Smith's use of a seer stone represented a critical component of the creation process that integrated his method of confirming the historical past with his own spiritual impressions and visions. As Richard L. Bushman argues, providing a helpful interpretive framework, Smith's "practice with the stone, looking for lost objects and probably for treasure, was an initiation into 'seeing' [i.e., visionary sight] that could be transferred to translation of the gold plates in the stones of the Urim and Thummim. In fact, as work on the Book of Mormon went on, a seerstone took the place of the Urim and Thummim, blending the culture of magic with the divine culture of translation."[33] In other words, Smith's use of a seer stone to envision lost and hidden objects taught him how to envision the translation of ancient historical texts. And while the leap from visionary images of lost objects to the translation of ancient records might seem strained, nineteenth-century conceptions of "peep stones," "scrying stones," "crystals," and "glasses" nevertheless offered such an option.

Along with locating lost objects and a variety of buried treasures, seer stones possessed several other purported powers, such as detecting witchcraft; identifying thieves and stolen property; revealing secrets and hidden knowledge; facilitating communication with angels, spirits, and demons; and revealing anything about the past, present, and future—a particular advantage if one were hoping to obtain information about the history of otherwise mysterious and unknown ancient American civilizations.[34] Moreover, these stones and crystals for divination were occasionally associated specifically with the biblical Urim and Thummim. For instance, John Aubrey (1626–97), the famous English antiquarian, equated the Urim and Thummim with divining crystals. After mentioning the use of the biblical Urim and Thummim as an implement for "Visions in the Stone of the Breast-plate" among priests in ancient Israel, Aubrey went on to claim that, "the Magicians, now, use a Crystal-Sphere, or Mineral-Pearl for this purpose," later describing how one magician had a "Glass" that revealed "things past, and to come."[35]

A more detailed description appears in *The Astrologer of the Nineteenth Century* (1825), a handbook of occult sciences by the London-based society known as "the Members of the Mercurii." The work describes a modern (homemade) version of the ancient Urim and Thummim, consisting of "an oval *chrystal*, or polished surface set in gold."[36] When describing "the hidden mystery of the *urim and thummim*," the author claims that, by sitting still and looking into the object, "whatever thou desirest or wishest to see or know, shall be manifested unto thee, and thou shalt become acquainted with all hidden things, *and wilt be enablad* [enabled] *to see anything that is being done in any part of the world, no matter how distant, or whether past, present, or future.*"[37] Readers of the Book of Mormon might recognize how the Jaredite/Nephite "interpreters"—an object that Smith would later describe as "spectacles" and "Urim and Thummim"—shared these same properties.

When describing how the interpreters could translate languages, Ammon, the Nephite explorer who discovered the people of Zeniff, added (Mosiah 8:13,17), "Whosoever is commanded to look in them, the same is called seer. . . . a seer can know of things which has past, and also of things which is to come;

and by them shall all things be revealed, or rather, shall secret things be made manifest, and hidden things shall come to light, and things which is not known, shall be made known by them."[38] Similarly, according to an 1870 account by Fayette Lapham, who spoke with Joseph Smith's father (Joseph Sr.) in 1830, Joseph Jr. "one day tried the spectacles ["interpreters"], and found that, by looking through them, he could see everything—past, present, and future—and could also read and understand the characters written on the plates."[39] From Smith's nineteenth-century perspective, the "interpreters" and the "Urim and Thummim" therefore had the same properties as his seer stone, which would offer the same point of access into the history of the ancient people recorded on the gold plates.

Finally, another lesser-known power of seer stones involved both the instruction and revelatory translation of languages. If, for example, diviners wanted to learn another language, which usually meant learning the "tongue of angels," they might conjure into their seer stone one of several spirits that instructed inquirers in another tongue, such as the spirit Agares, who "teacheth presently all manner of tongues"; Forneus, who taught "the knowledge of tongues"; or Ronove, who also taught the "knowledge of tongues."[40] John Dee (1527–1608/1609), one of the most famous early modern polymaths and Christian occult practitioners, for example, actively sought to rediscover the original Adamic language, which, as Deborah E. Harkness observes, Dee described as "'celestial speech,' the 'language of the angels,' the 'speech of angels,' the 'speech of God,' and the 'language of Adam.'"[41] Through his scryer Edward Kelly (aka "Kelley"; 1555–1597), known even in the nineteenth century as Dee's "prophet or seer," Dee purportedly contacted angels, who "began delivering characters, words, and names in the divine language in March 1582 when Dee began his relationship with Edward Kelly."[42] Such efforts would eventually lead to the revelatory translation of angelic works.

According to Harkness, "The first revealed book conveyed to Dee and Kelly was the *Liber Logaeth*, or 'the Book of the Speech of God,'" adding that, "It conveyed the angelic language and emphasized the role that language would play in perfecting the world and returning it to its original state."[43] The next revealed book, *De heptarchia mystica*, "contained prayers to specific angels," along with "the seals for forty-nine elemental angels with powers over aspects of the natural world." Unfortunately, as Harkness notes, "Dee's translation of the calls [prayers of invocation] has been lost."[44] Another work, *48 Claves angelicae*, "contained verses in both English and the angels' language, and Dee translated the keys with the angels' assistance."[45] Other works included *Liber scientiae auxilii et victoriae terrestris* and *Tabula bonorum angelorum invocationes*, as well as other books now lost or destroyed.[46] In his study on Christian Platonism in early Mormon thought, Stephen Fleming further adds that "Dee and Kelley's angel conversations at one point took on the element of translating an ancient text in an unknown language: the Book of Enoch."[47] As such, Smith's use of a seer stone to translate texts, though uncommon, was not unprecedented.

Whether or not he knew the titles or the specifics of Dee's angelic texts, Smith likely had some exposure to Dee and Kelly through popular culture, reference works, biographies of notable people, and published materials on esoteric practices.[48] Samuel Butler's famous satiric poem *Hudibras* (1684), enormously popular since the late seventeenth century and frequently reprinted well into the nineteenth, openly mocked Edward Kelly's scrying: "Kelly did all his feats upon / The devil's looking glass, a stone; / Where playing with him at bo-peep, / He solv'd all problems ne'er so deep."[49] Zachary Grey, the editor of an 1806 edition of *Hudibras*, notes, "This Kelly was chief seer (or, as Lilly calls him, Speculator) to Dr. Dee. . . . He pretended to see apparitions in a chrystal or beryl looking-glass (or a round stone like a chrystal)."[50] In a preceding section in the work, Grey provides readers with a substantial biography of Dee, in which he mentions that, "He [Dee] had a round stone like a crystal brought him (as he said) by angels, in which others saw apparitions, and from whence they heard voices, which he carefully wrote down from their mouths."[51] While such descriptions appeared in popular culture, other biographies of Dee and Kelly have more direct links to Smith. According to D. Michael Quinn, for example, Smith owned a magical Jupiter talisman specifically patterned after talismans described in Francis Barrett's *The Magus* (1801), a book that also contained "several pages about Dee and Kelley."[52] Given Smith's well-documented preoccupations with Western esotericism, it would be highly unusual for him to have been completely unaware of John Dee and his scryer, Edward Kelly.

In terms of translation, however, perhaps the most direct reference appears in Adam Clarke's New Testament notes on the meaning of "the tongues of men and of angels" in Paul's famous address on faith, hope, and charity (1 Cor. 13). As previously mentioned, Smith may have used Clarke's Commentary during the period when he produced the Book of Mormon (see chapter 4). When addressing the different interpretations regarding the language of angels, Clarke observes that, "probably the apostle refers to a notion that was common among the Jews, that there was a language by which angels might be invoked, adjured, collected, and dispersed: and, by the means of which, many secrets might be found out: and curious arts and sciences known." Clarke then adds that "*Cornelius Agrippa's* occult philosophy abounds" in this search to discover the language of angels, "and it was the main object of Dr. *Dee's* actions with spirits, to get a complete vocabulary of this language."[53] Dee's use of a seer stone to create a dictionary with a "complete vocabulary" of the angelic language would, of course, involve translation. Thus, whether or not Smith knew that Dee also translated entire texts of angelic books, Clarke's Commentary nevertheless paved the way for readers to consider how seer stones could both reveal and translate the language of angels. With this framework available to Smith, the step to translating ancient records would hardly be a step at all.

Smith's use of a seer stone to translate the Book of Mormon therefore alerts us to his esoteric preoccupations that reached beyond the isolated task of creating a history of ancient American people. Critical to understanding Smith's translation process is the recognition that, throughout his life, as Samuel Morris Brown observes, Smith sought to recover "the language of primitive humanity spoken in the Garden of Eden and the sacred names by which language first touched creation."[54] That lifetime concern ranged from his taking lessons in Hebrew (believed to be the closest living language to the language of Adam) to attempting the translation of Egyptian papyri.[55] Thus, as Brown has demonstrated, Smith's "translation activities" should be contextualized within his "broader quest for pure Adamic language."[56] Moreover, given the content of the Book of Mormon, Smith's interest certainly began before he started the production of the work. As Brown also argues, "the quest for linguistic purity represented a significant motif in the overall Book of Mormon narrative," indicating a recurrent concern that reached back, at the very least, to the period when he claimed to have had conversations with the angel Moroni.[57]

Likewise, the "tongue of angels" (equated with, and other times differentiated from, the Adamic language) emerges as one of Smith's topics of interest in the Book of Mormon. "Do ye not remember," asks the prophet Nephi of his auditors, "that I said unto you, that after ye had received the Holy Ghost, ye could speak with the tongue of Angels? And now, how could ye speak with the tongue of Angels, save it were by the Holy Ghost? Angels speak by the power of the Holy Ghost" (2 Nephi 32:2–3).[58] Here, among the many contemporary theories regarding the actual nature of the angelic language and the interpretation of Paul's tongue of angels in 1 Corinthians 13:1, Smith reveals a conception that requires the presence of the Holy Ghost as a facilitator. Rather than being a language that relied solely on the mechanical apparatus of a mortal body, the tongue of angels involved the direct communication of thoughts and ideas from one spirit to another. This is the same process described in the revelation to Oliver Cowdery regarding the nature of the revelatory translation involved in the production of the Book of Mormon:

"Yea, behold, I will tell you [i.e., tell you the correct translation] in your mind and in your heart, *by the Holy Ghost, which shall come upon you and which shall dwell in your heart.* Now, behold, *this is the spirit of revelation.*"[59]

This explicit articulation of the revelatory translation process and its reliance on the interpretation of Paul's passage (the phrase "the tongues of men and of angels" only appears in the Bible in 1 Corinthians 13:1) reflect an understanding of angelic communication that also featured prominently in Western esotericism. Clarke's reference to "*Cornielus Agrippa's* occult philosophy," noted above, offers a pertinent example. According to Henry Cornelius Agrippa (1486–1535), in his popular *Three Books of Occult Philosophy* (1531), the angelic language did not require a "tongue . . . jaws, palate, lips, teeth, throat, lungs, the aspera arteria, and muscles of the breast." Rather, angels and demons spoke directly from one spirit to another, "by impressing the conception of the speech in those to whom they speak, after a better manner then [sic] if they should express it by an audible voyce." He further adds, "That instrument, whatsoever the vertue be [i.e., whatever the process is], by which one spirit makes known to another spirit what things are in his minde, is called by the Apostle *Paul* the tongue of Angels."[60] In *The Magus* (1801), the book noted earlier in connection with Smith and his family's magical implements, Francis Barrett quoted this same passage from Agrippa, even using the original title for the section "Of the Tongue of Angels, and of Their Speaking amongst Themselves and with Us."[61] Smith's abiding interest in a pure and undefiled language thus resulted in a deep entanglement of his process of revelation with his method of revelatory translation. At the nexus of these inspired practices, the seer stone acted as a necessary prop to gain access to hidden information and to facilitate the process of revealing and translating the content of the gold plates.

Smith's seer stone therefore offered a potential way, from his point of view, to peer into the past and discover the history of the ancient inhabitants of the Americas, long before any translation work would begin. As such, his preliminary work on the Book of Mormon could be viewed as a form of training in the use of the seer stone. For example, after the angel Moroni's first visit to Smith in 1823, Smith claimed that Moroni directed him to return to the Hill Cumorah, the location of the buried plates, once a year to receive instructions. "Accordingly, as I had been commanded," Smith recalled, "I went at the end of each year, and at each time I found the same messenger [Moroni] there, and received instruction and intelligence from him at each of our interviews, respecting what the Lord was going to do, and how and in what manner His kingdom was to be conducted in the last days."[62] Given these annual visits and lessons, we might consider the possibility that Smith also received instructions on how to use the seer stone.

According to Moroni's first message to Smith, the gold plates would be translated into English with an object called "interpreters" (later described as "Urim and Thummim"), which he had buried with the gold plates. Yet, without access to the interpreters until he finally retrieved all the buried objects in 1827, Smith would not have had the opportunity to practice using the device before the translation needed to begin. Nevertheless, because Smith's seer stone had the same capacity to translate languages as the ancient interpreters, Moroni could arguably take the opportunity to instruct Smith on the process of revelatory translation using his seer stone. Indeed, as already noted, Smith would eventually abandon the "interpreters" found with the gold plates and use his familiar and much used seer stone to dictate the text of the Book of Mormon.

Moreover, whatever a person chooses to believe about the reality of Smith's conferences with the angel Moroni, the historical evidence suggests that Smith did, after all, need some measure of guidance in the correct use of his seer stone. After Moroni's first visit in September of 1823, for example, as Dan Vogel points out, Smith continued to use his seer stone on a number of treasure-seeking projects, none of which was successful.[63] If Smith's purported visits with Moroni took place, then the argument could be made that the angel's messages also included, by necessity, some detailed instructions and sober advice about the proper use of seer stones. Thus, instead of Smith's self-directed visualizations of lost and hidden treasures as the method of learning how to translate the gold plates with a seer stone, what better way, from Moroni's point of view, to instruct the young prophet in the translation of Reformed Egyptian into English than to have him actually initiate preliminary translations of Reformed Egyptian into English.

If such were the case, the fact that the gold plates were still buried in the Hill Cumorah would have posed no obstacle. Even after he obtained the plates, Smith rarely (if ever) directly consulted them during the translation process, but rather produced the work by focusing on his seer stone, while the plates themselves lay covered with a cloth or hidden out of sight.[64] Isaac Hale, Joseph's father-in-law and an observer of the process, famously proclaimed, "The manner in which he [Joseph] pretended to read and interpret, was the same as when he looked for the money-diggers, with the stone in his hat, and his hat over his face, while the Book of Plates were at the same time hid in the woods!"[65] Given the mystical properties of his seer stone, Smith could have initiated preliminary translations of the gold plates, with direct visionary access to the buried text, from the moment Moroni first informed him of their existence in September of 1823.

With this perspective in mind, Smith's preliminary work on the Book of Mormon—the construction of narrative skeletons and his familiarization with its stories—would have been a necessary and integral part of the translation process. Furthermore, it would help to explain Smith's reticence about sharing the details of his method or making a formal statement about its precise operations to his fellow church members. In order to avoid potential misunderstandings about his actual process and extensive preparations, Smith may well have found it easier in informal settings to give a shorthand account to inquirers—that is, he simply saw the translated words on the surface of the stone—than to belabor such situations with a time-consuming description of the actual and more complicated interactive process that he had already revealed to Oliver Cowdery.

In contrast to these informal comments to his followers (which may or may not have actually occurred), Smith never provided an official description of his translation process. When asked to provide a formal account during an October 1831 conference, for example, Smith declined. Cowdery, the clerk of the conference, noted that, "Brother Joseph Smith, Jun., said that it was not intended to tell the world all the particulars of the coming forth of the Book of Mormon; and also said that it was not expedient for him to relate these things."[66] Yet, if Smith had already been describing to family, friends, and other eyewitnesses that he translated the Book of Mormon by seeing words on the surface of his seer stone, sharing the same information with a gathering of church leaders and devoted followers would hardly be scandalous.

Thus, it could be argued that Smith, when speaking in casual settings, merely simplified his description of the translation process in order to reflect the understanding and intellect of his inquirers by adopting Paul's strategy for communication in such situations: "I have fed you with milk, and not with meat: for hitherto ye were not able to bear it, neither yet now are ye able" (1 Cor. 3:2). The same might be said of modern interpretations of Smith's process, which often rely too heavily on accounts of eyewitnesses, who, though present to observe Smith's process, never actually saw for themselves the seer stone producing luminous letters.

Emma Smith and David Whitmer Statements

In the research surrounding the questions concerning Smith's possible use of written materials during the composition of the Book of Mormon—specifically, whether or not he consulted a Bible, commentaries, story notes, books, or manuscripts—the accounts of two eyewitnesses seem central: an 1879 interview with Emma Smith and two interviews, one in 1881 and the other in 1884, with David Whitmer. These statements, though ostensibly straightforward, nevertheless prove to be too problematic and ambiguous to support many of the scholarly interpretations built upon them, leading to several unsustainable assertions. Because Whitmer's statements rely on Emma's account, this review necessarily begins with her depiction.

In February of 1879, Joseph and Emma's oldest son, Joseph Smith III, approached Emma for an interview, which was intended, among other issues, as a response to various controversial rumors and accusations surrounding Mormonism.[67] In the section addressing the origins of the Book of Mormon, Emma gave the following answers:

> [EMMA] A[NSWER]: . . . In writing for your father I frequently wrote day after day, often sitting at the table close by him, he sitting with his face buried in his hat, with the stone in it, and dictating hour after hour with nothing between us.
>
> [JOSEPH III] Q[UESTION]: Had he not a book or manuscript from which he read, or dictated to you?
>
> A: He had neither manuscript nor book to read from.
>
> Q: Could he not have had, and you not know it?
>
> A: If he had anything of the kind he could not have concealed it from me.

In response to another question from Joseph III, Emma later added:

> Q: Could not father have dictated the Book of Mormon to you, Oliver Cowdery and the others who wrote for him, after having first written it, or having read it out of some book?
>
> A: Joseph Smith . . . could neither write nor dictate a coherent and well-worded letter, let alone dictating a book like the Book of Mormon.[68]

Citing Emma's responses, many scholars have argued that Smith never used written materials of any kind during the translation process. Hardy offers a typical example of this position, arguing that "Joseph Smith's wife—the person who had the longest and closest view of the production of the text—explicitly denied that he had written something out beforehand that he either had memorized or consulted as he translated." He subsequently adds, "Joseph's wife, Emma, asserted that he never worked from a book or manuscript (which would have included the Bible)."[69] A closer examination of the context of Emma's statements, however, indicates that such interpretations reach beyond the scope of the actual evidence and overgeneralize very specific claims and contexts.

For example, left out of such interpretations are key questions in the 1879 interview that frame Emma's answers and lead into her responses. Earlier in the interview, after a brief history of Emma's marriage and early family life, Joseph III raises the issue of the Book of Mormon with the following segue:

> [JOSEPH III] Q: When did you first know Sidney Rigdon? Where?
> [EMMA] A: I was residing at father Whitmer's, when I first saw Sidney Rigdon. I think he came there.
> Q: Was this before or after the publication of the Book of Mormon?
> A: The Book of Mormon had been translated and published some time before.[70]

After additional information about the scribes who worked on the project, Joseph III changed the topic by asking Emma about polygamy in the church (more on this below), after which he asked for her opinion about "the truth of Mormonism." In her response to this last question, Emma redirected the discussion back to the Book of Mormon, where she made the statements that scholars have usually isolated from the context of the full interview—that is, Emma's claim that Joseph did not use a book or manuscript in the production of the work.

Thus, when viewing Emma's answers within the context of the entire interview, we find that her responses were explicitly prompted by and framed within the issue of Sidney Rigdon's alleged involvement in the creation of the Book of Mormon. That framework both established the topic and set the parameters for the questions that followed. An accurate interpretation of Emma's comments therefore requires an acknowledgment of the full context in which she made her statements, and an understanding of how those statements relate to Sidney Rigdon. In brief, some early critics of Smith argued that Sidney Rigdon (1793–1876), an early leader in the nascent Mormon faith, was the real mastermind behind the composition of the Book of Mormon. The criticism usually took one of two forms: either that Rigdon wrote or coordinated the writing of the book and passed it off as Smith's work, or that Rigdon provided Smith with a stolen manuscript, which the two of them purportedly modified and plagiarized.[71]

The latter theory is known today as the Spalding theory of plagiarism.[72] According to this theory, Rigdon allegedly obtained a copy of a romance novel written by a man named Solomon Spalding (1761–1816; aka Spaulding). Rigdon then gave the manuscript to Smith, who supposedly plagiarized Spalding's work to create the Book of Mormon. This theory gained notoriety with the publication of Eber D. Howe's anti-Mormon exposé, *Mormonism Unvailed* (1834).[73] "By the early 1840's," observes historian Lester C. Bush Jr., the Spalding theory "became the accepted explanation of the origin of the Book of Mormon."[74] Indeed, as Paul C. Gutjahr notes, "the Spalding theory of plagiarism became the single most dominant strain in anti-Mormon apologetics throughout the nineteenth century."[75] Joseph III's questions and Emma's answers therefore took place when the Spalding theory was at its height of popularity and cultural circulation, and the context of the interview explicitly demonstrates that Joseph III was attempting to challenge and discredit this specific theory.

The issue of whether or not Joseph occasionally consulted a Bible to assist in the dictation of certain passages in the Book of Mormon was never raised in the interview. Indeed, there is no evidence to suggest that either Joseph III or Emma even implied such a scenario. Joseph III's recollection of the interview provides further support of this view. In a 14 February 1879 letter, written less than two weeks after the interview, Joseph III responded to the criticisms of James T. Cobb, an antagonist of Smith and the Mormon faith.[76] Joseph III affirmed that, "during no part" of the dictation process "did Joseph Smith have any Mss. [manuscript] or Book of any kind from which to read, or dictate, except the metalic plates, which she [Emma] knew he had. Every argument advanced by you in support of the theory, that Sidney Rigdon was the responsible 'Black Pope' behind the throne moving upon the pliant mind of Joseph Smith, it seems to me, is defeated by this plain statement."[77] Note that Joseph III's description of a "Book of any kind" is specifically couched within the context of any book or manuscript connected to Rigdon.

Moreover, lest the argument be made that Joseph III was somehow including a Bible or commentary in this sweeping denial, the remainder of the letter clarifies his meaning. After spending the next two paragraphs talking about the actual timing of Rigdon's first appearance among the Mormons (proving that Rigdon arrived after the Book of Mormon had already been published), Joseph III gives a direct and precise statement about the issue at hand, arguing, "that there was no collusion between Joseph Smith and Sidney Rigdon in palming off a fraud upon the people, and also that Joseph had no Spaulding Mss [manuscript] from which the B[ook] of M[ormon] was plagiarized."[78] Joseph III's letter and the full context of Emma's interview thereby provide ample evidence that Emma was specifically referring to books and manuscripts that Joseph purportedly plagiarized—that is, Spalding's manuscript, or any other book, manuscript, or romance novel that someone else had already written. Whether or not Emma would have extended her observations to include a Bible or a biblical commentary remains unknown; the issue was never raised. Using Emma's statement to cast a wider net that includes any and all written materials, above and beyond Spalding's manuscript or any other similar and potentially plagiarized work, results in an interpretation that strains against the actual evidence and builds an argument on decidedly unstable foundations.

Overgeneralizing Emma's statements is not the only problematic issue with interpreting her claims. For example, when she describes how Joseph dictated the text "hour after hour with nothing between us," Emma was explicitly describing her experience as one of the scribes when she assisted with the initial 116 pages of the manuscript in Harmony, Pennsylvania.[79] Martin Harris, however, subsequently lost those same pages, and no evidence suggests that they contained extensive quotations of biblical passages. Thus, Joseph may never have consulted a Bible when Emma was acting as his scribe in Harmony. Moreover, as the project continued, Emma and Joseph relocated to Fayette, New York, where Joseph completed the translation project in an upstairs room in the home of Peter Whitmer Sr., secluded from the hustle and bustle of regular household business and the casual observations by nonparticipants. By the time the Smiths arrived in this new location, Cowdery had become the primary scribe on the project, and Emma's participation in the process significantly decreased.

Nevertheless, it remains possible that Emma occasionally participated as a backup scribe, though the evidence is sparse. According to David Whitmer, Cowdery apparently received additional but minor support from Christian Whitmer, John Whitmer, and Emma.[80] Whitmer's claim, however, requires caution. His description, given fifty years after the fact, lacks evidentiary support; the extant portions of the original scribal manuscript do not contain Emma's handwriting.[81] Perhaps more tellingly, when asked "Who were scribes for father when translating the Book of Mormon," Emma responded, "Myself, Oliver Cowdery, Martin Harris, and my brother, Reuben Hale."[82] Emma's statement refers exclusively to the scribes who worked on the project in Harmony, Pennsylvania, and she makes no reference to the additional scribes in Fayette. Such omissions suggest that Emma's testimony dealt with her experience as a scribe in Pennsylvania, but not in New York. They further suggest that her presence at dictation sessions in Fayette was infrequent and intermittent—enough so, in fact, that she may never have witnessed anyone other than Cowdery acting as the scribe. Thus, in this period when Emma's possible participation would have been minimal at best (if she ever acted as scribe at all in this new location), Joseph translated the internal books of the Book of Mormon that contained the most extensive biblical citations, such as 2 Nephi and 3 Nephi. Given such circumstances, Joseph may never have consulted a Bible during the dictation sessions that Emma attended, whether in Pennsylvania or New York.

Indeed, the situation in the Whitmer household in New York suggests that Emma likely did not witness the majority of the translation project after she and Joseph moved there. With so many visitors and new boarders, Mary Whitmer, Peter Sr.'s wife, faced additional household responsibilities. As David Whitmer, Peter Sr. and Mary's son, observed, "My father and mother had a large family of their own, the addition to it therefore of Joseph, his wife Emma and Oliver very greatly increased the toil and anxiety of my mother."[83] Given such conditions, Emma more than likely spent a significant amount of time assisting Mary with household business; the idea that she would avoid helping in such circumstances is not consistent with historical accounts of her character.

Furthermore, in a more specific account, David Whitmer directly states that Emma and several of the other eyewitnesses to Smith's translation process were not present during every dictation session. In an interview published 5 June 1881 in the *Kansas City Journal*, the reporter claimed that Whitmer stated, "I, as well as all of my father's family, Smith's wife, Oliver Cowdery, and Martin Harris were present during the translation."[84] After the article appeared, however, Whitmer wrote a 13 June 1881 letter to the editor to correct some errors in the original article. Among his critiques, Whitmer explicitly stated, "I did not wish to be understood as saying that those referred to as being present [the Whitmer family, Emma, Oliver, and Martin] were all of the time in the immediate presence of the translator, but were at the place and saw how the translation was conducted."[85] With eyewitnesses wandering in and out of the dictation sessions, none of them apparently witnessing the entire process from start to finish, the interpretations of their statements about Smith's use of a Bible, a biblical commentary, or even notes are all contingent accounts. The issue is significant: scholars who cite Emma Smith's and David Whitmer's accounts to justify the assertion that Joseph never used any written materials, of any kind, and at any time in the process, are assuming that Emma's and David's experiences for *some* of the days therefore apply to *all* of the days, building such assertions on demonstrably faulty overgeneralizations.

Other problematic interpretations of Emma's account concern her knowledge of any preexisting notes that Joseph may have had, as well as her ability to know what Joseph had or had not memorized. When describing the actual dictation sessions, Emma stated that Joseph did not use a manuscript, book, or "anything of the kind" (which presumably includes the use of notes *during dictation*), but she never addresses the idea, nor does it seem to have crossed her mind, that Joseph, *prior to dictation*, may have privately consulted a page or two of short notes with skeletal outlines and mnemonic cues.[86] In fact, Emma never specifically mentions "notes" in her account at all. When Joseph III asked if his father could have dictated the work "after having first written it, or having read it out of some book," Emma denied the possibility that Joseph made use of a fully written text.[87] But neither she nor Joseph III addresses the possibility that Joseph might have been following an entirely different method, one of oral composition that involved the use of private notes and the semi-extemporaneous amplification of skeletal narrative outlines. Moreover, even if such a question had been raised (or inferred), we would need to ask if Emma were even aware of the existence of such notes, particularly if Joseph had kept them concealed among his private papers. No evidence suggests that Emma rifled through Joseph's papers in a suspicious hunt for notes or manuscripts that might have revealed his prior work on the Book of Mormon. In fact, she presented herself as quite indifferent to such a pursuit.

According to her son Joseph III, Emma said that the gold plates, covered with a cloth, "lay on a small table in their living room in their cabin on her father's farm, and she would lift and move them when she swept and dusted the room and furniture. She even thumbed the leaves as one does the leaves of a book, and they rustled with a metalic sound."[88] In spite of thumbing the leaves in such tempting proximity, Emma never bothered to remove the cloth and look directly at the gold plates, stating, "I did not attempt to handle the plates, other than I have told you, nor uncover them to look at them."[89] Indeed, when describing how she moved the plates "from place to place on the table, as it was necessary in doing my work," Emma flatly stated that she "was not specially curious about them."[90] Emma's statement is consistent with an 1877 interview with Nels Madson and Parley P. Pratt Jr., in which she stated that the gold plates "lay under our bed for a few months but I never felt the liberty to look at them."[91] As such, whatever her reasons, Emma never presented herself as being particularly anxious to view any of the objects related to the translation project in her husband's private possession (gold plates, Urim and Thummim, or breastplate).

Moreover, even if Emma had stumbled across any possible notes, they would likely have consisted of truncated outlines and cryptic mnemonic cues. And given that her experience as a scribe pertained to the beginning of the translation process, she arguably would not have known if any such notes had anything to do with the work: the Book of Mormon, after all, had not yet been produced. Furthermore, many of the notes, particularly notes for sermon out-lines, would have appeared as nothing more than common scripture annota-tions for personal study. When publishing the Reverend Abraham Marshall's short notes for sermons (see chapter 4), his son Jabez described the sermon skeletons as "Scripture Annotations," for the use of "the Christian and the preacher, who are not above endeavouring to collect knowledge."[92] Including such notes for nonpreachers as well as preachers, and describing them as "scripture annotations," suggests that Jabez did not realize that such notes were actually brief sermon outlines for semi-extemporaneous expansion and deliv-ery. The question therefore needs to be asked if Emma would have recognized similar brief notes and short mnemonic cues as scripts for semi-extemporaneous oral performances.

Perhaps the most obvious problem with Emma's claims, however, is the as-sertion that Joseph had not memorized anything in advance of the dictation sessions. According to Hardy's interpretation, for example, Emma "explicitly denied that he had written something out beforehand that he either had mem-orized or consulted as he translated."[93] Apart from the dubious assumption that Emma monitored Joseph's every move during the translation period, we might ask how Emma had the ability to know what Joseph had or had not *mem-orized* during his private time. The uncritical interpretation of Emma's claims requires the acceptance of an unstated premise that Emma literally had the abil-ity to read Joseph's mind.

Smith's 1823 announcement of the gold plates and his stories about ancient Native Americans further complicate such claims. Emma and Joseph did not apparently meet until November of 1825, when Joseph boarded at the home of Emma's parents during a treasure hunting expedition.[94] After this brief initial meeting, Joseph returned a little over a year later and eloped with Emma, marrying her on 18 January 1827.[95] Thus, by the time Emma had the opportunity to observe her husband's day-to-day behavior, Joseph would al-ready have had more than three years to prepare, memorize, and internalize material for the translation work. Accepting Emma's claim that she knew what Joseph had or had not written or memorized results in precarious inter-pretations and unstable assumptions.

Another challenge to Emma's account concerns the timing and reliability of her recollections. Her 1879 statement is *fifty years* removed from the actual translation events in 1828 and 1829, and the distance shows. When asked if Jo-seph ever forbade her from examining the gold plates, for example, Emma responded, "I do not think he did."[96] Yet virtually all other accounts by family members and eyewitnesses indicate that people were forbidden from viewing the objects directly, without casings or coverings, under the threat of God's wrath and certain death for both Joseph and any unauthorized viewers.[97] Joseph himself claimed that the angel Moroni commanded him that "I should not show them to any person; neither the breast plate with the Urim and Thummim; only to those to whom I should be commanded to show them; if I did I should be destroyed."[98] Emma's vague recollection remains inconsistent with other firsthand accounts about the same issue.

While her imperfect memory might account for some of the inconsistencies in her reminiscence, Emma also appears to have deliberately altered historical facts in order to reframe interpretations of the past. This appears to be the case with her statements about Joseph's practice of polygamy. In the course of the same interview, Joseph III asks Emma, "What about the revelation on Polygamy? Did Joseph Smith have anything like it? What of spiritual wifery?" Emma responds, "There was no revelation on either polygamy, or spiritual wives. . . . No such thing as polygamy, or spiritual wifery, was taught, publicly or privately, before my husband's death, that I have now, or ever had any knowledge of. . . . He had no other wife but me."[99] This revisionist assertion sent shockwaves through the Latter Day Saint movement, which had already split into several factions. When the interview was published on 1 October 1879, Emma was living in Nauvoo, Illinois, and was a member of the Reorganized Church of Jesus Christ of Latter Day Saints (formerly RLDS, now "Community of Christ"). Within weeks, the article reached Salt Lake City, Utah, where it roused the ire of the members of the Church of Jesus Christ of Latter-day Saints (LDS), another Mormon faction that followed Brigham Young out west, where they continued the practice of polygamy. Emma's denials therefore struck at the heart of the LDS, or "Brighamite," community's doctrine and identity.

In a 17 October 1879 letter (published on 22 October) to the editor of *The Deseret News*, Joseph F. Smith, Emma's nephew and the son of Hyrum and Mary Smith, refuted his Aunt Emma's claims and included in his article "the sworn statements and affidavits of a few reliable persons [witnesses to Smith's practice of polygamy]—among whom are two of the wives of the Prophet Joseph Smith."[100] Immediately following this letter and its affidavits, another letter to the editor appears, sent by Eliza R. Snow, who signed her piece as "A wife of Joseph Smith the Prophet." Her anger at Emma's attempt to rewrite history resonated with great force: "If what purports to be her 'last testimony' was really her testimony, she died with a libel on her lips—a libel against her husband—against his wives—against the truth, and a libel against God. . . . It is a *fact* that Sister Emma, of her own free will and choice, gave her husband four wives, two of whom are now living, and ready to testify that she, not only gave them to her husband, but that she taught them the doctrine of plural marriage and urged them to accept it."[101] As Vogel notes, in a carefully worded and understated observation, Emma's "denial of her husband's practice of polygamy is considered untruthful by most historians."[102] The timing of Emma's interview, however, potentially sheds light on her responses to her son.

Within three months of the interview, Emma, apparently unwell at the time of the interview, died on 30 April 1879, at the age of seventy-four. Throughout her life she had endured an extraordinary number of heartrending shocks and exceptional difficulties, which no doubt shaped her perceptions and sensitivities. As such, her interview might best be described as a widow's defense, in which she was attempting to restructure the past in an effort to find resolutions for the present, while leaving a more hopeful legacy to her children and the believers of her faith. Even so, no matter how one decides to interpret Emma's statements and to acknowledge the difficulties of her life, the issue of her objectivity remains highly problematic. As much as her descriptions reveal important information about the past, their uncritical acceptance equally obscures historical realities.

Along with Emma's description of the translation process, David Whitmer provided oft-cited statements that initially appear to corroborate some of her claims. Such citations, however, likewise fall prey to problematic interpretations. For example, in an effort to distance Joseph from the use of a Bible or any other written materials during the translation process, Terryl L. Givens quotes the following July 1884 interview published in the *St. Louis Republican*: "Father Whitmer, who was present very frequently during the writing of this manuscript affirms that Joseph Smith had no book or manuscript, before him from which he could have read as is asserted by some that he did, he (Whitmer) having every opportunity to know."[103] Givens omitted the final segment of the complete sentence, however, which clarifies the original scope of the statement: "he (Whitmer) having every opportunity to know *whether Smith had Solomon Spaulding's or any other persons' romance to read from*."[104] Whitmer's statement thus specifically addressed the ongoing controversies regarding the supposed plagiarism of Spaulding's manuscript or some other manuscript of a romance novel. Whitmer was not, however, speaking about the separate issue of Joseph's possible use of a Bible or biblical commentaries during the dictation of the Book of Mormon (assuming that Whitmer had even been present for such usage).

Additionally, in an earlier 14 October 1881 interview with the *Chicago Times*, the reporter stated that (letters in all caps being part of an internal heading),

"Mr. Whitmer emphatically asserts, as did [Martin] Harris and [Oliver] Cowdrey [*sic*], that while Smith was dictating the translation he had NO MANUSCRIPT NOTES OR OTHER MEANS OF KNOWLEDGE save the seer-stone and the characters as shown on the plates, he being present and cognizant how it was done."[105] The very next sentence, however, provides the context for his claim: "In regard to the statement that Sidney Rigden [*sic*] had purloined the work of one Spaulding . . . Mr. Whitmer says there is no foundation for such an assertion."[106] Moreover, Whitmer specifically described what he saw "while Smith was dictating the translation," indicating that his observation only addressed Smith's actions during the dictation sessions that he personally witnessed.[107] His comment does not attempt to provide an account for Smith's actions or whereabouts throughout the entire course of each day.

Another challenge to Whitmer's 1881 and 1884 statements concerns the timing of his descriptions. Rather than being independent corroborating sources, Whitmer's depictions were almost certainly influenced by Emma's 1879 statement. Emma's October 1879 interview with Joseph III appeared in two different publications: the *Saints' Herald* and the *Saints' Advocate*.[108] The same month, in a 13 October 1879 letter to the editor of the *Saints' Herald*, John L. Traughber, "described as 'an old friend of David Whitmer,'" referenced Emma's interview, as it appeared in the 1 October edition of the same publication.[109] Traughber's purpose was to correct the faulty notion that Smith used the Urim and Thummim (specifically, the "interpreters" or "spectacles" buried with the plates) to translate the Book of Mormon, instead of the seer stone. In support of his argument, Traughber specifically quoted Emma's 1879 claim that Smith sat "with his face buried in his hat, with the stone in it, and dictating hour after hour with nothing between us."[110] When asserting that Smith used the seer stone, Traughber declared, "With the sanction of David Whitmer, and by his authority, I now state that he does not say that Joseph Smith ever translated in his presence by aid of Urim and Thummim; but by means of one dark colored, opaque stone, called a 'Seer Stone.'"[111] Traughber's letter strongly suggests that Whitmer was not only aware of Emma's statement but that it influenced his own depiction of events.

Aside from such influence, Whitmer nevertheless provides additional information about the translation project that offers greater insight into Joseph Smith's process and further destabilizes the argument that he could not have consulted or memorized notes, reference works, or any other materials. Such assertions rely on the assumption that Smith was under constant surveillance, with friends and family continuously monitoring his whereabouts and literally never having him out of their sight. Contradicting these assumptions, however, Whitmer provides evidence that Smith was frequently alone when preparing for dictation sessions.

In an 1881 *Saints' Herald* interview with William H. Kelley and George A. Blakeslee, two leaders in the RLDS faith, Whitmer states that Smith "could not translate unless he was humble and possessed the right feelings towards every one."[112] He then tells of a time when Joseph and Emma once had a disagreement, which troubled Joseph's mind and prevented him from translating. In order to calm down, he "went down stairs, out into the orchard and made supplication to the Lord; *was gone about an hour*—came back to the house, asked Emma's forgiveness and then came up stairs *where we were* and the translation went on all right."[113] With Joseph in the orchard and Whitmer upstairs, Whitmer obviously could not know what Joseph was doing during his hour-long absence. Whether or not Smith was simply meditating and praying, or also involved in reviewing notes and/or mentally rehearsing the narratives that he was about to produce, his actions remained out of sight.

Neither was Joseph's argument with Emma the only time he left the home on solo excursions before dictation sessions. In an 1887 pamphlet titled *An Address to All Believers in Christ*, Whitmer further stated, "At times when Brother Joseph would attempt to translate, [and] he would look into the hat in which the stone was placed, he found he was spiritually blind and could not translate. He told us that his mind dwelt too much on earthly things, and various causes would make him incapable of proceeding with the translation."[114] Whitmer did not state how often these moments of spiritual blindness occurred, though his description clearly indicates multiple events. "When in this condition," Whitmer added, Smith "*would go out and pray,* and when he became sufficiently humble before God, he could then proceed with the translation."[115] Debates over what Joseph may or may not have done during these private excursions will no doubt continue. Nevertheless, Whitmer's accounts indicate that Smith, at the very least, had the opportunity to review and prepare work in private, and none of the historical sources provides, or even claims to provide, a detailed account of all of Smith's activities when he was alone.

Translating the Book of Mormon

Whether one chooses to believe that the Book of Mormon emerged exclusively from Smith's mind and creative powers or as the translation of an authentic historical record, an examination of the textual and historical evidence suggests that Smith engaged in advance preparation for the work. The text reveals a process of careful and thoughtful planning, and the specific structuring method that underpins the composition of the entire work centers on the introductory technique of laying down heads to create sketch outlines and mnemonic cues. Because this contemporary technique was ubiquitous in the early nineteenth century, and because Smith himself used this same technique to structure his other compositions, the presence of this common introductory and organizational method points to Smith as the most likely source.

Moreover, the textual evidence clearly reveals that these structural tools, most obviously in the form of anticipatory narrative outlines, prompted and guided the semi-extemporaneous oral production of the work. These "prompts" allowed Smith the ability to move directly and fluently from carefully prepared mental "skeletons" and familiar mnemonic cues to the rapid dictation of the full text. Indeed, the process of combining these specific structuring devices with efficient oral performance techniques reflects the same compositional and semi-extemporaneous delivery methods in popular use among the evangelical preachers in Smith's own vibrant sermon culture. Whether he constructed the narrative outlines through divine inspiration or from his own creative imagination, Smith's actual execution of the project followed the same well-known sermonizing techniques that existed among his contemporaries.

When combined together, the textual evidence and historical accounts favor a scenario in which Smith began thinking about the Book of Mormon narratives sometime before 22 September 1823, when he first announced the appearance of the angel Moroni and the existence of an ancient record. In the years that followed, Smith carefully developed his ideas about the narratives through a process of revelatory translation, which may or may not have involved the use of his seer stone. Through a meticulous process of testing out narrative patterns against his affective spiritual responses, Smith produced, revised, and honed the narratives over several years, becoming intimately familiar with the stories and characters during the process. By the time he actually started dictating the text, Smith would have required only a small handful of notes containing brief outlines and narrative cues, which he could keep private among his personal papers. Such preparations would have provided him with a guiding framework of story patterns, which he could then expand rapidly and extemporaneously in the moment of oral performance, allowing himself the flexibility to improvise new topics and tangents along the way. Alternatively, depending on his level of increasing familiarity with the overall narrative, he may not have required any notes at all, relying exclusively on his memory of the historical structures he had formulated and his semi-extemporaneous expansion of them.

In the end, however one chooses to understand Smith's involvement in the production of the Book of Mormon, his method of revelatory translation complicates easy characterizations of the process. Because Smith's approach involved meditating on narrative possibilities, while seeking spiritual confirmation about their truthfulness and historical authenticity, the work emerged from some form of dialectical process, which, nuanced according to one's beliefs, might be understood as involving the participation of the Holy Spirit in connection with Smith's inspired imagination or as a complex matrix of Smith's affective and spontaneous responses to conscious narrative creations and subconscious elaborations in his mind. Whatever we may choose to believe, the historical record strongly suggests that Joseph Smith genuinely felt that his project emerged from divine inspiration and guidance.

Moreover, Smith's dialectical process of translation—in essence, an act of coauthorship with the divine utterances of God—offers a potential explanation concerning what initially appears to be a contradiction in his own descriptions of his role(s) in the production of the Book of Mormon. In the 1830 first edition of the work, Smith identified himself as the "author" in the copyright registration and as the "AUTHOR AND PROPRIETOR" on the title page of the book.[116] As scholars have argued, Smith was not claiming to be the sole originator of the work but rather was adhering to statutory language for legal compliance with current copyright laws.[117] In fact, in the preface of the same edition, Smith insists that he "translated" the Book of Mormon, specifically doing so "by the gift and power of God."[118] At the same time, however, in an immediate and apparent contradiction, Smith signed this same explanatory preface as "THE AUTHOR."[119]

While the conventions of copyright law may well explain Smith's use of "author" in both the registration and on the title page, the law did not require Smith to identify himself as "the author" in the preface of the work. Here then, we might consider that Smith's third description of himself as the "author" may indicate his personal conception of what it meant to be an author *of divine utterances*. His self-referential label suggests that he viewed his process within the cooperative framework provided by Paul: "All scripture is given by inspiration of God" (2 Tim. 3:16). Thus, as with the prophets and apostles of old, Smith became an instrument in God's hands, working as an inspired collaborator in the production of scriptural texts, plotting out storylines and dictating the Book of Mormon according to the impulses of the Holy Ghost and the spirit of revelation. Smith would later provide evidence of his perception of this dialectical framework, as recorded by an audience member listening to one of his discourses in 1840.

In a 6 February 1840 letter to his wife, Matthew L. Davis, a reporter from New York, described his experience watching Smith deliver a presentation on Mormonism to an attentive audience in Washington, DC. According to Davis, Smith offered a revealing characterization of his role in the translation of the Book of Mormon, stating that Smith claimed the work "was communicated to him, *direct from heaven*. If there was such a thing on earth, as the author of it, then he (Smith) was the author; but the idea that he wished to impress was, that he had penned it as dictated by God."[120] This idea of an "author" on earth recording a dictation "by God" in heaven thereby erodes the boundaries between mortal contributions and divine utterances. And the resulting process, involving the symbiotic exchange between a mortal man and an immortal God, reveals Smith's understanding of the nature of divine collaboration.

Even so, in spite of his efforts to answer what must have been for him a complex question, Smith's response carries a measure of imprecision and conveys a somewhat awkward ambiguity. The question of authorship in such a divine collaboration resists any effort to draw a distinct line of separation between the specific contributions of each coauthor. Smith's response hints at his own uncertainty about the precise details of such an interactive and divinely engaged process. Indeed, Smith himself may well have been astounded by the final text of his virtuoso oral performance, as he witnessed the emergence of full-blown religious histories from little more than a few years of preliminary meditations and, possibly, a handful of brief narrative sketches. As Taves has observed, individuals constructing narratives involving spiritual methods or supernatural conditions often believe that the resulting stories originate outside themselves and are historically true.[121]

Thus, Smith's inconclusive and somewhat vague references to translation and authorship suggest his own indeterminacy about the exact nature and process involved in the creation of the Book of Mormon. He literally may not have known, consciously or otherwise, how much or how little his own contributions influenced the language and shape of the final text. In the end, we are left with the attempt to recover "Smith's subjective experience," which, in spite of efforts to recuperate the past, will always remain elusive.[122] Indeed, given Smith's own indeterminacy, such a perspective may never have been possible to discover. When drawing his King Follett sermon to a close, Smith paused, looked over his audience, and then announced, "You don't know me—you never will. You never knew my heart. No man knows my history."[123] Given the spiritual and dialectical process he adopted for his revelatory translation, Smith may well have included himself among those who never fully understood his process, or, indeed, who never fully knew his own heart and soul.

Epilogue

For nearly two centuries Joseph Smith's ambitious creation of the Book of Mormon has captured the attention of a vast and diverse audience. Yet many of the details surrounding the techniques of oral performance involved in its construction have remained largely unexplored. Smith's oral composition of the Book of Mormon occurred in a time and place where people regularly gathered together around firesides at home and in public spaces like town halls and literary debate societies to tell stories, exchange news, participate in communal readings, deliver memorized and semi-extemporaneous recitations, engage in political discourse, barter, and debate. Moreover, the fraught culture of revivalism, filled with sermons, prayers, and exhortations—all governed by the concept of speaking according to divine inspiration and by the guidance of the Holy Spirit—instilled in Smith a fluency in extemporaneous and semi-extemporaneous speaking, delivered in a linguistic register that interwove a heightened biblical-style English with the colloquial idiolect of local speakers. As these cultural streams of oral performance converged in the torrential flow of the Book of Mormon text, Smith found his prophetic voice and launched his career as a prophet of God.

This study has sought to answer some of the questions surrounding the origins of the Book of Mormon through an examination of the relationship between Smith's work and the sermon culture of his time and place. Nevertheless, this exploration remains incomplete. Within the complex tapestry of nineteenth-century oral performance genres and cultural locations, several additional issues contributing to Smith's ability to produce the Book of Mormon reach beyond the scope of this work. These issues include the dynamics of storytelling culture in early nineteenth-century America, the role of memory in an intensely oral culture and its development and training, the significance of orality in education and beginning composition instruction, the oral-formulaic nature of the Book of Mormon text and what it reveals about Smith's informal training and the eventual composition of the work, Smith's use of contemporary performance conventions, and the source materials that Smith used and adapted to formulate many of his stories. Smith's nineteenth-century oratorical culture thereby offers several promising and richly interrelated issues that present new directions and important insights for future studies.

Such lines of inquiry, however, especially when considering Smith's avenues of formal and informal education, immediately confront a traditional and often unquestioned perception in the Mormon cultural imagination: the enduring and self-promoted myth that Smith was an uneducated, illiterate, unschooled child of nature, whose skills and intellectual capacities would have prevented him from composing a text like the Book of Mormon. As this study has sought to demonstrate, however, Smith's method of composition reveals an advanced understanding of nineteenth-century compositional strategies and a fluency in their techniques. Such evidence undermines the hagiographical accounts of Smith as an ignorant farm boy and further uncovers the presence of a familiar (and constricting) trope: the humble and illiterate but righteous man, who, in spite of his lack of formal training and education, is chosen by God to reveal important truths to mankind and to confound the wise and cynical men of the world.

This popular and ancient trope carries the palimpsestic imprint of sacred biblical narratives in the Judeo-Christian imagination: young Joseph, sold into Egypt as a slave, yet chosen by God to save his family from famine and to ensure the survival of the Hebrew nation; the bucolic story of young David, the humble shepherd boy, chosen by God to become the King of Israel; several of Christ's apostles, illiterate fishermen, chosen by God to lead the Christian movement; and even Jesus Christ himself, born into the humble home of a poor carpenter, yet chosen by God from the foundation of time to die on the cross and redeem the world. In fact, Smith explicitly positioned himself within this trope during one of his earliest interactions with critics of his movement.

In the latter part of 1831, Nancy Towle, a Freewill Baptist itinerant preacher visiting the newly formed Mormon community in Kirtland, Ohio (one of the towns where Smith and his followers first settled after leaving New York), recounted Smith's self-identification with Christ's humble and illiterate apostles. After observing the dynamics of the community under Smith's leadership, Towle became convinced that the group was deceived and openly challenged Smith's claims: "I turned to Smith and said, 'Are you not ashamed, of such pretensions? You, who are no more than any ignorant plough-boy of our land! . . . He [Smith] only replied, by saying, 'The gift, has returned back again, as in former times, to illiterate fishermen.'"[1] The simple but effective retort immediately evoked a powerful biblical precedent, aligning Smith with Christ's apostles, as men called of God and not by man. Smith's strategic use of this trope therefore offers insight into Smith's self-perception and identification for himself and for his movement, even though the trope equally cloaks the actual history of his formal and informal educational background.

A reexamination of Smith's early life and educational opportunities therefore requires a search that reaches beyond the well-worn paths of unquestioned assumptions.[2]

Legacy

Within weeks of publishing the Book of Mormon, Smith officially organized the "Church of Christ," later renamed "The Church of Jesus Christ of Latter-day Saints."[3] Soon afterward, he and his small but growing band of followers joined the flood of migrants pushing further into the interior of the continent, where they would establish communities in Ohio, Illinois, and Missouri. According to Smith, now the Prophet Joseph Smith, the Mormon faith presented itself as Christ's original church. As the church grew, so did Smith's vision for the future of the organization. Amidst the political, religious, economic, and cultural disruptions of early nineteenth-century America, Smith created an extraordinary religious worldview that not only provided stability to his followers but also elevated their status to dizzying heights of eternal significance.

At a time when the hopes of prosperous idealism confronted the realities of rural and frontier economic hardship, when the dreams of the proverbial self-made man were undermined by the adversities of unending and often hopeless toil and debt, Smith introduced a new story about the value and significance of the human soul: God's true followers were destined to become kings and priests, queens and priestesses, in eternity. They would progress in faith, knowledge, and righteousness until they would "inherit thrones, kingdoms, principalities, and powers, dominions, all heights and depths." And in an eternal destination unrivaled by any of the other contemporary Christian sects in the American frontier, Smith revealed that his righteous followers would become "gods. . . . from everlasting to everlasting. . . . then shall they be above all, because all things are subject unto them. Then shall they be gods, because they have all power, and the angels are subject unto them."[4] Smith's expansive cosmology conjured up a new and soaring reality for the lives of his followers and offered breathtaking promises of eternal progression. Instilled with such a majestic view of their future potential and spiritual dignity, Smith's flock would follow him anywhere.

Sitting at the heart of this magnificent vision rested the Book of Mormon. In an 1841 council with the leaders of his nascent faith, Smith declared that "the Book of Mormon was the most correct of any book on earth, and the keystone of our religion."[5] And as the "keystone" of the new movement, Smith's religious innovations, revelations, and authority all rested on the validity and authenticity of the text. Several years earlier, in 1834, Smith had asserted the claim more pointedly. "Take away the Book of Mormon and the revelations," Smith announced, "and where is our religion? We have none."[6] Everything in Smith's developing cosmology hinged on the book—an epic oral narrative initiated within the claustrophobic walls of a rural farmhouse in Harmony, Pennsylvania, and a work that would soon accompany Mormon missionaries across the globe in their proselytizing efforts. Yet, no matter how the book would be received and evaluated by its many audiences, whether as an authentic sacred text or an artifact of early nineteenth-century America, the oral features within the text would tell the story of its own creation. As the script of an extended oral performance, derived from a kaleidoscope of contemporary cultural practices, the Book of Mormon reveals critical insights into the centrality of the spoken word and the prominence of oratorical culture in the early American republic.

Notes

Abbreviations

AAP   William Buell Sprague, ed. *Annals of the American Pulpit; or, Commemorative Notices of Distinguished American Clergyman of Various Denominations.* 9 vols. New York: Robert Carter & Brothers, 1856–69.

BM   Joseph Smith. *The Book of Mormon.* 1st ed. Palmyra, NY: E. B. Grandin, 1830.

D&C   Joseph Smith. *The Doctrine and Covenants of the Church of Jesus Christ of Latter-day Saints.* Salt Lake City, UT: Church of Jesus Christ of Latter-day Saints, 1991.

D&D   *The Doctrines and Discipline of the Methodist Episcopal Church in America, with Explanatory Notes by Thomas Coke and Francis Asbury.* Philadelphia: The Methodist Episcopal Church, 1798.

EMD   Dan Vogel, ed. *Early Mormon Documents.* 5 vols. Salt Lake City, UT: Signature Books, 1996–2003.

HC   Joseph Smith. *History of the Church of Jesus Christ of Latter-Day Saints,* edited by B. H. Roberts. 7 vols. Salt Lake City, UT: Church of Jesus Christ of Latter-day Saints, 1902–32.

JSP   The Joseph Smith Papers. http://josephsmithpapers.org/.

Preface

1. HC, 4:461.

2. Paul C. Gutjahr, *The Book of Mormon: A Biography,* Lives of Great Religious Books (Princeton, NJ: Princeton University Press, 2012), 151.

3. Laurie F. Maffly-Kipp, ed., *The Book of Mormon: Translated by Joseph Smith Jr.* (1830; New York: Penguin Books, 2008), viii.

4. Throughout this study, I use "Latter Day Saint movement" as an umbrella term that recognizes the many different organizations that spring from Joseph Smith's original restoration movement. I also often use the acronym "LDS" and the term "Mormon" to describe people and issues of the Church of Jesus Christ of Latter-day Saints. This usage, though recently fallen out of favor within the organization, is an attempt to preserve economy of space. For further information on the various denominations of the Latter Day Saint movement, see Newell G. Bringhurst and John C. Hamer, eds., *Scattering of the Saints: Schism within Mormonism* (Independence, MO: John Whitmer Books, 2007).

5. For further reading on the academic study of Mormonism and the role of devotional studies and apologetics, see *Mormon Studies Review* 1, no. 1 (2014), which devoted its first issue to discussions on these topics. See also Blair G. Van Dyke and Loyd Isao Ericson, eds., *Perspectives on Mormon Theology: Apologetics* (Salt Lake City, UT: Greg Kofford Books, 2017).

6. Royal Skousen observes, "Witnesses seemed to have believed that Joseph actually saw an English text in the interpreters [Urim and Thummim/seer stone], but it is possible that Joseph saw the text, so to speak, in his 'mind's eye.'" "How Joseph Smith Translated the Book of Mormon: Evidence from the Original Manuscript," *Journal of Book of Mormon Studies* 7, no. 1 (1998): 24. For "tight control" and "loose control," see Skousen, "How Joseph Smith Translated," 24; Brant A. Gardner, *The Gift and Power: Translating the Book of Mormon* (Salt Lake City, UT: Greg Kofford Books, 2011), 147–56.

7. Grant Hardy, ed., *The Book of Mormon: Another Testament of Jesus Christ*, Maxwell Institute Study Edition (Provo, UT: Neal A. Maxwell Institute for Religious Scholarship and the Religious Studies Center, Brigham Young University, 2018), 623.

8. See Skousen, "How Joseph Smith Translated," 24; Gardner, *Gift and Power*, 147–56.

Introduction

1. In the 1830 first edition of the Book of Mormon, Smith identified himself as the "author" in the copyright registration, title page, and preface. I discuss this further in chapter 7.

2. HC, 1:16.

3. Time estimates vary. In 1984 W. Cleon Skousen suggested "approximately 65 working days." *Isaiah Speaks to Modern Times* (Salt Lake City, UT: Ensign Publishing, 1984), 102n66. In 1986 John W. Welch and Tim Rathbone proposed "a span of no more than sixty-five to seventy-five total days." "How Long Did It Take to Translate the Book of Mormon?," in *Reexploring the Book of Mormon*, ed. John W. Welch (Salt Lake City, UT: Deseret Book and the Foundation for Ancient Research and Mormon Studies, 1992), 3. Using the same research, John W. Welch revised his estimate to "only about sixty-five working days." "How Long Did It Take Joseph Smith to Translate the Book of Mormon?" *Ensign* 20, no. 1 (January 1988), https://www.lds.org/study/ensign/1988/01/i-have-a-question/how-long-did-it-take -joseph-smith-to-translate-the-book-of-mormon?lang=eng. Later, Welch and Tim Rathbone lowered their figure to "less than sixty working days." "Book of Mormon Translation by Joseph Smith," in *Encyclopedia of Mormonism*, ed. Daniel H. Ludlow (New York: Macmillan, 1992), 210. Most recently, Welch estimates "a total of only 57 to 63 available full-time working days." "Timing the Translation of the Book of Mormon," *BYU Studies Quarterly* 57, no. 4 (2018): 34.

4. Regarding doctrinal changes, see, for example, Melodie Moench Charles, "Book of Mormon Christology," in *New Approaches to the Book of Mormon: Explorations in Critical Methodology*, ed. Brent Lee Metcalfe (Salt Lake City, UT: Signature Books, 1993), esp. 107–8.

5. For the word count, see Welch, "Timing the Translation," 22. The comparison between the Book of Mormon and Homer's epics quickly diverges, however, regarding questions of aesthetics, authorship, repetition, and transmission. For an overview of these issues with Homer, see Robert Fowler, "The Homeric Question," in *The Cambridge Companion to Homer*, ed. Robert Fowler (New York: Cambridge University Press, 2004), 220–32.

6. Scribal errors inevitably occurred.

7. For an effective description of orality in early American culture, see Robert A. Gross, "Reading for an Extensive Republic," in *A History of the Book in America: An Extensive Republic: Print, Culture, and Society in the New Nation, 1790-1840*, vol. 2, ed. Robert A. Gross

and Mary Kelley (Chapel Hill: American Antiquarian Society and the University of North Carolina Press, 2010), 518–24.

8. In one of the racially controversial passages in the Book of Mormon, God cursed Laman and Lemuel with dark skin, along with all their descendants, because of their wickedness; see 2 Nephi 5:19–24.

9. For further discussion on the usage and avoidance of the term "cult" in academic discourse, see for example, James T. Richardson, "Definitions of Cult: From Sociological-Technical to Popular-Negative," *Review of Religious Research* 34, no. 4 (June 1993): 348–56; Paul J. Olson, "The Public Perception of 'Cults' and 'New Religious Movements,'" *Journal for the Scientific Study of Religion* 45, no. 1 (2006): 97–106.

10. Arthur Versluis, *Magic and Mysticism: An Introduction to Western Esotericism* (Lanham, MA: Rowman & Littlefield, 2007), 2.

Chapter One

1. To my knowledge, Grant Hardy is the first to describe the Book of Mormon as an "extended oral performance," but he does not pursue the implications of Smith's oral composition. "Introduction," in *The Book of Mormon: The Earliest Text*, ed. Royal Skousen (New Haven, CT: Yale University Press, 2009), xx–xxi.

2. According to Smith, the ancient Nephite prophet Moroni buried a translation implement called "interpreters" with the gold plates (the object is mentioned in Mosiah 28:13–14, 20). Though the precise date remains unknown regarding the first use of the term "Urim and Thummim" to describe the "interpreters" and Smith's seer stone, H. Michael Marquardt shows that Orson Hyde and Samuel H. Smith used the term no later than 5 August 1832. See Marquardt, "Orson Hyde and Samuel H. Smith at Boston in 1832," http://user.xmission.com/%7Eresearch/central/hydesmith.htm. See also Michael Hubbard Mackay and Nicholas J. Frederick, *Joseph Smith's Seer Stones* (Salt Lake City, UT: Religious Studies Center at Brigham Young University and Deseret Book, 2016), 50. Dan Vogel suggests that "Urim and Thummim gradually came to replace the earlier term, perhaps to displace charges of Smith's early involvement as a treasure seer" (EMD, 1:52n1).

3. See Royal Skousen, "How Joseph Smith Translated the Book of Mormon: Evidence from the Original Manuscript," *Journal of Book of Mormon Studies* 7, no. 1 (1998): 24, 27.

4. See Stan Larson, "The Historicity of the Matthean Sermon on the Mount in 3 Nephi," in *New Approaches to the Book of Mormon: Explorations in Critical Methodology*, ed. Brent Lee Metcalfe (Salt Lake City, UT: Signature Books, 1993), 116. Larson counts Mormon scholars Hugh Nibley, Sidney B. Sperry, and B. H. Roberts among those who believe that Smith consulted a King James Version Bible. See also David P. Wright, "Isaiah in the Book of Mormon: Or Joseph Smith in Isaiah," in *American Apocrypha: Essays on the Book of Mormon*, ed. Dan Vogel and Brent Lee Metcalfe (Salt Lake City, UT: Signature Books, 2002), 157–234; H. Michael Marquardt, *The Rise of Mormonism: 1816–1844* (Longwood, FL: Xulon Press, 2005), 141.

5. EMD, 1:541.

6. D. Michael Quinn's *Early Mormonism and the Magic World View*, 2nd ed. (1987; Salt Lake City, UT: Signature Books, 1998) remains the most detailed and authoritative work on the subject. John L. Brooke's *The Refiner's Fire: The Making of Mormon Cosmology, 1644-1844*

(New York: Cambridge University Press, 1994) presents the most ambitious study tracing a broad intellectual history of Smith's esoteric thought. These works are not free from criticism; interested readers should consult responses to their studies.

7. James E. Johnson, "Burned-Over District," in *Dictionary of Christianity in America*, ed. Daniel G. Reid et al. (Downers Grove, IL: InterVarsity Press, 1990), 202.

8. Whitney R. Cross, *The Burned-over District: The Social and Intellectual History of Enthusiastic Religion in Western New York, 1800-1850* (Ithaca, NY: Cornell University Press, 1950), 3.

9. "Primitivism," in *Dictionary of Christianity in America*, ed. Daniel G. Reid et al. (Downers Grove, IL: InterVarsity Press, 1990), 940. "Seeker" was a label that covered a broad spectrum of belief. For a detailed description of Seekerism in the Smith family, see Dan Vogel, *Religious Seekers and the Advent of Mormonism* (Salt Lake City, UT: Signature Books, 1988), 8–11, 25.

10. Richard L. Bushman, *Joseph Smith: Rough Stone Rolling* (New York: Alfred A. Knopf, 2005), 55.

11. See, for example, Brooke, *Refiner's Fire*, xv–xvi, 145–46; Bushman, *Joseph Smith: Rough Stone*, 8–27; Donna Hill, *Joseph Smith: The First Mormon* (Garden City, NY: Doubleday, 1977), 47–49; Mark A. Scherer, *The Journey of a People: The Era of Restoration, 1820 to 1844* (Independence, MO: Community of Christ Seminary Press, 2013), xix–xx; Vogel, *Religious Seekers*, 25–30, 79, 88, 97–102, 181–86.

12. Bushman, *Joseph Smith: Rough Stone*, 26.

13. For overviews of these alternative pursuits, see Catherine L. Albanese, *A Republic of Mind and Spirit: A Cultural History of American Metaphysical Religion* (New Haven, CT: Yale University Press, 2007); Quinn, *Early Mormonism*.

14. Brooke, *Refiner's Fire*, 7.

15. Walter W. Woodward, *Prospero's America: John Winthrop, Jr., Alchemy, and the Creation of New England Culture, 1606-1676* (Chapel Hill: The Omohundro Institute of Early American History and Culture and the University of North Carolina Press, 2010), [1].

16. Richard T. Hughes and C. Leonard Allen, *Illusions of Innocence: Protestant Primitivism in America, 1630–1875* (Chicago: University of Chicago Press, 1988), 20–21.

17. For an overview of Smith's pursuit of the "Adamic" language, see Samuel Morris Brown, "Joseph (Smith) in Egypt: Babel, Hieroglyphs, and the Pure Language of Eden," *Church History: Studies in Christianity and Culture* 78, no. 1 (2009): 26–65.

18. Samuel Morris Brown, "The Language of Heaven: Prolegomenon to the Study of Smithian Translation," *Journal of Mormon History* 38, no. 1 (Summer 2012): 55.

19. All biblical references hereafter refer to the King James Version of the Bible. For Moses and Aaron's battle with Pharaoh's priests, see Exod. 7–10; for "faith as a grain of mustard seed," see Matt. 17:20; for use of the Urim and Thummim, see 1 Sam. 28:6 and Num. 27:21; for "the sign of the Son of man," see Matt. 24:29–30. For additional references to magic in the Bible, see Brian Copenhaver, *The Book of Magic: From Antiquity to the Enlightenment* (London: Penguin Classics, 2015), [5]–70.

20. Copenhaver, *Book of Magic*, [5].

21. While Christian theurgy focused on God's powers, an element of nervousness and danger always accompanied explorations of the unknown. Theurgical practices occasionally involved the controlled invocation, or warding off, of demons, either to gain insight into mysteries or to neutralize evil forces (such as when hunting for buried treasure). I have used a spare definition of theurgy here. For a detailed definition and discussion, see Claire Fanger,

"Introduction: Theurgy, Magic, and Mysticism," in *Invoking Angels: Theurgic Ideas and Practices, Thirteenth to Sixteenth Centuries,* ed. Claire Fanger (University Park: Pennsylvania State University Press, 2012), 1–33, esp. 15–27.

22. David D. Hall, *Worlds of Wonder, Days of Judgment: Popular Religious Belief in Early New England* (New York: Knopf, 1989), 100. For a discussion on the prevalence of magic, attitudes toward practitioners, and the cultural context in which such practices proliferated, see Alan Taylor, "The Early Republic's Supernatural Economy: Treasure Seeking in the American Northeast, 1780–1830," *American Quarterly* 38, no. 1 (1986): 6–34; and Jon Butler, *Awash in a Sea of Faith: Christianizing the American People* (Cambridge, MA: Harvard University Press, 1990), 67–97.

23. EMD, 1:457.

24. EMD, 1:285, with minor transcription modifications.

25. See, for example, Quinn, *Early Mormonism,* 68; William J. Hamblin, "That Old Black Magic," *FARMS Review of Books* 12, no. 2 (2000): 281-83; Samuel Morris Brown, "Reconsidering Lucy Mack Smith's Folk Magic Confession," *Mormon Historical Studies* 13, nos. 1 & 2 (Spring/Fall 2012): 1–4.

26. See Albanese, *Republic of Mind,* 137; Brooke, *Refiner's Fire,* 158; Quinn, *Early Mormonism,* 68–70; Brown, "Reconsidering Lucy Mack Smith," 5–7.

27. Taylor, "Early Republic's Supernatural Economy," 9–10.

28. Caleb Butler, *History of the Town of Groton* (Boston: T. R. Marvin, 1848), 256. See also Quinn, *Early Mormonism,* 26; Taylor, "Early Republic's Supernatural Economy," esp. 8–14.

29. Dan Vogel, "The Locations of Joseph Smith's Early Treasure Quests," *Dialogue: A Journal of Mormon Thought* 27, no. 3 (1994): 198.

30. See EMD, 3:147; Quinn, *Early Mormonism,* 70, 294–96.

31. See EMD, 1:553; Quinn, *Early Mormonism,* 32.

32. See EMD, 2:194–95; Quinn, *Early Mormonism,* 33.

33. Quinn, *Early Mormonism,* 67.

34. Quinn, *Early Mormonism,* 134–35.

Chapter Two

1. See, for example, D&C, 47:1, 3; 69:3; 85:1. For detailed discussions, see JSP, "Introduction to Histories: Volume 1," "Introduction to Histories: Volume 2," and "Joseph Smith's Historical Enterprise."

2. Williams transcribed the majority of the opening outline, though Smith wrote part of the last sentence (beginning with "the Kees of the Kingdom of God"). Apart from minor adjustments in spelling and punctuation, I am using the transcription by the editors of the Joseph Smith Papers; see JSP, "History, circa Summer 1832," 1.

3. JSP, "History, circa Summer 1832," 1–2.

4. JSP, "History, circa Summer 1832," 3.

5. For a recent essay addressing the different versions of Smith's account, see Gregory A. Prince, "Joseph Smith's First Vision in Historical Context: How a Historical Narrative Became Theological," *Journal of Mormon History* 41, no. 4 (2015): 74–94.

6. JSP, "History, circa Summer 1832," 3.

7. "Laying down heads" refers to two separate stages in the process of composition and delivery. In composition, "laying down heads" concerns the preparation of an outline. In delivery, "laying down heads" refers to a preacher's explicit announcement of his or her sermon outline in the opening of an oration. See John Claude, *An Essay on the Composition of a Sermon,* trans. Robert Robinson, 3rd ed. (London: T. Scollick, 1788), 1:45 footnotes. I address this further in chapter 4. See also Hugh Blair, *Lectures on Rhetoric and Belles Lettres* (Philadelphia: Robert Aitken, 1784), 291. Blair also refers to this process as "dividing a Sermon into heads" (291). John Quincy Adams describes it as "laying down . . . divisions" and "the proposition [main topic] is divided into several points by partition." *Lectures on Rhetoric and Oratory* (Cambridge, MA: Hilliard and Metcalf, 1810), 2:11, 2:6. Charles Simeon describes it as the "distribution" of a sermon "into its leading parts." *Helps to Composition; or, Six Hundred Skeletons of Sermons,* 1st American ed. (Philadelphia: William W. Woodward, 1810-11), 1:viii. George Campbell describes it as "*the partition,* or as it is more commonly termed the division of the subject into its constituent branches." *Lectures on Systematic Theology and Pulpit Eloquence* (London: T. Cadell and W. Davies, 1807), 432, (original italics).

8. Regarding the development of composition instruction, Robert J. Connors proposes that "much of what we have come to know as the pedagogy of explanation developed between 1801 and 1835." *Composition-Rhetoric: Backgrounds, Theory, and Pedagogy* (Pittsburgh: University of Pittsburgh Press, 1997), 218.

9. Joan C. Beal, "Walker, John (1732–1807)," in *Oxford Dictionary of National Biography,* ed. Michael Duffy, https://doi.org/10.1093/ref:odnb/28499.

10. Robert J. Connors suggests, "The first American edition seems to have been [George] Kline's of 1808." *Composition-Rhetoric,* 341n3. I have since located an earlier 1804 edition, also printed by Kline.

11. John Walker, *The Teacher's Assistant in English Composition* (Boston: J. T. Buckingham, 1810), chapter introduction ("Advertisement"), [156].

12. For Walker's explanation on how to apply his method, see *The Teacher's Assistant,* chapter introduction ("Advertisement"), [156].

13. Connors, *Composition-Rhetoric,* 218–19.

14. Connors, *Composition-Rhetoric,* 218.

15. Connors, *Composition-Rhetoric,* 219.

16. Daniel Defoe, *The Life and Adventures of Robinson Crusoe* (Edinburgh: John Ballantyne and Company, 1812), [1], original italics.

17. I have silently amended the manuscript for readability.

18. BM, [5].

19. For Willard Richards's notes, see JSP, "Discourse, 29 January 1843, as Reported by Willard Richards–A," [153–56], [1]. Willard would use his notes to recreate a portion of Smith's sermon for publication; see JSP, "Discourse, 29 January 1843, as Reported by Willard Richards–B," [2].

20. The transcription follows the work of the Joseph Smith Papers editors. My notations [in brackets] are intended to clarify the punctuation and meaning. JSP, "Discourse, 29 January 1843, as Reported by Franklin D. Richards," [11–12].

21. JSP, "Revelations, Letters, Reports," 1.

22. William V. Smith, "Joseph Smith's Sermons and the Early Mormon Documentary Record," in *Foundational Texts of Mormonism: Examining Major Early Sources*, ed. Mark Ashurst-McGee, Robin Scott Jensen, and Sharalyn D. Howcroft (New York: Oxford University Press, 2018), 212.

23. Smith, "Joseph Smith's Sermons," 203; see also 212–13.

24. See, for example, Adams, *Lectures on Rhetoric and Oratory*, 2:[3]–4, 6, 20; Blair *Lectures on Rhetoric and Belles Lettres*, 291–93; Claude, *Essay on the Composition of a Sermon*, 1:85; John Wilkins, *Ecclesiastes: Or, a Discourse Concerning the Gift of Preaching*, 6th ed. (London: Samuel Gellibrand, 1675), 20.

25. Smith's handwriting begins with the phrase, "the Kees of the Kingdom of God." The editors of the Joseph Smith Papers provide a helpful transcription; see JSP, "History, circa Summer 1832," 1.

26. Dean C. Jessee, ed., *Personal Writings of Joseph Smith* (Salt Lake City, UT: Deseret Book and Brigham Young University Press, 2002), 2.

27. EMD, 1:541.

28. David Williamson, *Reflections on the Four Principal Religions* (London: John Richardson, 1824), 2:390. Williamson was specifically describing the general practice of reading sermon notes among the clergy of the Church of England, though the practice was the same for "sermon readers" across denominations.

29. For a description of long notes in colonial New England, see Harry S. Stout, *The New England Soul: Preaching and Religious Culture in Colonial New England* (New York: Oxford University Press, 1986), 219.

30. Williamson, *Reflections*, 2:391.

31. Williamson, *Reflections*, 2:391.

32. Williamson, *Reflections*, 2:391–92.

33. Williamson, *Reflections*, 2:394.

34. D&C, 84:85.

35. Brian Jackson, "'As a Musician Would His Violin': The Oratory of the Great Basin Prophets," in *A New History of the Sermon: The Nineteenth Century*, ed. Robert H. Ellison (Leiden, Netherlands: Brill, 2010), 508. Jackson offers an excellent overview of the development of oratorical performance in early Mormon preaching, particularly among the Mormon settlers in the Utah Territory. See also Davis Bitton, "Strange Ramblings: The Ideal and Practice of Sermons in Early Mormonism," *BYU Studies* 41, no. 1 (2002): 5–28. To these studies, I would add that the absence of formal homiletic training among most Mormon missionaries and preachers did not equate to the absence of traditional preaching patterns. Though the formal divisions of Greco-Roman rhetoric were never held as models for sermon construction in the development of Mormon sermonizing, the variations of the popular "plain style" sermon, along with the theological justifications undergirding the approach, deeply informed Mormon preaching.

36. Harry S. Stout observes how the notes of some colonial sermons "could contain three to five hundred words per page" and take up "six to twelve pages" per sermon; see *New England Soul*, 34, 151–52. Regarding short notes, Phyllis M. Jones and Nicholas R. Jones observe that Thomas Shepard's and John Davenport's sermon notes were "small pages (about five by seven inches), densely covered on both sides with very small handwriting;

the divisions of the sermon clearly marked (doctrines, reasons, and uses); texts of Scripture cited and often copied in full; and the contents of each division swiftly detailed in a few complete sentences." *Salvation in New England* (Austin: University of Texas Press, 1977), 17.

37. Solomon Stoddard, *The Defects of Preachers Reproved in a Sermon Preached at Northampton, May 19th, 1723* (New London, CT: T. Green, 1724), 24.

38. See William Perkins, *The Arte of Prophecying: Or, a Treatise Concerning the Sacred and Onely True Manner and Methode of Preaching* (1592, Latin; London: Felix Kyngston for E. E., 1607); Richard Bernard, *The Faithfull Shepheard* (1607, 1609; London: Thomas Pavier, 1621); John Wilkins, *Ecclestiastes* (originally published 1651); and Gilbert Burnet, *A Discourse of the Pastoral Care*, 5th ed. (1692; London: C. Bathurst et al., 1766.).

39. Meredith Marie Neuman, *Jeremiah's Scribes: Creating Sermon Literature in Puritan New England* (Philadelphia: University of Pennsylvania Press, 2013), 14–15.

40. For an analysis of the differences between these two styles, see Neuman, *Jeremiah's Scribes*, 14–15.

41. Sandra M. Gustafson, *Eloquence Is Power: Oratory & Performance in Early America* (Chapel Hill: The Omohundro Institute of Early American History and Culture and the University of North Carolina Press, 2000), 17.

42. George Whitefield, *Letters of George Whitefield: For the Period 1734-1742* (Chatham, UK: The Banner of Truth Trust, 1976), 446.

43. Stout, *New England Soul*, 189.

44. For a comparison of the development of Puritan and Anglican sermons, see Perry Miller, *The New England Mind: The Seventeenth Century* (Cambridge, MA: Harvard University Press, 1954), 332–33.

45. For Harry S. Stout's overview of Whitefield's characteristics, see *The Divine Dramatist: George Whitefield and the Rise of Modern Evangelicalism* (Grand Rapids, MI: W.B. Eerdmans, 1991), 39–44, 93–95, 153–54. For Benjamin Franklin's observations, see Kenneth Silverman, ed., *Benjamin Franklin: The Autobiography and Other Writings* (1986; Harmondsworth: Viking Penguin, 2003), 108–9. See also Jon Butler, Grant Wacker, and Randall Balmer, *Religion in American Life: A Short History* (New York: Oxford University Press, 2008), 120.

46. Iain Murray, ed., *George Whitefield's Journals*, 7th ed. (1960; Edinburgh: Banner of Truth Trust, 1998), 205.

47. George Whitefield, *A Letter to the Rev. The President, and Professors, Tutors, and Hebrew Instructor, of Harvard-College in Cambridge* (Boston: S. Kneeland and T. Green, 1745), 14–15, original italics.

48. Harry S. Stout, "New Lights," in *Dictionary of Christianity in America*, ed. Daniel G. Reid et al. (Downers Grove, IL: InterVarsity Press, 1990), 816.

49. Harry S. Stout, "Old Lights," in *Dictionary of Christianity in America*, ed. Daniel G. Reid et al. (Downers Grove, IL: InterVarsity Press, 1990), 841.

50. Stout, *New England Soul*, 219.

51. Stout, *New England Soul*, 220.

52. For Whitefield's influence on Wheelock and other Yale graduates, see Stout, *New England Soul*, 200; John Fea, "Wheelock's World: Letters and the Communication of Revival

in Great Awakening New England," *Proceedings of the American Antiquarian Society: A Journal of American History and Culture through 1876* 109, no. 1 (April 1999): 107.

53. David McClure and Elijah Parish, *Memoirs of the Rev. Eleazar Wheelock, D.D.* (Newburyport, MA: Edward Little, 1811), 170.

54. McClure and Parish, *Memoirs of the Rev. Eleazar Wheelock*, 119. McClure and Parish's use of "extemporaneous" offers an example of how "extempore" and "extemporaneous" could be used interchangeably, without clarification.

55. AAP, 1:402.

56. See, for example, Richard K. Behrens, "From the Connecticut Valley to the West Coast: The Role of Dartmouth College in the Building of the Nation," *Historical New Hampshire* 63, no. 1 (Spring 2009): 45–68.

57. AAP, 1:396.

58. AAP, 1:575.

59. Bradford Kingman, *Epitaphs from Burial Hill, Plymouth, Massachusetts, from 1657-1892* (Brookline, MA: New England Illustrated Historical Publishing Company, 1892), 82.

60. AAP, 1:368.

61. Fea, "Wheelock's World," 99.

62. AAP, 1:410 (Bellamy), 1:433 (Hopkins), 1:605 (Huntington), 1:552-553 (West).

63. Bushman, *Joseph Smith: Rough Stone Rolling*, 20, 95; Richard K. Behrens, "Dartmouth Arminianism and Its Impact on Hyrum Smith and the Smith Family," *John Whitmer Historical Association* 26 (2006): 172.

64. Walker's *Rhetorical Grammar* remained part of the curriculum until at least 1825. See, for example, *Catalogue of the Officers and Students of Dartmouth College* (Concord, NH: Dartmouth College, 1825), [18].

65. John Walker, *A Rhetorical Grammar: In Which the Common Improprieties in Reading and Speaking Are Detected,* 3rd ed. (London: John Walker, 1801), see esp. 261–67, 307–9.

66. See *Catalogue of Books Belonging to the Library of the Social Friends, September, 1813* (Hanover, NH: Charles Spear, 1813), 13. The Social Friends was one of several student organizations at Dartmouth that served as literary and debate societies.

67. Blair, *Lectures on Rhetoric and Belles Lettres*, 269, 285–95, esp. 291–93.

68. Bushman, *Joseph Smith: Rough Stone Rolling*, 19.

69. See, for example, Richard Lloyd Anderson, *Joseph Smith's New England Heritage: Influences of Grandfathers Solomon Mack and Asael Smith* (1971; Salt Lake City, UT: Deseret Book and Brigham Young University Press, 2003), 10, 33, 35, 115–18, 195; Bushman, *Joseph Smith: Rough Stone Rolling*, 10–27. Several family members pursued spiritual paths outside of Congregationalism, such as Universalism and Seekerism. See, for example, Anderson, *Joseph Smith's New England Heritage*, 133–35; Dan Vogel, *Religious Seekers and the Advent of Mormonism* (Salt Lake City, UT: Signature Books, 1988).

Chapter Three

1. Whitney R. Cross, *Burned-over District: The Social and Intellectual History of Enthusiastic Religion in Western New York, 1800-1850* (Ithaca, NY: Cornell University Press, 1950), 13. See also 9–13.

2. Cross, *Burned-over District*, 11. For Cross's account of the Mormon faith, see also 138–50.

3. HC, 1:2.

4. HC, 1:3.

5. HC, 1:3.

6. EMD, 1:494-95.

7. See Richard L. Bushman, *Joseph Smith: Rough Stone Rolling* (New York: Alfred A. Knopf, 2005), 37. For William's statement (which omits Sophronia), see EMD, 1:495.

8. EMD, 3:259.

9. EMD, 3:259.

10. EMD, 1:513.

11. John Wesley, *Sermons on Several Occasions* (London: W. Strahan, printer; T. Trye, Bookseller, 1746), 1:v–vii, original italics. John 7:17 reads, "If any man will do his will, he shall know of the doctrine."

12. HC, 1:4.

13. H. Michael Marquardt, *The Rise of Mormonism: 1816–1844* (Longwood, FL: Xulon Press, 2005), 22–24. See also William Smith's reminiscence in EMD, 1:494–95.

14. Quoted in Marquardt, *Rise of Mormonism*, 23. For Cowdery's full text, see EMD, 2:422–25. For further information on George Lane, see Marquardt, *Rise of Mormonism*, 22–27.

15. HC, 1:3.

16. EMD, 3:94.

17. D&D, 67.

18. EMD, 3:50. See also Orsamus Turner, *History of the Pioneer Settlement of Phelps & Gorham's Purchase* (Rochester, NY: William Alling, 1852), 214.

19. Marquardt, *Rise of Mormonism*, 50. See also D&D, 72.

20. For contemporary descriptions of Methodist services, see *The Beauties of Methodism* (London: J. Fielding, n.d., early 1780s), xi; Robert Adam, *The Religious World Displayed* (Philadelphia: Moses Thomas, 1818), 3:127; D&D, 120–21, 132–45.

21. D&D, 67.

22. The advice to preachers was equally applicable to exhorters; see D&D, 84–89.

23. See Marquardt, *Rise of Mormonism*, 49.

24. D&D, 85.

25. D&D, "Notes," 85.

26. D&D, 89.

27. D&D, "Notes," 85–87.

28. For short biographies of exhorters who became preachers, see the accounts of Edward Jackson and George Shadford in *The Experience and Ministerial Labours of Several Methodist Preachers, Who Laboured in Connection with the Late Rev. John Wesley* (New York: Daniel Hitt, 1812), esp. 202, 330–33.

29. D&C, 11:21, italics mine.

30. Vicki Tolar Burton, *Spiritual Literacy in John Wesley's Methodism: Reading, Writing, and Speaking to Believe* (Waco, TX: Baylor University Press, 2008), 111.

31. Burton, *Spiritual Literacy*, 111.

32. See, for example, AAP, volume 7 (1861): 69–70, 77, 88, 115, 139, 251–52, 270, 273, 291, 300, 327–28, 359, 367, 388, 395, 405, 431, 477, 493, 508, 525, 566, 571, 585, 604, 606, 625, 693–94, 725, 730, 735, 757, 785.

33. Methodist Episcopal Church, *A Form of Discipline for the Ministers, Preachers, and Members of the Methodist Episcopal Church in America* (New York: Methodist Episcopal Church, 1787), 28.

34. Methodist Episcopal Church, *Form of Discipline*, 27. See also D&D, 106–7.

35. Isaac Watts, *A Guide to Prayer; or, a Free and Rational Account of the Gift, Grace and Spirit of Prayer* (1716; Aberdeen: J. Boyle, 1792), 146, original italics.

36. John Newton, *Cardiphonia: Or, the Utterance of the Heart,* 4th ed. (1781; London: J. Buckland and J. Johnson, 1787), 2:61.

37. Newton, *Cardiphonia*, 2:61.

38. See, for example, "T.C. Strong, Book-Seller & Printer," *Palmyra Register*, 29 September 1818, 1; "T.C. St[r]ong . . . Books, and Stationary," *Palmyra Register*, 17 May 1820, 4; "Palmyra Book Store," *Wayne Sentinel*, 5 May 1824, 3 ("Newton's Letters").

39. D&D, 78.

40. Adam Clarke, *A Letter to a Methodist Preacher, on His Entrance to the Work of the Ministry,* 3rd ed. (1800; Portland, ME: A. & J. Shirley, 1816), 23, original italics.

41. Clarke, *Letter to a Methodist Preacher*, 3rd ed., 22.

42. Clarke, *Letter to a Methodist Preacher*, 3rd ed., 23.

43. Clarke, *Letter to a Methodist Preacher*, 3rd ed., 24, original italics.

44. Adam Clarke, *A Letter to a Methodist Preacher, on His Entrance to the Work of the Ministry* (London: J. Butterworth; W. Baynes; and R. Edwards, 1800), Dedication, typography modified.

45. William Perkins, *The Arte of Prophecying: Or, a Treatise Concerning the Sacred and Onely True Manner and Methode of Preaching* (London: Felix Kyngston for E. E., 1607), 28, typography lightly modified.

46. Perkins, *Arte of Prophecying*, 32, typography lightly modified.

47. Perkins, *Arte of Prophecying*, 30, typography lightly modified.

48. Perkins, *Arte of Prophecying*, 131.

49. Gilbert Burnet, *A Discourse of the Pastoral Care,* 5th ed. (London: C. Bathurst et al., 1766), 208.

50. D&D, 78; John Claude, *An Essay on the Composition of a Sermon,* trans. Robert Robinson, 3rd ed. (London: T. Scollick, 1788), 1:101.

51. See John Wilkins, *Ecclesiastes: Or, a Discourse Concerning the Gift of Preaching,* 6th ed. (London: Samuel Gellibrand, 1675), 3–4, 45–114.

52. Maldwyn L. Edwards, "Adam Clarke, the Man," *Methodist History* 9, no. 4 (July 1971): 55; Wilbur F. Tillett, "Part First," in *The Doctrines and Polity of the Methodist Episcopal Church, South*, ed. Wilbur F. Tillett and James Atkins (Nashville, TN: Methodist Episcopal Church, South, 1905), 8. For the dates of composition, see Edwards, "Adam Clarke, the Man," 54.

53. D. W. Riley, "Tegg v. Everett: The Publication of the Second Edition of Adam Clarke's Commentary," *Proceedings of the Wesley Historical Society* 44 (September 1984): 145.

54. Edwards, "Adam Clarke, the Man," 54.

55. Stan Larson, "The Historicity of the Matthean Sermon on the Mount in 3 Nephi," in *New Approaches to the Book of Mormon: Explorations in Critical Methodology*, ed. Brent Lee Metcalfe (Salt Lake City, UT: Signature Books, 1993), 128.

56. John Beauchamp, "Wesleyan-Methodist Literature," *The Wesleyan-Methodist Magazine* 8 (January 1884): 66.

57. On Smith's revision of the Bible, see Robert J. Matthews, "Joseph Smith Translation of the Bible (JST)," in *Encyclopedia of Mormonism*, ed. Daniel H. Ludlow (New York: Macmillan, 1992), 763–69. For Smith's possible use of Clarke's Commentary during his revision of the Bible and/or the creation of the Book of Mormon, see Haley Wilson and Thomas Wayment, "A Recently Recovered Source: Rethinking Joseph Smith's Bible Translation," *Journal of Undergraduate Research* [Brigham Young University] (March 2017), http://jur.byu.edu/?p=21296, especially note 3. Wilson and Wayment suggest that Smith's use of Clarke's Commentary was a result of Sidney Rigdon's influence (after the composition of the Book of Mormon). Yet, they also note an alteration to Matt. 5:22, which also occurs in 3 Nephi 12:22. This modification suggests the possibility that Smith was exposed to Clarke's Commentary before or during the production of the Book of Mormon. For related studies, see Larson, "Historicity of the Matthean Sermon," 127–29; Ronald V. Huggins, "'Without a Cause' and 'Ships of Tarshish': A Possible Contemporary Source for Two Unexplained Readings from Joseph Smith," *Dialogue: A Journal of Mormon Thought* 36, no. 1 (Spring 2003): 165-79; Seth Perry, "The Many Bibles of Joseph Smith: Textual, Prophetic, and Scholarly Authority in Early-National Bible Culture," *Journal of the American Academy of Religion* 84, no. 3 (September 2016): 763.

58. EMD, 4:294; for background, see also 4:293.

59. EMD, 4:333. Peck gave this account in 1860, but he also reported the same event in 1843. See EMD, 4:328–30.

60. EMD, 4:329.

61. Adam Clarke, ed., *The Holy Bible, Containing the Old and New Testaments*, vol. 1 (London: Joseph Butterworth and Son, 1825), Advertisement, original italics.

62. William V. Smith, "Joseph Smith's Sermons and the Early Mormon Documentary Record," in *Foundational Texts of Mormonism: Examining Major Early Sources*, ed. Mark Ashurst-McGee, Robin Scott Jensen, and Sharalyn D. Howcroft (New York: Oxford University Press, 2018), 199.

63. Bunting, *The Life*, 1:134. For additional information on Disney Alexander, see Paul W. Chilcote, *The Methodist Defense of Women in Ministry: A Documentary History* (Eugene, OR: Cascade Books, 2017), 41–42.

64. Disney Alexander, *Christian Holiness Illustrated and Enforced* (Halifax, UK: T. Wills and J. Johnson, 1800), 4–5.

65. Methodist Episcopal Church, *A Form of Discipline*, 24.

66. D&D, 88.

67. D&D, iv. Pomeroy Tucker advertised copies of *The Doctrine and Discipline* (listed as "Methodist Discipline") in his local Palmyra newspaper. See, for example, "Palmyra Book Store," *Wayne Sentinel*, 2 June 1824, 4.

68. D&D, 71.

69. Clarke, *Letter to a Methodist Preacher* (1800), 11, 18–19, original italics.

70. Clarke, *Letter to a Methodist Preacher*, 3rd ed., preface, original italics.

71. *Pulpit Elocution: Or, Characters and Principles of the Most Popular Preachers, of Each Denomination* (London: J. Wade, 1782), 53.

72. William Myles, *A Chronological History of the People Called Methodists*, 3rd ed. (London: William Myles, 1803), 6, original italics.

73. William Gibson, "The British Sermon 1689–1901: Quantities, Performance, and Culture," in *The Oxford Handbook of the British Sermon 1689-1901*, ed. Keith A. Francis and William Gibson (Oxford: Oxford University Press, 2012), 22.

74. Quoted in Myles, *Chronological History*, 54–55, original italics.

75. For Wesley's advice to young preachers, see Wesley, *Directions Concerning Pronunciation and Gesture* (Bristol: William Pine, 1770).

76. See, for example, "T.C. Strong, Book-Seller & Printer," *Palmyra Register*, 22 September 1818, 1 ("Wesley's sermons"); "T.C. Strong, Book-Seller & Printer," *Palmyra Register*, 17 November 1818, 1; "New Books," *Ontario Repository*, 9 March 1825, 4. Wesley's *Sermons* appeared in several different versions under the same title. My dating of 1746 follows one of the earliest publications to use the title *Sermons on Several Occasions*, printed and published in London by W. Strahan.

77. John Wesley, *Sermons on Several Occasions* (Philadelphia: J. Crukshank; John Dickins, 1794), 1:91-92, original italics.

78. David Williamson, *Reflections on the Four Principal Religions* (London: John Richardson, 1824), 2:391–92.

79. Charles Grandison Finney, *Lectures on Revivals of Religion*, 2nd ed. (New York and Boston: Leavitt, Lord; Crocker & Brewster, 1835), "Advertisement by the Reporter, [Joshua Leavitt]" [v].

80. AAP, 7:477 (Chase); 7:566 (Covell); 6:688, original italics (Rodgers).

81. For descriptions of "without notes" and "extempore," see, respectively, *Pulpit Elocution*, 53, and Myles, *Chronological History*, 6.

82. AAP, 6:250 (Stanford); 3:557 (Paxton).

83. AAP, 7:455, 462 (Capers).

84. AAP, 3:508–9 (Lacy); 7:292 (Dougharty).

85. AAP, 4:672 (Foot); 7:405 (Parker); 6:418, 426 (Vardeman).

86. AAP, 7:747 (Ninde); 7:649 (Summerfield); 7:681 (Sherman).

87. AAP, 7:818, 824–25 (Hinman); 7:809 (Waterman); 7:375 (Smith).

88. AAP, 7:522, original italics (Lybrand); 7:604 (Pitman); 7:539, original italics (Bascom).

89. See Bushman, *Joseph Smith: Rough Stone Rolling*, 37; EMD, 1:495, 513.

90. AAP, 4:145 (Williston); 3:569 (Hill); 3:187–88 (Duffield); 4:341, original italics (Rice).

91. AAP, 3:631 (Lyle); 4:194, 197, original italics (Baxter); 3:532 (Henderson); 3:119 (Blair); 3:380 (Taggart).

92. For additional Presbyterian preachers and their sermon methods, see AAP, volumes 3 and 4 (Presbyterians). Volume 3: John Anderson (1767–1835), 590; James Blythe (1765–1842), 596; David Bostwick (1721–63), 134; David Caldwell (1725–1824), 267; John Moorhead (ca. 1703–73), 46; Jonathan Parsons (1705–76), 51; Thomas Reese (1742–96), 332; John Rosbrugh (1717–77), 256; Caleb Smith (1723–62), 147; James Turner (1759–1828), 586. Volume 4: John Breckenridge (1797–1841), 649–50; James Gallaher (1792–1853), 536; Henry Kollock (1778–1819), 271; Samuel Martin (1767–1845), 120; John Mitchell Mason (1770–1829), 23; Samuel Kelsey Nelson (1787–1827), 417; William Stephens Potts (1802–52), 727; John Brodhead Romeyn (1777–1825), 221; James Long Sloss (1791–1841), 583, 588; James Patriot Wilson (1769–1830), 355; Samuel Gover Winchester (1805–41), 757.

93. AAP, 6:215 (Baldwin); see also Daniel Chessman, *Memoir of Rev. Thomas Baldwin, D.D.* (Boston: True & Greene, 1826), 54, 67; AAP, 6:325 (Batchelder).

94. AAP, 6:101 (Smith); 6:513 (Palmer); 6:241 (Leland); 6:451 (Kerr).

95. For additional Baptist preachers and their methods, see AAP, volume 6 (Baptists): Lott Cary (ca. 1780–1828), 585; Joseph Cook (ca. 1749–90), 187; Elisha Cushman (1788–1838), 564; James Manning (1738–91), 96–97; Abraham Marshall (1748–1819), 170; Samuel Lamkin Straughan (1783–1821), 517.

96. For information on the Baptist "whine," see Bruce A. Rosenberg, *Can These Bones Live? The Art of the American Folk Preacher* (1970; Urbana: University of Illinois Press, 1988), 16, 19, 50. For the Methodist "groan," see Edward Jerningham, "An Essay on the Eloquence of the Pulpit in England," in *The Pulpit Orator; Being a New Selection of Eloquent Pulpit Discourses, Accompanied with Observations on the Composition and Delivery of Sermons* (Boston: Joseph Nancrede, 1804), 93–94.

97. EMD, 1:513. See also Cross, *Burned-over District*, 41–42.

Chapter Four

1. For information on audience size and length of time, see Donald Q. Cannon, "The King Follett Discourse: Joseph Smith's Greatest Sermon in Historical Perspective," *BYU Studies* 18, no. 2 (1978): 182 and 182n15. For the word count, I am using Stan Larson's amalgamated text; see Stan Larson, "The King Follett Discourse: A Newly Amalgamated Text," *BYU Studies* 18, no. 2 (1978): 193–208. None of the record keepers kept pace with Smith's delivery, so the actual word count is likely higher than this estimate.

2. Larson, "King Follett Discourse," 200–201. Unless otherwise noted, words in italics represent language found only in Wilford Woodruff's account, which he constructed from his notes and memory.

3. Larson, "King Follett Discourse," 201.

4. Larson, "King Follett Discourse," 201.

5. Larson, "King Follett Discourse," 199, italics mine.

6. Larson, "King Follett Discourse," 198. Smith also referred to earlier speeches in the closing of his oration, saying (207, italics Woodruff's), *"There have also been remarks made* [earlier in the conference] *concerning all men being redeemed from hell."* This reference again reveals how Smith was responding to earlier claims.

7. William V. Smith, "Joseph Smith's Sermons and the Early Mormon Documentary Record," in *Foundational Texts of Mormonism: Examining Major Early Sources*, ed. Mark Ashurst-McGee, Robin Scott Jensen, and Sharalyn D. Howcroft (New York: Oxford University Press, 2018), 215.

8. Van Hale, "The Doctrinal Impact of the King Follett Discourse," *BYU Studies* 18, no. 2 (1978): 213–20, 224.

9. HC, 6:326.

10. Cannon, "King Follett Discourse," 181.

11. For details, see Cannon, "King Follett Discourse," 182–84; Larson, "King Follett Discourse," 193–96.

12. Larson, "King Follett Discourse," 194.

13. Larson, "King Follett Discourse," 194.

14. Calvin Smith, "A Critical Analysis of the Public Speaking of Joseph Smith, First President of the Church of Jesus Christ of Latter-Day Saints." PhD diss., Purdue University, 1965. (Purdue Doc. No. 66-5304)," 75. See also Brian Jackson, "'As a Musician Would His Violin': The Oratory of the Great Basin Prophets," in *A New History of the Sermon: The Nineteenth Century*, ed. Robert H. Ellison (Leiden, Netherlands: Brill, 2010), 507.

15. William Perkins, *The Arte of Prophecying: Or, a Treatise Concerning the Sacred and Onely True Manner and Methode of Preaching* (London: Felix Kyngston for E. E., 1607), 148, original italics, typography lightly modified. For "*Doctrine* and *Use*," see John Wilkins, *Ecclesiastes: Or, a Discourse Concerning the Gift of Preaching*, 6th ed. (London: Samuel Gellibrand, 1675), 7, original italics. For "Doctrines and Vses," see Richard Bernard, *The Faithfull Shepheard* (London: Thomas Pavier, 1621), 290. For "doctrine, reasons, and uses," see Perry Miller, *The New England Mind: The Seventeenth Century* (Cambridge, MA: Harvard University Press, 1954), 335. Harry S. Stout describes the pattern as "the distinctive text-doctrine-application formula of the plain style sermon." *The New England Soul: Preaching and Religious Culture in Colonial New England* (New York: Oxford University Press, 1986), 34.

16. Phyllis M. Jones and Nicholas R. Jones, *Salvation in New England* (Austin: University of Texas Press, 1977), 9.

17. Perkins, *Arte of Prophecying*, 148, original italics, typography lightly modified.

18. Wilkins, *Ecclesiastes*, 7, original italics.

19. Jean Claude taught that "there are in general *five* parts of a sermon, the exordium, the connection, the division, the discussion, and the application: but, as connection and division are parts which ought to be extremely short, we can properly reckon only *three* parts; exordium, discussion, and application." *An Essay on the Composition of a Sermon*, trans. Robert Robinson, 3rd ed. (London: T. Scollick, 1788), 1:1–2, original italics. For terminology, I am adopting Nan Johnson's categories for the six-part scheme; see Nan Johnson, *Nineteenth-Century Rhetoric in North America* (Carbondale: Southern Illinois University Press, 1991), 181.

20. Dee E. Andrews, *The Methodists and Revolutionary America, 1760-1800: The Shaping of an Evangelical Culture* (Princeton, NJ: Princeton University Press, 2000), 79.

21. Larson, "King Follett Discourse," 199.

22. George Campbell, *Lectures on Systematic Theology and Pulpit Eloquence* (London: T. Cadell and W. Davies, 1807), 434–35; see also 452–53.

23. Claude, *An Essay*, 1:45, original italics.

24. Quoted in Stout, *New England Soul*, 153.

25. See Hugh Blair, *Lectures on Rhetoric and Belles Lettres* (Philadelphia: Robert Aitken, 1784), 291; John Quincy Adams, *Lectures on Rhetoric and Oratory* (Cambridge, MA: Hilliard and Metcalf, 1810), 2:20.

26. Charles Simeon, *Helps to Composition; or, Six Hundred Skeletons of Sermons.* 1st American ed. (Philadelphia: William W. Woodward, 1810–11), 1:viii, original italics. The first reference to Simeon's multivolume work appears in a 1796 sermon he preached at Cambridge, titled *The Gospel Message* (Cambridge, UK: John Burges). The title page indicates that it was "*intended as an APPENDIX to Claude's Essay and the Hundred Skeletons before published*," suggesting that Simeon may have published an earlier unknown work. From 1801 to 1802, Simeon published *Helps to Composition, or, Five Hundred Skeletons of Sermons* (Cambridge: John Burgess, Printer, 1801–2). The second edition that followed added one

hundred more sermons skeletons, resulting in the revised title, *Helps to Composition; or, Six Hundred Skeletons of Sermons* (London: T. Cadell and W. Davies, 1808). I am using the 1801–2 date to identify the work.

27. The practice of explicitly announcing heads in sermons was often criticized. Archbishop of Cambray François Fénelon (1651–1715), whose *Dialogues Concerning Eloquence* frequently appeared in treatises on sermons, argued, "Divisions give only a *seeming* Order; while they really mangle and clog a Discourse, by separating it into two or three Parts. . . . There remains no true Unity after such Divisons." *Dialogues Concerning Eloquence in General; and Particularly, That Kind Which Is Fit for the Pulpit,* trans. William Stevenson (London: J. Walthoe Jr., 1722), 114, original italics. For Blair's response to Fénelon, see *Lectures on Rhetoric and Belles Lettres,* 291–93.

28. Blair, *Lectures on Rhetoric and Belles Lettres,* 291.

29. Adams, *Lectures on Rhetoric and Oratory,* 2:9–10. See also 11-12, 20.

30. Adams, *Lectures on Rhetoric and Oratory,* 2:10.

31. AAP, 3:467. Tentative descriptions of a preacher's techniques are common, such as (AAP, 3:628, italics mine) "He [John Poage Campbell] preached without notes, and *apparently* extempore," and (AAP, 3:596, italics mine), "He [James Blythe] preached sometimes from short notes, which lay before him, or were held in his hand; sometimes, *I believe,* without any written preparation at all."

32. Quoted in Whitney R. Cross, *The Burned-over District: The Social and Intellectual History of Enthusiastic Religion in Western New York, 1800-1850* (Ithaca, NY: Cornell University Press, 1950), [2], original italics.

33. Blair, *Lectures on Rhetoric and Belles Lettres,* 292.

34. Blair, *Lectures on Rhetoric and Belles Lettres,* 292. Blair's footnote provides the translation.

35. Wilkins, *Ecclesiastes,* 6, original italics.

36. Blair, *Lectures on Rhetoric and Belles Lettres,* 241. Here, Blair is addressing "all kinds of Public Speaking," rather than focusing exclusively on pulpit orations.

37. Henry Ware, *Hints on Extemporaneous Preaching* (Boston: Cummings and Hilliard, 1824), 73–74.

38. AAP, 4:355, italics mine.

39. John A. Roche, *The Life of John Price Durbin, D.D., LL.D., with an Analysis of His Homiletic Skill and Sacred Oratory* (New York: Phillips & Hunt; Cranston & Stowe, 1889), 278–79.

40. James Glazebrook, *The Practice of What Is Called Extempore Preaching Recommended* (London: J. Mathews, 1794), 17, footnote.

41. Roche, *Life of John Price Durbin,* 288, original italics.

42. Ware, *Hints on Extemporaneous Preaching,* 75–76.

43. Larson, "King Follett Discourse," 199.

44. For Larson's use of italics for Woodruff's notes, see Larson, "King Follett Discourse," 198.

45. Larson, "King Follett Discourse," 199–200.

46. For a detailed discussion on resumptive repetition and editorial practices in biblical texts, see Burke O. Long, "Framing Repetitions in Biblical Historiography," *Journal of Biblical Literature* 106, no. 3 (1987): 385–99.

47. Brant A. Gardner, "Literacy and Orality in the Book of Mormon," *Interpreter* 9 (2014): 69.

48. Gardner, "Literacy and Orality," 69.

49. Larson, "King Follett Discourse," 200.

50. JSP, "History, circa Summer 1832," 1, spelling and punctuation lightly modified.

51. Ann Taves, *Revelatory Events: Three Case Studies of the Emergence of New Spiritual Paths* (Princeton, NJ: Princeton University Press, 2016), 253.

52. AAP, 6:170.

53. Jabez P. Marshall, *Memoirs of the Late Rev. Abraham Marshall* (Mount Zion, GA: Jabez P. Marshall, 1824), 82, original italics.

54. Marshall, *Memoirs*, 95–96.

55. Marshall, *Memoirs*, 81–82, original italics.

56. AAP, 6:169. According to his son Jabez (Marshall, *Memoirs*, 8), Marshall, whose education in his early life was overseen by his mother and father, "never received forty days education in his life, from a school-master."

57. Ware, *Hints on Extemporaneous Preaching*, 29–30.

58. AAP, 3:586.

59. AAP, 4:650.

60. AAP, 4:727.

61. AAP, 3:414.

62. AAP, 3:414–15, italics mine.

63. Andrews, *The Methodists*, 79.

64. Campbell, *Lectures on Systematic Theology*, [497]–98.

65. Campbell, *Lectures on Systematic Theology*, 502–3.

66. Campbell, *Lectures on Systematic Theology*, 503–4.

67. Campbell, *Lectures on Systematic Theology*, 505.

68. Claude, *An Essay*, 1:81–82, original italics.

69. Andrews, *The Methodists*, 196.

70. See D. Bruce Hindmarsh, *The Evangelical Conversion Narrative: Spiritual Autobiography in Early Modern England* (Oxford: Oxford University Press, 2005), 233–34. See also Andrews, *The Methodists*, 196.

71. Hindmarsh, *Evangelical Conversion Narrative*, 234.

72. For biographies of individual Methodist preachers, Hindmarsh (*Evangelical Conversion Narrative*, 234) mentions Silas Told, Thomas Walsh, John Nelson, John Pawson, John Haime, Thomas Mitchell, and Thomas Taylor.

73. See, for example, *The Experience of Several Eminent Methodist Preachers* (Philadelphia: Parry Hall for John Dickins, 1791); and *The Experience and Ministerial Labours of Several Methodist Preachers* (New York: Daniel Hitt for the Methodist Connection in the United States, 1812). Additional publishers of *The Experience and Ministerial Labours* included Thomas Yeats and Thomas Johns (Chambersburg, PA, 1812), and John Dix (Barnard, VT, 1812).

74. Hindmarsh, *Evangelical Conversion Narrative*, 228.

75. Hindmarsh, *Evangelical Conversion Narrative*, 242.

76. Hindmarsh, *Evangelical Conversion Narrative*, 242; see also 248.

77. JSP, "History, circa Summer 1832," 1. Spelling and punctuation lightly modified.

78. *Experience and Ministerial Labours*, 124. See also Robert Miller, "Experience of Mr. Robert Miller," *The Methodist Magazine for the Year 1801*, Vol. 24: part 2 (February), 55.

79. *Experience and Ministerial Labours*, 194, original italics.

80. For a summary of Olivers's life, see J. R. Watson, "Olivers, Thomas (bap. 1725, d. 1799), Methodist Preacher and Hymn Writer," in *Oxford Dictionary of National Biography* (Oxford: Oxford University Press, 2004), http://www.oxforddnb.com/view/10.1093/ref:odnb /9780198614128.001.0001/odnb-9780198614128-e-20738.

81. *Experience and Ministerial Labours*, 97.

82. *Experience and Ministerial Labours*, 103.

83. John Mason, *The Student and Pastor; or, Directions How to Attain to Eminence and Usefulness in Those Respective Characters* (London: J. Noon et al., 1755), 50.

84. Mason, *Student and Pastor*, 50–51.

85. Mason, *Student and Pastor*, 51.

86. See, for example, John Mason, *The Student and Pastor; or, Directions How to Attain to Eminence and Usefulness in Those Respective Characters* (London: H. D. Symonds, 1807), 43. See also Samuel T. Armstrong, ed., *The Young Minister's Companion; or, a Collection of Valuable and Scarce Treatises on the Pastoral Office* (Boston: Samuel T. Armstrong, 1813), 35.

87. Nathaniel Hawthorne, "A Fellow-Traveller," in *Selected Tales and Sketches*, ed. Michael J. Colacurcio (New York: Penguin Books, 1987), 85.

Chapter Five

1. For 269,510 words, see John W. Welch, "Timing the Translation of the Book of Mormon," *BYU Studies Quarterly* 57, no. 4 (2018): 22. For my figure of 108,099, see the end of this chapter.

2. King Benjamin enumerates the obligations of his auditors to God: "And now, *in the first place*, he hath created you. . . . *And secondly*, he doth require." BM, 158 (Mosiah 2:23–24), italics added. This listing of points, though common in nineteenth-century sermons, does not function as a prefatory outline.

3. BM, [123], italics mine.

4. See, for example, James Cook, *A Voyage to the Pacific Ocean* (London: C. Stalker; Scatcherd & Whitaker, 1788), 3:202–3. For a variant (touching on "points" rather than "heads"), see Miguel D. Cervantes, *The Life and Exploits of the Ingenious Gentleman Don Quixote De La Mancha,* trans. Charles Jarvis, 5th ed. (London: J. Dodsley, 1788),3: bk. 1, pt. 2, 15–16.

5. Brian Jackson, "As a Musician Would His Violin': The Oratory of the Great Basin Prophets," in *A New History of the Sermon: The Nineteenth Century*, ed. Robert H. Ellison (Leiden, Netherlands: Brill, 2010), 505. See BM, 62.

6. Jackson, "'As a Musician,'" 505, emphasis Jackson's; see also Helaman 5:18.

7. BM, 289.

8. BM, 244–45.

9. BM, 441.

10. BM, 10.

11. D&C, 20:26.

12. D&C, 18:32–35, emphasis mine.

13. D&C, 100:5–6, emphasis mine.

14. Jackson, "'As a Musician,'" 505.

15. D&C, 11:21–22, 26, italics mine. See also D&C, 84:85.

16. Stan Larson, "The King Follett Discourse: A Newly Amalgamated Text," *BYU Studies* 18, no. 2 (1978): 199, italics mine.

17. BM, 74, italics mine.

18. BM, 74–85. For a detailed analysis of Isa. 48 and 49 in Jacob's sermon, see David P. Wright, "Joseph Smith's Interpretation of Isaiah in the Book of Mormon," *Dialogue: A Journal of Mormon Thought* 31, no. 4 (1998): esp. 190–96.

19. BM, 240, emphasis mine. Also, the prophet Abinadi was slain because he "prophesied of *many things which is to come*, yea, even the coming of Christ." BM, 171, emphasis mine; Mosiah 7:26. See also Mosiah 8:17; 13:10; 16:14; Alma 5:44; 10:12; 3 Nephi 15:7.

20. BM, 78, emphasis mine.

21. BM, 83, emphasis mine.

22. BM, 83, emphasis mine.

23. BM, 74, emphasis mine.

24. For a helpful overview of the scholastic sermon structure and the medieval texts that taught variations of the form, see Siegfried Wenzel, *Medieval Artes Praedicandi: A Synthesis of Scholastic Sermon Structure* (Toronto: Medieval Academy of America, University of Toronto Press, 2015), esp. [xv], 47–86.

25. John Quincy Adams, *Lectures on Rhetoric and Oratory* (Cambridge, MA: Hilliard and Metcalf, 1810), 2:19.

26. John Claude, *An Essay on the Composition of a Sermon,* trans. Robert Robinson, 3rd ed. (London: T. Scollick, 1788), 1:43.

27. Claude, *An Essay,* 1:43n1.

28. For example, King Benjamin announces the topic of his famous oration with two cues: "I shall proclaim unto this my people . . . that [1] thou [Mosiah] art a king, and a ruler" and "[2] moreover, I shall give this people a name [the name of Christ], that thereby they may be distinguished." BM, 154; Mosiah 1:10–11. King Limhi also described Abinadi's exhortations and prophecies with two cues: "a Prophet of the Lord have they slain . . . [1] who told them of their wickedness and abominations, and [2] prophesied of many things which is to come, yea, even the coming of Christ." BM, 171; Mosiah 7:26.

29. BM, 74.

30. BM, 74.

31. BM, 74.

32. BM, 74.

33. BM, 124. For the full sermon, see BM, 124–29 (Jacob 1–3).

34. BM, 124.

35. BM, 125.

36. BM, 126, italics mine.

37. BM, 126.

38. BM, 577.

39. BM, 578.

40. Smith appears to have conflated temporarily Moroni's voice with that of Mormon's. While alternative interpretations are possible, such speculations require the reader to make assumptions regarding unwritten circumstances external to the narrative, rather than evidence within the text itself.

41. BM, 580.

42. Along with Paul's formula, Smith borrows extensively from the entire chapter (compare 1 Cor. 13:3–8 with Moroni 7:44-46). In 1967 Hugh Nibley argued that Paul's text was not original, but influenced by earlier writers perhaps as far back as "Babylonian times." Nibley limited his comments to "the well-known 'Pauline' *formula*, 'faith, hope, and love,'" citing the work of Adolf Harnack, Johannes Weiss, and Richard Reitzenstein. *Since Cumorah: The Book of Mormon in the Modern World* (Salt Lake City, UT: Deseret Book, 1967), 128, italics mine. Later, however, Nibley incorrectly argued that the "whole passage" on faith, hope, and charity "originated not with Paul at all" but existed in "some older but unknown source: Paul is merely quoting from the record." *The Prophetic Book of Mormon*, vol. 8 of *The Collected Works of Hugh Nibley* (Salt Lake City, UT: Deseret Book and Foundation for Ancient Research and Mormon Studies, 1989), 216. Nibley's claim, however, misconstrued the research of these scholars. Harnack, Reitzenstein, and Weiss were addressing the origins of the *single-phrase formula* "faith, hope, charity" in 1 Cor. 13:13. None of them was proposing, or even implying, that Paul borrowed his "whole passage" from an earlier source. Indeed, the structure of Paul's passage is framed according to Greco-Roman rhetorical models (long postdating Lehi's departure to the Americas), and the language of the Book of Mormon passage demonstrates unequivocal dependence on the King James Bible. For a helpful overview of the debate among these early nineteenth-century scholars, see James Brennan, "The Exegesis of 1 Cor. 13," *Irish Theological Quarterly* 21, no. 3 (July 1954): 270–78. For additional commentary and scholarship on Paul's passage, see Joseph A. Fitzmyer, *First Corinthians: A New Translation with Introduction and Commentary*, The Anchor Yale Bible (New Haven, CT: Yale University Press, 2008), 32: 487–507. See also Richard Reitzenstein, "Die Entstehung Der Formel 'Glaube, Liebe, Hoffnung,'" in *Historische Zeitschrift* (Munich: Druck und Verlag von R. Oldenbourg, 1916), 189–208; and Reitzenstein, "Die Formel Glaube, Liebe, Hoffnung Bei Paulus," *Nachrichten von der Königlichen Gesellschaft der Wissenschaften zu Göttingen*, Philologisch-historische Klasse aus dem Jahre 1917, Heft 1 (1917–18): 130–51.

43. BM, 580.

44. BM, 577.

45. John Wesley occasionally provided models for progressive heads. In his "Sermon LV. On the Use of Money," for example, Wesley announces that, "perhaps all the instructions, which are necessary for this [topic], may be reduced to three plain rules," but he does not immediately reveal what those rules are. Rather, he reveals each rule as he progresses through the sermon: "Gain all you can"; "Save all you can"; and "Give all you can." *Sermons on Several Occasions*, 5th ed. (London: G. Whitfield, 1799), 4:112-130, esp. 115, 122, 126. See also Wesley's "Advice to the People called Methodist, with Regard to Dress" (*Sermons*, 1799, 4:131–48). Hugh Blair's popular five-volume *Sermons* (London, Edinburgh: W. Strahan and T. Cadell; William Creech, 1777–1801) also provided numerous examples of such progressive heads.

46. BM, 323.

47. BM, 332, italics mine.

48. For the heads, see BM, 333, 336–37.

49. George Campbell, *Lectures on Systematic Theology and Pulpit Eloquence* (London: T. Cadell and W. Davies, 1807), 16.

50. John Pawson, *A Serious and Affectionate Address to the Junior Preachers in the Methodist Connection* (London: 1798), 23.

51. Adam Clarke, *A Letter to a Methodist Preacher, on His Entrance to the Work of the Ministry,* 3rd ed. (Portland, ME: A. & J. Shirley, 1816), 11, original italics.

52. Campbell, *Lectures on Systematic Theology,* 10. For Campbell's explanation of "sacred history" and "christian system," see 10–13.

53. Campbell, *Lectures on Systematic Theology,* 12.

54. BM, 286.

55. Philip L. Barlow, *Mormons and the Bible: The Place of the Latter-Day Saints in American Religion,* Religion in America (1991; New York: Oxford University Press, 2013), xxxii Preface (2013).

56. See, for example, James Fordyce, *The Eloquence of the Pulpit,* 4th ed. (Glasgow: R. Banks, 1755), 22.

57. Campbell, *Lectures on Systematic Theology,* 19. See also John Newton, *Cardiphonia: Or, the Utterance of the Heart,* 4th ed. (London: J. Buckland and J. Johnson, 1787), 2:61.

58. Campbell, *Lectures on Systematic Theology,* 20.

59. Alexander Campbell, "Delusions: An Analysis of the Book of Mormon," *The Millennial Harbinger* 2, no. 2 (February 1831): 93.

60. JSP, "History, circa Summer 1832," 1–2. I have slightly modified the editorial notations for reading and comprehension.

61. For Smith family and relatives with current or former ties to the Congregational church, see Richard Lloyd Anderson's *Joseph Smith's New England Heritage: Influences of Grandfathers Solomon Mack and Asael Smith* (1971; Salt Lake City, UT: Deseret Book and Brigham Young University Press, 2003), esp. 10, 33, 35, 115–18, 195. For Sunday school at the Presbyterian church, see EMD, 2:127. For joint revivals, see EMD, 1:513. For "intimate acquaintance," see JSP, "History, circa Summer 1832," 2. For Smith's participation as a lay exhorter at Methodist class meetings, see EMD, 3:50.

62. For a description of the various forms of exhortations, see Ann Taves, *Fits, Trances, & Visions: Experiencing Religion and Explaining Experience from Wesley to James* (Princeton, NJ: Princeton University Press, 1999), 59–60.

63. BM, 154.

64. BM, 154.

65. Mark D. Thomas, *Digging in Cumorah: Reclaiming Book of Mormon Narratives* (Salt Lake City, UT: Signature Books, 2003), 137; BM, 155–56.

66. King Benjamin's digression does not provide a crisp example of resumptive repetition, yet the progression of ideas presents a clear point of departure and return: first, the prosperity of those who obey the commandments (Mosiah 2:31); second, the "awful situation" of those who do not obey the commandments (Mosiah 2:32–40); and third, a return to the prosperity of those who obey the commandments (Mosiah 2:41).

67. BM, 159.

68. For Smith's use of revival language, see Mark D. Thomas, "The Meaning of Revival Language in the Book of Mormon," *Sunstone* 8, no. 3 (May–June 1983): 19–25. For Smith's revival language in relation to evangelical conversion narratives and camp meetings, see Grant H. Palmer, *An Insider's View of Mormon Origins* (Salt Lake City, UT: Signature Books, 2002), 95–133; Thomas, *Digging in Cumorah,* 123–47.

69. For "the demands of divine justice," see, for example, Hosea Ballou, *A Series of Lecture Sermons, Delivered at the Second Universalist Meeting* (Boston: Henry Bowen, 1818), 59; "The

Doctrine of the Atonement," *The Christian's Magazine* 3, no. 12 (December 1810): 682; Samuel Walker, *The Christian: Being a Course of Practical Sermons,* 3rd ed. (London: Edward Dilly and Barnabas Thorn, 1759), 58. For "immortal soul" and its ubiquitous variants, see Richard Baxter, *A Call to the Unconverted* (1658; Philadelphia: W. W. Woodward, 1806), xvii, 42, 119, 149, 275, 279, 285, 296; Lorenzo Dow, *The Chain of Lorenzo* (Augusta, GA: G. F. Randolph, ca. 1803), 8. For "awaken . . . soul," see Dow, *Chain of Lorenzo,* [1]; Isaac Watts, *An Extract from the Works of the Pious, and Laborious, Isaac Watts, D. D.* (New Brunswick, NJ: A. Blauvelt, 1812), 15. For "a lively sense" of "guilt" and other variants, see John Henry Hobart, *A Companion for the Altar* (New York: Peter A. Mesier, 1804), 40, 74, 120, 122; John Wesley, *Sermons, on Several Occasions* (New York: The Methodist Connection in the United States, 1810), 1:168. For variants of "shrink with" or "from" emotional or spiritual experiences, see Timothy Dwight, *The Charitable Blessed; a Sermon, Preached in the First Church in New-Haven* (New Haven, CT: Sidney's Press, 1810), 14; Robert Hindmarsh, *A Seal upon the Lips of Unitarians, Trinitarians, and All Others* (Philadelphia: Johnson Taylor, 1815), 20; Joseph Swain, "Lo, He Comes, Array'd in Veng'ance (The Coming of Christ to Judgment)," in *A New Selection of Seven Hundred Evangelical Hymns, for Private, Family, and Public Worship,* ed. John Dobell (Morristown, NJ: Peter A. Johnson, 1810), 382. For variants of "fill the breast," see Enoch Mudge, "Hymn 57, Joy in Attending on Public Worship," in *The American Camp-Meeting Hymn Book,* ed. Enoch Mudge (Boston: Joseph Burdakin, 1818), 74; "Fragment of a Vision," in *Evangelicana; or, Gospel Treasury,* ed. William Collier (Boston: Hastings, Etheridge, and Bliss, 1809), 301; Lindley Murray, *The English Reader* (1799; Albany, NY: Websters and Skinners, 1814), 115. For variants of "no claim" on "mercy," see Charles Chauncy, *Twelve Sermons* (Boston: Thomas Leverett, 1765), 157; Jonathan Dickinson, *The True Scripture-Doctrine Concerning Some Important Points of Christian Faith* (Chambersburg, PA: Robert and George K. Harper, 1800), 125, 136. "Doom," "final doom," and "never-ending torment" are ubiquitous in nineteenth-century religious discourse. For "doom" and "final doom," coupled with "torment," "never ending torment," and "eternal torment," see Thomas Hersey, *A Voice from the Grave* (Morgantown, VA: J. Campbell, 1806), [3], 4, 6; John Murray, *The Justification of Believers by Imputed Righteousness* (Newburyport, MA: John Mycall, 1789), 135.

70. BM, 162. For "falling exercises" in relation to the Book of Mormon, see Thomas, "Meaning of Revival Language," 20. See also Thomas, *Digging in Cumorah,* 131.

71. BM, 162.

72. BM, 160, italics mine.

73. See, for example, 2 Nephi 6:4 and Alma 7:7.

74. BM, 160–61.

75. Determining an exact number of words is not the purpose of this exercise. Rather, these are conservative estimates intended to provide the reader with an illustration of how religious orations saturate the text of the Book of Mormon. Word counts are based on the 1981 edition. I have sought to remove phrases extraneous to orations, such as "And I, Nephi, said unto them" (1 Nephi 22:2), and similar introductory verses (e.g., 1 Nephi 22:1). I have also purposefully left out many passages with mixed genres (e.g., historical narratives intertwined with religious themes and biblical phraseology) that could have contributed to this estimate, but not without intensive untangling. As such, the overall amount of text within these oral genres is actually much higher than the numbers offered here.

76. Phyllis M. Jones and Nicholas R. Jones, eds., *Salvation in New England* (Austin: University of Texas Press, 1977), 5.

77. Jones and Jones, *Salvation*, 188n10.

78. Jones and Jones, *Salvation*, 9. Hooker would have likely delivered his sermon series from his notes, while the final printed version would have undergone editing for publication (often the result of a mix of preacher notes, auditor notes, preacher revisions, and publisher revisions). For an excellent study on the cultural production of printed sermons, see Meredith Marie Neuman, *Jeremiah's Scribes: Creating Sermon Literature in Puritan New England* (Philadelphia: University of Pennsylvania Press, 2013).

79. John Mason, *The Student and Pastor; or, Directions How to Attain to Eminence and Usefulness in Those Respective Characters* (1755; London: H. D. Symonds, 1807), 43–44.

Chapter Six

1. BM, [5], original italics.

2. JSP, "History, circa Summer 1832," 1, transcription lightly modified.

3. Seth Perry, "The Many Bibles of Joseph Smith: Textual, Prophetic, and Scholarly Authority in Early-National Bible Culture," *Journal of the American Academy of Religion* 84, no. 3 (September 2016): 752. See also Seth Perry, *Bible Culture & Authority in the Early United States* (Princeton, NJ: Princeton University Press, 2018), 111.

4. Adam Clarke, *The Holy Bible, Containing the Old and New Testaments* (London: Joseph Butterworth and Son, 1825), Genesis 12, chapter heading, original italics.

5. For a popular example, see Matthew Poole, *Annotations upon the Holy Bible,* 4 vols. (Edinburgh: Thomas and John Turnbull, 1800–1801).

6. Clarke, *Holy Bible*, general preface, xxvii, original italics.

7. See Hugh Nibley, *Since Cumorah: The Book of Mormon in the Modern World* (Salt Lake City, UT: Deseret Book, 1967), 157, 170–71.

8. For a list of Mesopotamian characteristics, see, for example, Earl Leichty, "The Colophon," in *Studies Presented to A. Leo Oppenheim*, ed. R. D. Biggs and J. A. Brinkman, (Chicago: University of Chicago Press and the Oriental Institute of the University of Chicago, 1964), 147–54; Hermann Hunger, *Babylonische und Assyrische Kolophone,* ed. Kurt Bergerhof, Manfred Dietrich, and Oswald Loretz (Neukirench-Vluyn, Germany: Neukirchener Verlag des Erziehungsvereins; Butzon & Bercker Kevelaer, 1968), [1]–24.

9. For a discussion on ancient Semitic modifications of Mesopotamian colophons (e.g., scribes adding the name of a text's author), along with possible "extended colophons" and colophons moved to the beginning of a narrative segment, see H. M. I. Gevaryahu, "Biblical Colophons: A Source for the 'Biography' of Authors, Texts and Books," *Vetus Testamentum: Supplement* 28, Congress Volume, Edinburgh (1974): 42–59. For further samples and discussion, see J. R. Lundbom, "Baruch, Seraiah, and Expanded Colophons in the Book of Jeremiah," *Journal for the Study of the Old Testament* 11, no. 36 (1986): 89–114.

10. John A. Tvedtnes, "Colophons in the Book of Mormon," in *Rediscovering the Book of Mormon*, ed. John L. Sorenson and Melvin J. Thorne (Salt Lake City, UT: Deseret Book and Foundation for Ancient Research and Mormon Studies, 1991), 32.

11. See, for example, Thomas W. Mackay, "Mormon as Editor: A Study in Colophons, Headers, and Source Indicators," *Journal of Book of Mormon Studies* 2, no. 2 (1993): 90–109.

12. Hardy, *Understanding the Book of Mormon: A Reader's Guide* (New York: Oxford University Press, 2010), 63. See also Brant A. Gardner, "Nephi as Scribe," *Mormon Studies Review* 23, no. 1 (2011): 45–55.

13. Portions of the manuscript also show Smith's handwriting; see JSP, "History, circa Summer 1832."

14. Royal Skousen, ed., *The Original Manuscript of the Book of Mormon: Typographical Facsimile of the Extant Text* (Provo, UT: Foundation for Ancient Research and Mormon Studies and Brigham Young University, 2001), 18. See also 6–7.

15. Royal Skousen, ed., *The Book of Mormon: The Earliest Text* (New Haven, CT: Yale University Press, 2009), 507; for Skousen's discussion on "sense-lines," see xlii–xliv.

16. BM, 407, original italics.

17. Skousen, *Original Manuscript of the Book of Mormon*, [487].

18. According to Skousen's typographical facsimile (*Original Manuscript of the Book of Mormon*, [487n17]), only the number "I" in the heading "Chapter I" is written "with heavier ink flow," indicating one of the few places where Cowdery returned to add information at a later time.

19. For examples of summaries composed in the course of dictation, prior to the actual composition of the narratives, see Skousen, *Original Manuscript of the Book of Mormon*, 164, 319, 335, 339, 372.

20. Skousen, *The Book of Mormon: The Earliest Text*, xlv. Skousen's description of the summaries occurs in the context of his explanation for his decision to italicize the Book of Mormon summaries in his work.

21. Hardy, *Understanding the Book of Mormon*, 124.

22. Skousen states, "Basically, the original text refers to the English-language text that Joseph Smith saw by means of the interpreters and the seer stone. Although I myself believe that Joseph actually saw words of English, it is also possible that the English-language text he saw was in his mind's eye rather than literally in the physical instruments." *Analysis of Textual Variants of the Book of Mormon: Part One, 1 Nephi 1 - 2 Nephi 10*, vol. 4 of *The Critical Text of the Book of Mormon* (Provo, UT: Foundation for Ancient Research and Mormon Studies, 2004), 3. See also Royal Skousen, "How Joseph Smith Translated the Book of Mormon: Evidence from the Original Manuscript," *Journal of Book of Mormon Studies* 7, no. 1 (1998): 31.

23. Skousen, "How Joseph Smith Translated," 28.

24. Skousen, "How Joseph Smith Translated," 23; for the quote in the brackets, see 24. For further discussion on "tight control" and other theories of translation, see Brant A. Gardner, *The Gift and Power: Translating the Book of Mormon* (Salt Lake City, UT: Greg Kofford Books, 2011), 147–56.

25. Skousen, "How Joseph Smith Translated," 28.

26. Skousen, *Analysis of Textual Variants, Part 1*, 44.

27. Skousen, "How Joseph Smith Translated," 28.

28. Hardy observes, "The story of the Book of Mormon is told, to a large extent, as a series of interlocking biographies." *Understanding the Book of Mormon*, 31.

29. Skousen, *Analysis of Textual Variants, Part 1*, 44.

30. BM, 221–30.

31. BM, 230–32.

32. BM, 232–42.

33. BM, 242–45.

34. BM, 245–66.

35. Skousen, "How Joseph Smith Translated," 28.

36. Grant Hardy, "Textual Criticism and the Book of Mormon," in *Foundational Texts of Mormonism: Examining Major Early Sources*, ed. Mark Ashurst-McGee, Robin Scott Jensen, and Sharalyn D. Howcroft (New York: Oxford University Press, 2018), 64.

37. The history surrounding Smith's composition of these short books introduces further complications. After Smith completed the opening portion of the Book of Mormon, a manuscript of 116 pages that contained 1 Nephi through the Book of Mosiah, Martin Harris, a supporter of Smith, lost the manuscript. According to the chronology of the work, the books of Enos, Jarom, and Omni occurred before the Book of Mosiah, suggesting the possibility that earlier versions of these three shorter texts may have been lost with the 116 pages. As such, the original manuscript could have contained longer, multichapter versions of these three books. Smith's inclusion of "Chapter I" for these works could therefore be a residual artifact of these earlier lost books.

38. Skousen, "How Joseph Smith Translated," 28.

39. For the background on the loss of the 116 pages, see Richard L. Bushman, *Joseph Smith: Rough Stone Rolling* (New York: Alfred A. Knopf, 2005), 66–68. See also William J. Critchlow III, "Manuscript, Lost 116 Pages," in *Encyclopedia of Mormonism*, ed. Daniel H. Ludlow (New York: Macmillan, 1992), 854–55.

40. The original manuscript supports this interpretation. Not only did Smith (or his scribe Cowdery) delete the word "Chapter" and replace it with the title "the Second Book of Nephi," the word "Second" was yet an even later addition. In other words, the evidence indicates that in his initial dictation of this replacement text, Smith apparently reverted to his original headings and said, "The Book of Nephi," even though the title was now supposed to be "The Second Book of Nephi" (suggesting that this is the location in the lost 116 pages where Lehi's book ended and Nephi's first book originally began). Only later did Smith realize that he needed to assign the "First" and "Second" distinctions to Nephi's works, resulting in the subsequent insertion of "Second" into the title.

41. BM, 59, italicized in original.

42. Hardy, *Understanding the Book of Mormon*, 50. See also Genesis 48 and 49.

43. BM, 69.

44. BM, 69, italics mine.

45. For further commentary, see Richard Dilworth Rust, *Feasting on the Word: The Literary Testimony of the Book of Mormon* (Salt Lake City, UT: Deseret Book and Foundation for Ancient Research and Mormon Studies, 1997), 71–75; Hardy, *Understanding the Book of Mormon*, 55–57. For an analysis of Nephi's Psalm in relation to Old Testament "individual laments," see Matthew Nickerson, "Nephi's Psalm: 2 Nephi 4:16–35 in the Light of Form-Critical Analysis," *Journal of Book of Mormon Studies* 6, no. 2 (1997): 26–42. For an analysis of the structural components, see Steven P. Sondrup, "The Psalm of Nephi: A Lyric Reading," *BYU Studies* 21, no. 3 (1981): 357–72.

46. BM, 71, italics mine.

47. Though he does not address resumptive repetition for this passage, Hardy (*Understanding the Book of Mormon*, 56) nevertheless notes the position of Nephi's Psalm as appearing

"exactly between the arguments among the brothers that broke out within a few days of Lehi's death."

48. BM, 71, italics mine.

49. BM, 71–72, italics mine.

50. Hardy, *Understanding the Book of Mormon*, 50.

51. All word counts are based on the 1981 modern edition.

52. BM, 73.

53. For a recent work on racial issues within the nascent Mormon cosmology, see Max Perry Mueller, *Race and the Making of the Mormon People* (Chapel Hill: The University of North Carolina Press, 2017).

54. BM, 323, italics mine.

55. For the headings, see BM, 323, 330, 332, original italics.

56. Gilles Fauconnier and Mark Turner, *The Way We Think: Conceptual Blending and the Mind's Hidden Complexities* (New York: Basic Books, 2002), 103.

57. Fauconnier and Turner, *The Way We Think*, 103.

58. Fauconnier and Turner's use of "mental spaces" and "frames" should be understood within the definitions they provide for their theory. They define (*The Way We Think*, 40, original italics) "mental spaces" as "small conceptual packets constructed as we think and talk, for purposes of local understanding and action," adding that these mental spaces "are connected to long-term schematic knowledge called 'frames,' such as the frame of *walking along a path*, and to long-term specific knowledge, such as a memory of the time you climbed Mount Rainier in 2001."

59. Fauconnier and Turner, *The Way We Think*, 103.

60. BM, 232, 239, original italics.

61. BM, 441, [574]–75, 581, 583, original italics. See also 514, 575–76, original italics: "*An account of the people of Nephi, according to his Record*" (4 Nephi 1); "The manner of administering the wine" (Moroni 5:1); "And now I speak concerning baptism" (Moroni 6:1).

62. BM, 50.

63. BM, 201, 216, 323, 410–11, 476, and 493.

64. Hardy, *Understanding the Book of Mormon*, 112–13, 97–98. See also Hardy's discussion on Mormon's editorial previews, 146–47. See also 106–7, 191.

65. BM, 123 (Jacob 1); 202 (Mosiah 23); 221 (Alma 1); 245 (Alma 9); 348 (Alma 45); 426 (Helaman 7); 476 (3 Nephi 11); 538–39 (Ether 1:1, 5); original italics.

66. BM, [452], original italics.

67. Hardy, *Understanding the Book of Mormon*, [31]. Hardy later suggests (107) that the Book of Mormon is structured as "almost a lineage history."

68. BM, 173, original italics (Mosiah 9, heading).

69. BM, 169.

70. BM, 170–71.

71. BM, 216, italics mine.

72. BM, 269, original italics.

73. BM, 282, original italics.

74. BM, 285, italics mine.

75. BM, 288–89. The "I" apparently refers to the narrator, Mormon.

76. BM, 302.

77. *The Experience and Ministerial Labours of Several Methodist Preachers* (New York: Daniel Hitt for the Methodist Connection in the United States, 1812), 103.

78. See Brent Lee Metcalfe, "Priority of Mosiah: A Prelude to Book of Mormon Exegesis," in *New Approaches to the Book of Mormon*, ed. Brent Lee Metcalfe (Salt Lake City, UT: Signature Books, 1993), 395–444.

79. BM, 26–28.

80. BM, 441–49.

81. In approximately 92 B.C.E., the Nephites changed their government from a monarchy to a system of chief judges; see Mosiah 29. For the next one hundred years, the Nephites marked time according to the "reign of the judges" (Mosiah 29:44).

82. BM, [123].

Chapter Seven

1. Ann Taves, *Revelatory Events: Three Case Studies of the Emergence of New Spiritual Paths* (Princeton, NJ: Princeton University Press, 2016), 245.

2. David Henige, *Historical Evidence and Argument* (Madison: University of Wisconsin Press, 2005), 43, original italics.

3. For the December 1827 start date, see Mark Scherer, *The Journey of a People: The Era of Restoration, 1820 to 1844* (Independence, MO: Community of Christ Seminary Press, 2013), 81. For 1828, see Richard L. Bushman, *Joseph Smith: Rough Stone Rolling* (New York: Alfred A. Knopf, 2005), 69.

4. Larry E. Morris, *A Documentary History of the Book of Mormon* (New York: Oxford University Press, 2019), 3.

5. Royal Skousen argues that the nonstandard English in the original translation may have been intentionally inserted by God. "The Original Language of the Book of Mormon: Upstate New York Dialect, King James English, or Hebrew?" *Journal of Book of Mormon Studies* 3, no. 1 (1994): 31–32. See also Grant Hardy, *The Book of Mormon: Another Testament of Jesus Christ*, Maxwell Institute Study Edition (Provo, UT: Neal A. Maxwell Institute for Religious Scholarship and the Religious Studies Center, Brigham Young University, 2018), 623. If God inserted Smith's New York dialect into the text, then it stands to reason that God could also insert the structures of nineteenth-century compositions and sermons.

6. Hardy, *The Book of Mormon: Another Testament*, 621.

7. For Emma's statement, see EMD, 1:541-42. For Whitmer's, see EMD, 5:86. Only Whitmer referred to "notes" in his account. Emma referred to manuscripts and books.

8. See HC, 1:12.

9. Scherer, *Journey of a People*, 81; Bushman, *Joseph Smith: Rough Stone Rolling*, 69.

10. EMD, 1:295–96.

11. EMD, 1:496.

12. Quoted in Morris, *Documentary History*, 28–29.

13. JSP, "Joseph Smith's Historical Enterprise," 1.

14. HC, 1:12.

15. EMD, 1:170. As Dan Vogel notes (EMD, 1:169), Smith apparently used Orson Pratt's pamphlet *A Interesting Account of Several Remarkable Visions* (1840) "as a model" for his

description of Moroni's message in the Wentworth letter. Nonetheless, Smith did not simply copy or paraphrase Pratt's description. Citing historian Dean C. Jessee, Vogel (EMD, 1:149) adds that Pratt's narrative was dependent on his relationship with Smith and exposure to his earlier writings (thus pointing to Smith as the ultimate source of Pratt's material). Additionally, Smith modified Pratt by eliding ideas, revising language, and adding new information (e.g., Book of Mormon "civilization, laws, governments"). Such revisions suggest that Smith adapted and refined Pratt's description in order to convey a more complete and accurate account of his version of Moroni's message.

16. EMD, 1:295, italics mine.

17. EMD, 1:296.

18. See Royal Skousen, "How Joseph Smith Translated the Book of Mormon: Evidence from the Original Manuscript," *Journal of Book of Mormon Studies* 7, no. 1 (1998): 22–31; Brant A. Gardner, *The Gift and Power: Translating the Book of Mormon* (Salt Lake City, UT: Greg Kofford Books, 2011), [137]–56.

19. See HC, 1:220, footnote. For an overview of translation accounts, see Richard Van Wagoner and Steve Walker, "Joseph Smith: 'The Gift of Seeing,'" *Dialogue: A Journal of Mormon Thought* 15, no. 2 (1982): 49–68.

20. D&C, 8:2–3.

21. D&C, 9:7–10, italics mine.

22. Taves, *Revelatory Events*, 247. Taves's description refers to the revelation to Oliver Cowdery in D&C, 8, but the observation is equally applicable to D&C, 9.

23. For Taves's analysis of these positions, see *Revelatory Events*, 245–47.

24. Taves, *Revelatory Events*, 247.

25. For further discussion on Smith's pneumatology, see Lynne Savage Hilton Wilson, "Joseph Smith's Doctrine of the Holy Spirit Contrasted with Cartwright, Campbell, Hodge, and Finney," PhD diss., Marquette University, 2010, 260–67. For additional information on "dialogic revelation," see Terryl Givens, *By the Hand of Mormon: The American Scripture That Launched a New World Religion* (New York: Oxford University Press, 2002), 209–39.

26. D&C, 128:18.

27. For "the Bible alone," I am following Seth Perry's description in *Bible Culture and Authority in the Early United States* (Princeton, NJ: Princeton University Press, 2018), 5. See also Paul C. Gutjahr, *The Book of Mormon: A Biography*, Lives of Great Religious Books (Princeton, NJ: Princeton University Press, 2012), 14.

28. W. S. Barker, "Priesthood of Believers," in *Dictionary of Christianity in America*, ed. Daniel G. Reid et al. (Downers Grove, IL: InterVarsity Press, 1990), 939.

29. Perry, *Bible Culture*, 5.

30. Edward Bickersteth, *A Scripture Help, Designed to Assist in Reading the Bible Profitably*, 5th ed. (London: L. B. Seeley, 1816), 17.

31. Stan Larson, "The King Follett Discourse: A Newly Amalgamated Text," *BYU Studies* 18, no. 2 (1978): 203, Larson's italics.

32. Graham St. John Stott makes a related point when contrasting Smith's rapid dictation with Cowdery's failed attempt at translation. Stott argues that Smith's preliminary study and preparation were necessary components of his translation that allowed him to dictate quickly, while Cowdery's lack of such preparations resulted in his failure to perform. "The Seer Stone

Controversy: Writing the 'Book of Mormon,'" *Mosaic: An Interdisciplinary Critical Journal* 19, no. 3, Literature and Altered States of Consciousness, Part I (Summer 1986): 41–42.

33. Richard L. Bushman, "Joseph Smith as Translator," in *The Prophet Puzzle: Interpretive Essays on Joseph Smith*, ed. Bryan Waterman (Salt Lake City, UT: Signature Books, 1999), 79.

34. See, for example, Keith Thomas, *Religion and the Decline of Magic* (1971; London: Penguin Books, 1991), 219–20, 256–57, 273–74; John Aubrey, *Miscellanies* (London: Edward Castle, 1696), 128–29; William Turner, *The History of All Religions in the World: From the Creation Down to This Present Time* (London: John Dunton, 1695), 32–33; Merlinus Anglicus, *The Astrologer of the Nineteenth Century; or, the Master Key of Futurity* (London: Knight and Lacey, 1825), 509–11. Crystal gazing might also include invoking spirits, many of which supposedly revealed information about the past, present, and future. See Reginald Scot, *Scot's Discovery of Witchcraft* (London: R.C. and Giles Calvert, 1651), 266–77.

35. Aubrey, *Miscellanies*, 128–29.

36. Anglicus, *Astrologer of the Nineteenth Century*, 509, original italics.

37. Anglicus, *Astrologer of the Nineteenth Century*, 511, original italics.

38. BM, 173.

39. EMD, 1:463.

40. Scot, *Scot's Discovery of Witchcraft*, 266, 271. Such spirits could be called using a magic circle or a crystal. For the incantation invoking spirits into a crystal, see 286–89.

41. Deborah E. Harkness, *John Dee's Conversations with Angels: Cabala, Alchemy, and the End of Nature* (New York: Cambridge University Press, 1999), 158.

42. Harkness, *John Dee's Conversations*, 166. For the description of Kelly, see James Granger, *A Biographical History of England*, 4th ed. London: W. Baynes et al., 1804), 1:272–74. See also D. Michael Quinn, *Early Mormonism and the Magic World View*, 2nd ed. (Salt Lake City, UT: Signature Books, 1998), 40.

43. Harkness, *John Dee's Conversations*, 41.

44. Harkness, *John Dee's Conversations*, 41.

45. Harkness, *John Dee's Conversations*, 43.

46. Harkness, *John Dee's Conversations*, 39, 44.

47. Stephen J. Fleming, "The Fulness of the Gospel: Christian Platonism and the Origins of Mormonism" (PhD diss., University of California, Santa Barbara, 2014), 192.

48. For Smith's access to materials on John Dee, see Fleming, "The Fulness," 94–96, 187–204; Noel A. Carmack, "The Curious Case of Joseph Howard, Palmyra's Seventeen-Year-Old Somnium Preacher," *Journal of Mormon History* 40, no. 3 (2014): 31–35.

49. Samuel Butler, *Hudibras, in Three Parts, Written in the Time of the Late Wars*, ed. Zachary Grey (1684; London: Vernor, Hood, and Sharpe et al., 1806), 2:61–62. For additional references to Kelly and Dee, see 2:16, 2:24–25.

50. Butler, *Hudibras*, 2:61, footnote v. 631, 632.

51. Butler, *Hudibras*, 2:24, footnote v. 235, 236.

52. Quinn, *Early Mormonism*, 40; see also 83–84.

53. Adam Clarke, *The New Testament of Our Lord and Saviour, Jesus Christ*, 1st American Royal Octavo ed., vol. 2 (New York: A. Paul et al., 1823); see note for "*And of angels*]" for 1 Cor. 13:1; original italics.

54. Samuel Morris Brown, "Joseph (Smith) in Egypt: Babel, Hieroglyphs, and the Pure Language of Eden," *Church History: Studies in Christianity and Culture* 78, no. 1 (2009): 27.

55. For Smith's study of Hebrew in relation to his translation projects, see, for example, Brown, "Joseph (Smith) in Egypt," 26–65; Bushman, *Joseph Smith: Rough Stone Rolling*, 290–93.

56. Samuel Morris Brown, "The Language of Heaven: Prolegomenon to the Study of Smithian Translation," *The Journal of Mormon History* 38, no. 1 (Summer 2012): 71.

57. Brown, "Joseph (Smith) in Egypt," 34.

58. BM, 120.

59. D&C, 8:2–3, italics mine.

60. Henry Cornelius Agrippa, *Three Books of Occult Philosophy*, trans. J. F. [John French?] (London: Gregory Moule, 1651), 413, original italics.

61. Francis Barrett, *The Magus; or, Celestial Intelligencer; Being a Complete System of Occult Philosophy* (London: Lackington, Allen, 1801), 2:53–54, typography modified.

62. HC, 1:16.

63. Vogel asks an important and relevant question: "If Smith translated and received revelations with his stone, did he also locate real buried treasure by the same means?" *Joseph Smith: The Making of a Prophet* (Salt Lake City, UT: Signature Books, 2004), x. For a detailed survey of Smith's money-digging projects, see Dan Vogel, "The Locations of Joseph Smith's Early Treasure Quests," *Dialogue: A Journal of Mormon Thought* 27, no. 3 (1994): 197–231.

64. During the period of Joseph's translation, for example, Emma stated that the plates were concealed under a cloth or stored under their bed; see EMD, 1:541, 546.

65. EMD, 4:287.

66. HC, 1:220, footnote.

67. For historical background, see EMD, 1:534–36.

68. EMD, 1:541–42. See Joseph Smith III, "Last Testimony of Sister Emma," *The Saints' Herald* 26, no. 19 (October 1879): 289–90. Like many of his colleagues, Smith's spelling was often nonstandard. Yet, he could certainly compose and dictate coherent letters. For a brief note on historian Dale Morgan's assessment of Smith's writing, together with Vogel's list of "letters in Joseph's own hand which seem inconsistent with Emma's statement," see EMD, 1:539n24. Elsewhere I have argued that Emma's statement was not a literal, objective description of Joseph's skills but a hyperbolic dismissal "to highlight her emphatic belief that Joseph could not have created the work [Book of Mormon] without divine assistance." William L. Davis, "Reassessing Joseph Smith Jr.'s Formal Education," *Dialogue: A Journal of Mormon Thought* 49, no. 4 (Winter 2016): 8.

69. Grant Hardy, *Understanding the Book of Mormon: A Reader's Guide* (New York: Oxford University Press, 2010), 7, 68.

70. EMD, 1:541.

71. See, for example, Gutjahr, *The Book of Mormon: A Biography*, 46–50.

72. For a detailed account of the theory, see Lester E. Bush Jr., "The Spalding Theory Then and Now," *Dialogue: A Journal of Mormon Thought* 10, no. 4 (Autumn 1977): 40–69; Gutjahr, *The Book of Mormon: A Biography*, 46–50; Eber D. Howe, *Mormonism Unvailed*, with critical commentary by Dan Vogel (1834; Salt Lake City, UT: Signature Books, 2015).

73. See Eber D. Howe, *Mormonism Unvailed* (Painesville, OH: E. D. Howe, 1834), 278–90. Howe did not originate the theory. Doctor Philatus Hurlbut ("Doctor" being his first name, not a title), collected affidavits from Spalding's family and friends, who believed that the Book of Mormon had been plagiarized. Howe purchased the documents and published the theory. See Bush, "Spalding Theory," 41–43.

74. Bush, "Spalding Theory," 44.

75. Gutjahr, *The Book of Mormon: A Biography*, 49.

76. For the letter and context, see EMD, 1:535–36, 543–45.

77. EMD, 1:544.

78. EMD, 1:545.

79. EMD, 1:541.

80. For David Whitmer's accounts of Emma, Christian Whitmer, and John Whitmer, see EMD, 5:60, 84, 105.

81. Only 28 percent of the original manuscript of the Book of Mormon exists, making it impossible to determine the number and identity of all the scribes. According to Skousen, the extant manuscript pages show the handwriting of Cowdery, Joseph Smith, and two unknown scribes. Emma's handwriting never appears. The possibility exists that Emma transcribed portions now lost, but without corroborating evidence the possibility remains speculative. Royal Skousen, *The Original Manuscript of the Book of Mormon: Typographical Facsimile of the Extant Text* (Provo, UT: Foundation for Ancient Research and Mormon Studies and Brigham Young University, 2001), 11.

82. EMD, 1:541.

83. EMD, 5:52. For details about Mary Whitmer's experience, see Amy Easton-Flake and Rachel Cope, "A Multiplicity of Witnesses: Women and the Translation Process," in *The Coming Forth of the Book of Mormon: A Marvelous Work and a Wonder*, ed. Dennis L. Largey et al. (Salt Lake City, UT: Brigham Young University Religious Studies Center and Deseret Book, 2015), 133–53.

84. Quoted in John W. Welch, "Documents of the Translation of the Book of Mormon," in *Opening the Heavens: Accounts of Divine Manifestations, 1820–1844*, ed. John Welch (Provo, UT: Brigham Young University Press and Deseret Book, 2017), 166.

85. EMD, 5:81.

86. EMD, 1:541.

87. EMD, 1:542.

88. EMD, 1:546–47.

89. EMD, 1:542.

90. EMD, 1:542.

91. EMD, 1:546.

92. Jabez P. Marshall, *Memoirs of the Late Rev. Abraham Marshall* (Mount Zion, GA: Jabez P. Marshall, 1824), 6, 80.

93. Hardy, *Understanding the Book of Mormon*, 7; see also 68.

94. EMD, "Circa 1–17 November 1825," 5:398.

95. Bushman, *Joseph Smith: Rough Stone Rolling*, 53.

96. EMD, 1:542.

97. See, for example, EMD, 1:497 (William Smith), 1:521 (Katherine Smith).

98. HC, 1:13.

99. Joseph Smith III, "Last Testimony," [289].

100. Joseph F. Smith, "Joseph the Seer's Plural Marriages," *Deseret News*, 22 October 1879, 604.

101. Eliza R. Snow, "Editors Deseret News," *Deseret News*, 22 October 1879, 605, original italics.

102. EMD, 1:535.

103. Givens, *By the Hand of Mormon*, 30–31, parenthesis in original. For Givens's context in relation to the Bible and notes, see 30–32. My quotation of Whitmer follows EMD, 5:128.

104. EMD, 5:128, parenthesis in original, italics mine.

105. EMD, 5:86. I have not located statements by Harris or Cowdery that deny the use of a Bible or biblical commentary. Their descriptions inevitably address the Spalding theory of plagiarism, such as Cowdery's statement: "That book [of Mormon] is true. Sidney Rigdon did not write it, Mr. Spaulding did not write it. I wrote it myself as it fell from the Lips of the prophet." EMD, 2:494.

106. EMD, 5:86.

107. EMD, 5:86.

108. EMD, 1:534.

109. EMD, 5:58.

110. EMD, 5:61.

111. EMD, 5:61.

112. EMD, 5:91.

113. EMD, 5:91, italics mine.

114. EMD, 5:197. See also David Whitmer, *An Address to All Believers in Christ* (Richmond, MO: David Whitmer, 1887), 30.

115. EMD, 5:197, italics mine. See also Whitmer, *An Address*, 30.

116. BM, [i–ii].

117. See John W. Welch and Miriam A. Smith, "Joseph Smith: 'Author and Proprietor,'" in *Reexploring the Book of Mormon*, ed. John W. Welch (Provo, UT: Foundation for Ancient Research and Mormon Studies and Deseret Book, 1992), 154–57.

118. BM, [v]—vi.

119. BM, vi.

120. HC, 4:79, original italics.

121. Taves, *Revelatory Events*, 250–51.

122. Taves, *Revelatory Events*, 245.

123. Larson, "King Follett Discourse," 208.

Epilogue

1. Nancy Towle, *Vicissitudes Illustrated, in the Experience of Nancy Towle, in Europe and America*, 2nd ed. (Portsmouth, NH: Nancy Towle, 1833), 157. On Towle, see Jon Butler, *Awash in a Sea of Faith: Christianizing the American People* (Cambridge, MA: Harvard University Press, 1990), 281.

2. For my preliminary research along these lines, see William L. Davis, "Performing Revelation: Joseph Smith and the Creation of the Book of Mormon" (PhD diss., University of

California, Los Angeles, 2016) and "Reassessing Joseph Smith Jr.'s Formal Education," *Dialogue: A Journal of Mormon Thought* 49, no. 4 (Winter 2016): 1–58.

3. H. Michael Marquardt, *The Rise of Mormonism: 1816–1844* (Longwood, FL: Xulon Press, 2005), 221–27; Paul C. Gutjahr, *The Book of Mormon: A Biography,* Lives of Great Religious Books (Princeton, NJ: Princeton University Press, 2012), 40.

4. D&C, 132:19–20.

5. HC, 4:461.

6. HC, 2:52.

Bibliography

Adam, Robert. *The Religious World Displayed*. 3 vols. Philadelphia: Moses Thomas, 1818.

Adams, John Quincy. *Lectures on Rhetoric and Oratory*. 2 vols. Cambridge, MA: Hilliard and Metcalf, 1810.

Agrippa, Henry Cornelius. *Three Books of Occult Philosophy*. Translated by J. F. [John French?]. London: Gregory Moule, 1651.

Albanese, Catherine L. *A Republic of Mind and Spirit: A Cultural History of American Metaphysical Religion*. New Haven, CT: Yale University Press, 2007.

Alexander, Disney. *Christian Holiness Illustrated and Enforced*. Halifax, UK: T. Wills and J. Johnson, 1800.

Anderson, Richard Lloyd. *Joseph Smith's New England Heritage: Influences of Grandfathers Solomon Mack and Asael Smith*. Salt Lake City, UT: Deseret Book and Brigham Young University Press, 2003. First published 1971.

Andrews, Dee E. *The Methodists and Revolutionary America, 1760–1800: The Shaping of an Evangelical Culture*. Princeton, NJ: Princeton University Press, 2000.

Anglicus, Merlinus [Robert Cross Smith?]. *The Astrologer of the Nineteenth Century; or, the Master Key of Futurity*. London: Knight and Lacey, 1825.

Armstrong, Samuel T., ed. *The Young Minister's Companion; or, a Collection of Valuable and Scarce Treatises on the Pastoral Office*. Boston: Samuel T. Armstrong, 1813.

Aubrey, John. *Miscellanies*. London: Edward Castle, 1696.

Ballou, Hosea. *A Series of Lecture Sermons, Delivered at the Second Universalist Meeting*. Boston: Henry Bowen, 1818.

Barker, W. S. "Priesthood of Believers." In *Dictionary of Christianity in America*, edited by Daniel G. Reid, Robert Dean Linder, Bruce L. Shelley, and Harry S. Stout. Downers Grove, IL: InterVarsity Press, 1990.

Barlow, Philip L. *Mormons and the Bible: The Place of the Latter-Day Saints in American Religion*. Religion in America. New York: Oxford University Press, 2013. First published 1991.

Barrett, Francis. *The Magus; or, Celestial Intelligencer; Being a Complete System of Occult Philosophy*. London: Lackington, Allen, 1801.

Baxter, Richard. *A Call to the Unconverted*. Philadelphia: W. W. Woodward, 1806. First published 1658.

Beal, Joan C. 2004. "Walker, John (1732–1807)." In *Oxford Dictionary of National Biography*, edited by Michael Duffy, https://doi.org/10.1093/ref:odnb/28499.

Beauchamp, John. "Wesleyan-Methodist Literature." *The Wesleyan-Methodist Magazine* 8 (January 1884): 64–69.

The Beauties of Methodism. London: J. Fielding; J. Scatcher & J. Whitaker; William Lane, n.d. (ca. 1780).

Behrens, Richard K. "Dartmouth Arminianism and Its Impact on Hyrum Smith and the Smith Family." *John Whitmer Historical Association* 26 (2006): 166–84.

———. From the Connecticut Valley to the West Coast: The Role of Dartmouth College in the Building of the Nation," *Historical New Hampshire* 63, no. 1 (Spring 2009): 45–68.

Bernard, Richard. *The Faithfull Shepheard.* London: Thomas Pavier, 1621.

Bickersteth, Edward. *A Scripture Help, Designed to Assist in Reading the Bible Profitably.* 5th ed. London: L. B. Seeley, 1816.

Bitton, Davis. "'Strange Ramblings': The Ideal and Practice of Sermons in Early Mormonism." *BYU Studies* 41, no. 1 (2002): 5–28.

Blair, Hugh. *Lectures on Rhetoric and Belles Lettres.* Philadelphia: Robert Aitken, 1784.

———. *Sermons.* 5 vols. London, Edinburgh: W. Strahan and T. Cadell; William Creech, 1777–1801.

Brennan, James. "The Exegesis of 1 Cor. 13." *Irish Theological Quarterly* 21, no. 3 (July 1954): 270–78.

Bringhurst, Newell G., and John C. Hamer, eds. *Scattering of the Saints: Schism within Mormonism.* Independence, MO: John Whitmer Books, 2007.

Brooke, John L. *The Refiner's Fire: The Making of Mormon Cosmology, 1644–1844.* New York: Cambridge University Press, 1994.

Brown, Samuel Morris. "Joseph (Smith) in Egypt: Babel, Hieroglyphs, and the Pure Language of Eden." *Church History: Studies in Christianity and Culture* 78, no. 1 (2009): 26–65.

———. "The Language of Heaven: Prolegomenon to the Study of Smithian Translation." *Journal of Mormon History* 38, no. 1 (Summer 2012): 51–71.

———. "Reconsidering Lucy Mack Smith's Folk Magic Confession." *Mormon Historical Studies* 13, nos. 1 & 2 (Spring/Fall 2012): 1–12.

Bunting, Thomas Percival. *The Life of Jabez Bunting, D.D.* Vol. 1. New York: Harper & Brothers, 1859.

Burnet, Gilbert. *A Discourse of the Pastoral Care.* 5th ed. London: C. Bathurst, J. Rivington, L. Hawes; R. Collins, R. Horsfield, T. Longman; the Executors of D. Midwinter and A. Ward, 1766.

Burton, Vicki Tolar. *Spiritual Literacy in John Wesley's Methodism: Reading, Writing, and Speaking to Believe.* Waco, TX: Baylor University Press, 2008.

Bush Jr., Lester E. "The Spalding Theory Then and Now." *Dialogue: A Journal of Mormon Thought* 10, no. 4 (Autumn 1977): 40–69.

Bushman, Richard L. *Joseph Smith: Rough Stone Rolling.* New York: Alfred A. Knopf, 2005.

———. "Joseph Smith as Translator." In *The Prophet Puzzle: Interpretive Essays on Joseph Smith,* edited by Bryan Waterman, 69–85. Salt Lake City, UT: Signature Books, 1999.

Butler, Caleb. *History of the Town of Groton.* Boston: T. R. Marvin, 1848.

Butler, Jon. *Awash in a Sea of Faith: Christianizing the American People.* Cambridge, MA: Harvard University Press, 1990.

Butler, Jon, Grant Wacker, and Randall Balmer. *Religion in American Life: A Short History.* New York: Oxford University Press, 2008.

Butler, Samuel. *Hudibras, in Three Parts, Written in the Time of the Late Wars,* edited by Zachary Grey. Vol. 2. London: Vernor, Hood, and Sharpe; Otridge and Son; Cuthell and Martin; et al., 1806. First published 1684.

Campbell, Alexander. "Delusions: An Analysis of the Book of Mormon." *The Millennial Harbinger* 2, no. 2 (February 1831): 85–96.

Campbell, George. *Lectures on Systematic Theology and Pulpit Eloquence.* London: T. Cadell and W. Davies, 1807.

Cannon, Donald Q. "The King Follett Discourse: Joseph Smith's Greatest Sermon in Historical Perspective." *BYU Studies* 18, no. 2 (1978): 179–92.

Carmack, Noel A. "The Curious Case of Joseph Howard, Palmyra's Seventeen-Year-Old Somnium Preacher." *Journal of Mormon History* 40, no. 3 (2014): 1–42.

Catalogue of Books Belonging to the Library of the Social Friends, September, 1813. Hanover, NH: Charles Spear, 1813.

Catalogue of the Officers and Students of Dartmouth College. Concord, NH: Dartmouth College, 1825.

Cervantes, Miguel de. *The Life and Exploits of the Ingenious Gentleman Don Quixote De La Mancha.* Translated by Charles Jarvis. 5th ed. 4 vols. London: J. Dodsley, 1788.

Charles, Melodie Moench. "Book of Mormon Christology." In *New Approaches to the Book of Mormon: Explorations in Critical Methodology*, edited by Brent Lee Metcalfe, 81–114. Salt Lake City, UT: Signature Books, 1993.

Chauncy, Charles. *Twelve Sermons.* Boston: Thomas Leverett, 1765.

Chessman, Daniel. *Memoir of Rev. Thomas Baldwin, D.D.* Boston: True & Greene, 1826.

Chilcote, Paul W. *The Methodist Defense of Women in Ministry: A Documentary History.* Eugene, OR: Cascade Books, 2017.

Clarke, Adam, ed. *The Holy Bible, Containing the Old and New Testaments.* Vol. 1. London: Joseph Butterworth and Son, 1825.

———. *A Letter to a Methodist Preacher, on His Entrance to the Work of the Ministry.* London: J. Butterworth; W. Baynes; and R. Edwards, 1800.

———. *A Letter to a Methodist Preacher, on His Entrance to the Work of the Ministry.* 3rd ed. Portland, ME: A. & J. Shirley, 1816.

———, ed. *The New Testament of Our Lord and Saviour, Jesus Christ.* First American Royal Octavo ed. Vol. 2. New York: A. Paul; N. Bangs and T. Mason; Martin Ruter; Armstrong and Plaskitt, 1823.

Claude, John [Jean]. *An Essay on the Composition of a Sermon.* Translated by Robert Robinson. 3rd ed. 2 vols. London: T. Scollick, 1788.

Connors, Robert J. *Composition-Rhetoric: Backgrounds, Theory, and Pedagogy.* Pittsburgh: University of Pittsburgh Press, 1997.

Cook, James. *A Voyage to the Pacific Ocean.* 4 vols. London: C. Stalker; Scatcherd & Whitaker, 1788.

Copenhaver, Brian. *The Book of Magic: From Antiquity to the Enlightenment.* London: Penguin Classics, 2015.

Critchlow William J., III. "Manuscript, Lost 116 Pages." In *Encyclopedia of Mormonism*, edited by Daniel H. Ludlow, 854–55. New York: Macmillan, 1992.

Cross, Whitney R. *The Burned-over District: The Social and Intellectual History of Enthusiastic Religion in Western New York, 1800-1850.* Ithaca, NY: Cornell University Press, 1950.

Davis, William L. "Performing Revelation: Joseph Smith and the Creation of the Book of Mormon." PhD diss., University of California, Los Angeles, 2016. ProQuest (Order No. 10243912).

———. "Reassessing Joseph Smith Jr.'s Formal Education." *Dialogue: A Journal of Mormon Thought* 49, no. 4 (Winter 2016): 1–58.

Defoe, Daniel. *The Life and Adventures of Robinson Crusoe.* Edinburgh: John Ballantyne and Company, 1812.

Dickinson, Jonathan. *The True Scripture-Doctrine Concerning Some Important Points of Christian Faith.* Chambersburg, PA: Robert and George K. Harper, 1800.

"The Doctrine of the Atonement." *The Christian's Magazine* 3, no. 12 (December 1810): 675–88.

The Doctrines and Discipline of the Methodist Episcopal Church in America, with Explanatory Notes by Thomas Coke and Francis Asbury. Philadelphia: The Methodist Episcopal Church, 1798.

Dow, Lorenzo. *The Chain of Lorenzo.* Augusta, GA: G. F. Randolph, n.d. (ca. 1803).

Dwight, Timothy. *The Charitable Blessed; a Sermon, Preached in the First Church in New-Haven.* New Haven, CT: Sidney's Press, 1810.

Easton-Flake, Amy, and Rachel Cope. "A Multiplicity of Witnesses: Women and the Translation Process." In *The Coming Forth of the Book of Mormon: A Marvelous Work and a Wonder,* edited by Dennis L. Largey, Andrew H. Hedges, John Hilton III, and Kerry Hull, 133–53. Salt Lake City, UT: Brigham Young University Religious Studies Center and Deseret Book, 2015.

Edwards, Maldwyn L. "Adam Clarke, the Man." *Methodist History* 9, no. 4 (July 1971): 50–56.

The Experience and Ministerial Labours of Several Methodist Preachers, Who Laboured in Connection with the Late Rev. John Wesley. New York: Daniel Hitt, 1812.

The Experience of Several Eminent Methodist Preachers. With an Account of Their Call to, and Success in the Ministry. Philadelphia: John Dickins, 1791.

Fanger, Claire. "Introduction: Theurgy, Magic, and Mysticism." In *Invoking Angels: Theurgic Ideas and Practices, Thirteenth to Sixteenth Centuries,* edited by Claire Fanger, 1–33. University Park: Pennsylvania State University Press, 2012.

Fauconnier, Gilles, and Mark Turner. *The Way We Think: Conceptual Blending and the Mind's Hidden Complexities.* New York: Basic Books, 2002.

Fea, John. "Wheelock's World: Letters and the Communication of Revival in Great Awakening New England." *Proceedings of the American Antiquarian Society: A Journal of American History and Culture through 1876* 109, no. 1 (April 1999): 99–144.

Fénelon, François de Salignac de La Mothe. *Dialogues Concerning Eloquence in General; and Particularly, That Kind Which Is Fit for the Pulpit.* Translated by William Stevenson. London: J. Walthoe Jr., 1722.

Finney, Charles Grandison. *Lectures on Revivals of Religion.* 2nd ed. New York and Boston: Leavitt, Lord; Crocker & Brewster, 1835.

Fitzmyer, Joseph A. *First Corinthians: A New Translation with Introduction and Commentary.* Vol. 32 of the Anchor Yale Bible. New Haven, CT: Yale University Press, 2008.

Fleming, Stephen J. "The Fulness of the Gospel: Christian Platonism and the Origins of Mormonism." PhD diss., University of California, Santa Barbara, 2014. ProQuest (Order No. 3645631).

Fordyce, James. *The Eloquence of the Pulpit.* 4th ed. Glasgow: R. Banks, 1755.

A Form of Discipline for the Ministers, Preachers, and Members of the Methodist Episcopal Church in America. New York: Methodist Episcopal Church, 1787.

Fowler, Robert. "The Homeric Question." In *The Cambridge Companion to Homer,* edited by Robert Fowler, 220–32. New York: Cambridge University Press, 2004.

"Fragment of a Vision." In *Evangelicana; or, Gospel Treasury*, edited by William Collier, 300–4. Boston: Hastings, Etheridge, and Bliss, 1809.

Gardner, Brant A. *The Gift and Power: Translating the Book of Mormon.* Salt Lake City, UT: Greg Kofford Books, 2011.

———. "Literacy and Orality in the Book of Mormon." *Interpreter* 9 (2014): 29–85.

———. "Nephi as Scribe." *Mormon Studies Review* 23, no. 1 (2011): 45–55.

Gevaryahu, H. M. I. "Biblical Colophons: A Source for the 'Biography' of Authors, Texts and Books." *Vetus Testamentum: Supplement* 28, Congress Volume, Edinburgh (1974): 42–59.

Gibson, William. "The British Sermon 1689–1901: Quantities, Performance, and Culture." In *The Oxford Handbook of the British Sermon 1689–1901*, edited by Keith A. Francis and William Gibson, 3–30. Oxford: Oxford University Press, 2012.

Givens, Terryl. *By the Hand of Mormon: The American Scripture That Launched a New World Religion.* New York: Oxford University Press, 2002.

Glazebrook, James. *The Practice of What Is Called Extempore Preaching Recommended.* London: J. Mathews, 1794.

Granger, James. *A Biographical History of England.* 4th ed. Vol. 1. London: W. Baynes; W. Clarke; J. White; T. Egerton; Hanwell and Parker; Deighton; J. Archer, 1804.

Gross, Robert A. "Reading for an Extensive Republic." In *A History of the Book in America: An Extensive Republic: Print, Culture, and Society in the New Nation, 1790–1840.* Vol. 2, edited by Robert A. Gross and Mary Kelley, 516–44. Chapel Hill: American Antiquarian Society and the University of North Carolina Press, 2010.

Gustafson, Sandra M. *Eloquence Is Power: Oratory & Performance in Early America.* Chapel Hill: The Omohundro Institute of Early American History and Culture and the University of North Carolina Press, 2000.

Gutjahr, Paul C. *The Book of Mormon: A Biography.* Lives of Great Religious Books. Princeton, NJ: Princeton University Press, 2012.

Hale, Van. "The Doctrinal Impact of the King Follett Discourse." *BYU Studies* 18, no. 2 (1978): 209–25.

Hall, David D. *Worlds of Wonder, Days of Judgment: Popular Religious Belief in Early New England.* New York: Knopf, 1989.

Hamblin, William J. "That Old Black Magic." *FARMS Review of Books* 12, no. 2 (2000): 225–393.

Hardy, Grant, ed. *The Book of Mormon: Another Testament of Jesus Christ.* Maxwell Institute Study Edition. Provo, UT: Neal A. Maxwell Institute for Religious Scholarship and the Religious Studies Center, Brigham Young University, 2018.

———. "Introduction." In *The Book of Mormon: The Earliest Text*, edited by Royal Skousen. New Haven, CT: Yale University Press, 2009.

———. "Textual Criticism and the Book of Mormon." In *Foundational Texts of Mormonism: Examining Major Early Sources*, edited by Mark Ashurst-McGee, Robin Scott Jensen, and Sharalyn D. Howcroft. New York: Oxford University Press, 2018.

———. *Understanding the Book of Mormon: A Reader's Guide.* New York: Oxford University Press, 2010.

Harkness, Deborah E. *John Dee's Conversations with Angels: Cabala, Alchemy, and the End of Nature.* New York: Cambridge University Press, 1999.

Hawthorne, Nathaniel. "A Fellow-Traveller." In *Selected Tales and Sketches,* edited by Michael J. Colacurcio. Penguin Classics, 80–85. New York: Penguin Books, 1987.

Henige, David. *Historical Evidence and Argument.* Madison: University of Wisconsin Press, 2005.

Hersey, Thomas. *A Voice from the Grave.* Morgantown, VA: J. Campbell, 1806.

Hill, Donna. *Joseph Smith: The First Mormon.* Garden City, NY: Doubleday, 1977.

Hindmarsh, D. Bruce. *The Evangelical Conversion Narrative: Spiritual Autobiography in Early Modern England.* Oxford: Oxford University Press, 2005.

Hindmarsh, Robert. *A Seal upon the Lips of Unitarians, Trinitarians, and All Others.* Philadelphia: Johnson Taylor, 1815.

Hobart, John Henry. *A Companion for the Altar.* New York: Peter A. Mesier, 1804.

Howe, Eber D. *Mormonism Unvailed.* Painesville, OH: E. D. Howe, 1834.

———. *Mormonism Unvailed.* With critical commentary by Dan Vogel. Salt Lake City, UT: Signature Books, 2015. First published 1834.

Huggins, Ronald V. "'Without a Cause' and 'Ships of Tarshish': A Possible Contemporary Source for Two Unexplained Readings from Joseph Smith." *Dialogue: A Journal of Mormon Thought* 36, no. 1 (Spring 2003): 157–79.

Hughes, Richard T., and C. Leonard Allen. *Illusions of Innocence: Protestant Primitivism in America, 1630–1875.* Chicago: University of Chicago Press, 1988.

Hunger, Hermann. *Babylonische und Assyrische Kolophone.* Alter Orient und Altes Testament, edited by Kurt Bergerhof, Manfred Dietrich, and Oswald Loretz. Neukirench-Vluyn, Germany: Neukirchener Verlag des Erziehungsvereins; Butzon & Bercker Kevelaer, 1968.

Jackson, Brian. "'As a Musician Would His Violin': The Oratory of the Great Basin Prophets." In *A New History of the Sermon: The Nineteenth Century,* edited by Robert H. Ellison, 489–520. Leiden, Netherlands: Brill, 2010.

Jerningham, Edward. "An Essay on the Eloquence of the Pulpit in England." In *The Pulpit Orator; Being a New Selection of Eloquent Pulpit Discourses, Accompanied with Observations on the Composition and Delivery of Sermons,* 54–123. Boston: Joseph Nancrede, 1804.

Jessee, Dean C., ed. *Personal Writings of Joseph Smith.* Salt Lake City, UT: Deseret Book and Brigham Young University Press, 2002.

Johnson, James E. "Burned-over District." In *Dictionary of Christianity in America,* edited by Daniel G. Reid, Robert D. Linder, Bruce L. Shelley, and Harry S. Stout. Downers Grove, IL: InterVarsity Press, 1990.

Johnson, Nan. *Nineteenth-Century Rhetoric in North America.* Carbondale: Southern Illinois University Press, 1991.

Jones, Phyllis M., and Nicholas R. Jones, eds. *Salvation in New England.* Austin: University of Texas Press, 1977.

The Joseph Smith Papers (JSP). http://josephsmithpapers.org/.

Kingman, Bradford. *Epitaphs from Burial Hill, Plymouth, Massachusetts, from 1657–1892.* Brookline, MA: New England Illustrated Historical Publishing Company, 1892.

Larson, Stan. "The Historicity of the Matthean Sermon on the Mount in 3 Nephi." In *New Approaches to the Book of Mormon: Explorations in Critical Methodology*, edited by Brent Lee Metcalfe, 115–63. Salt Lake City, UT: Signature Books, 1993.

———. "The King Follett Discourse: A Newly Amalgamated Text." *BYU Studies* 18, no. 2 (1978): 193–208.

Leichty, Erle. "The Colophon." In *Studies Presented to A. Leo Oppenheim*, edited by R. D. Biggs and J. A. Brinkman, 147–54. Chicago: University of Chicago Press and the Oriental Institute of the University of Chicago, 1964.

Long, Burke O. "Framing Repetitions in Biblical Historiography." *Journal of Biblical Literature* 106, no. 3 (1987): 385–99.

Lundbom, J. R. "Baruch, Seraiah, and Expanded Colophons in the Book of Jeremiah." *Journal for the Study of the Old Testament* 11, no. 36 (1986): 89–114.

Mackay, Michael Hubbard, and Nicholas J. Frederick. *Joseph Smith's Seer Stones*. Salt Lake City, UT: Religious Studies Center at Brigham Young University and Deseret Book, 2016.

Mackay, Thomas W. "Mormon as Editor: A Study in Colophons, Headers, and Source Indicators." *Journal of Book of Mormon Studies* 2, no. 2 (1993): 90–109.

Maffly-Kipp, Laurie F., ed. *The Book of Mormon: Translated by Joseph Smith Jr.* New York: Penguin Books, 2008. First published 1830 by E. B. Grandin (Palmyra, NY).

Marquardt, H. Michael. "Orson Hyde and Samuel H. Smith at Boston in 1832." http://user.xmission.com/%7Eresearch/central/hydesmith.htm.

———. *The Rise of Mormonism: 1816–1844*. Longwood, FL: Xulon Press, 2005.

Marshall, Jabez P. *Memoirs of the Late Rev. Abraham Marshall*. Mount Zion, GA: Jabez P. Marshall, 1824.

Mason, John. *The Student and Pastor; or, Directions How to Attain to Eminence and Usefulness in Those Respective Characters*. London: H. D. Symonds, 1807. First published 1755 by J. Noon; J. Buckland; J. Waugh and W. Fenner; and J. and S. Johnson (London).

Matthews, Robert J. "Joseph Smith Translation of the Bible (JST)." In *Encyclopedia of Mormonism*, edited by Daniel H. Ludlow, 763–69. New York: Macmillan, 1992.

McClure, David, and Elijah Parish. *Memoirs of the Rev. Eleazar Wheelock, D.D.* Newburyport, MA: Edward Little, 1811.

Metcalfe, Brent Lee. "The Priority of Mosiah: A Prelude to Book of Mormon Exegesis." In *New Approaches to the Book of Mormon*, edited by Brent Lee Metcalfe, 395–444. Salt Lake City, UT: Signature Books, 1993.

Miller, Perry. *The New England Mind: The Seventeenth Century*. Cambridge, MA: Harvard University Press, 1954.

Miller, Robert. "Experience of Mr. Robert Miller." Pts. 1 and 2. *The Methodist Magazine for the Year 1801*, Vol. 24 (January 1801): 3–10; (February 1801): 49–55.

Morris, Larry E. *A Documentary History of the Book of Mormon*. New York: Oxford University Press, 2019.

Mudge, Enoch. "Hymn 57, Joy in Attending on Public Worship." In *The American Camp-Meeting Hymn Book*, edited by Enoch Mudge. Boston: Joseph Burdakin, 1818.

Mueller, Max Perry. *Race and the Making of the Mormon People*. Chapel Hill: University of North Carolina Press, 2017.

Murray, Iain, ed. *George Whitefield's Journals*. 7th ed. Edinburgh: Banner of Truth Trust, 1998. First published 1960.

Murray, John. *The Justification of Believers by Imputed Righteousness*. Newburyport, MA: John Mycall, 1789.

Murray, Lindley. *The English Reader*. Albany, NY: Websters and Skinners, 1814. First published 1799 by Longman and Rees (York, UK).

Myles, William. *A Chronological History of the People Called Methodists*. 3rd ed. London: William Myles, 1803.

Neuman, Meredith Marie. *Jeremiah's Scribes: Creating Sermon Literature in Puritan New England*. Philadelphia: University of Pennsylvania Press, 2013.

Newton, John. *Cardiphonia: Or, the Utterance of the Heart*. 4th ed. Vol. 2. London: J. Buckland and J. Johnson, 1787. First published 1781.

Nibley, Hugh. *The Prophetic Book of Mormon*. Vol. 8 of *The Collected Works of Hugh Nibley*. Salt Lake City, UT: Deseret Book and Foundation for Ancient Research and Mormon Studies, 1989.

———. *Since Cumorah: The Book of Mormon in the Modern World*. Salt Lake City, UT: Deseret Book, 1967.

Nickerson, Matthew. "Nephi's Psalm: 2 Nephi 4:16–35 in the Light of Form-Critical Analysis." *Journal of Book of Mormon Studies* 6, no. 2 (1997): 26–42.

Olson, Paul J. "The Public Perception of 'Cults' and 'New Religious Movements.'" *Journal for the Scientific Study of Religion* 45, no. 1 (2006): 97–106.

Palmer, Grant H. *An Insider's View of Mormon Origins*. Salt Lake City, UT: Signature Books, 2002.

Pawson, John. *A Serious and Affectionate Address to the Junior Preachers in the Methodist Connection*. London, 1798.

Perkins, William. *The Arte of Prophecying: Or, a Treatise Concerning the Sacred and Onely True Manner and Methode of Preaching*. London: Felix Kyngston for E. E., 1607.

Perry, Seth. *Bible Culture and Authority in the Early United States*. Princeton, NJ: Princeton University Press, 2018.

———. "The Many Bibles of Joseph Smith: Textual, Prophetic, and Scholarly Authority in Early-National Bible Culture." *Journal of the American Academy of Religion* 84, no. 3 (September 2016): 750–75.

"Primitivism." In *Dictionary of Christianity in America*, edited by Daniel G. Reid, Robert Dean Linder, Bruce L. Shelley, and Harry S. Stout. Downers Grove, IL: InterVarsity Press, 1990.

Prince, Gregory A. "Joseph Smith's First Vision in Historical Context: How a Historical Narrative Became Theological." *Journal of Mormon History* 41, no. 4 (2015): 74–94.

Pulpit Elocution: Or, Characters and Principles of the Most Popular Preachers, of Each Denomination. London: J. Wade, 1782.

Quinn, D. Michael. *Early Mormonism and the Magic World View*. 2nd ed. Salt Lake City, UT: Signature Books, 1998. First published 1987.

Reitzenstein, Richard. "Die Entstehung Der Formel 'Glaube, Liebe, Hoffnung.'" In *Historische Zeitschrift*, 189–208. Munich and Berlin: Druck und Verlag von R. Oldenbourg, 1916.

———. "Die Formel Glaube, Liebe, Hoffnung Bei Paulus." *Nachrichten von der Königlichen Gesellschaft der Wissenschaften zu Göttingen.* Philologisch-historische Klasse aus dem Jahre 1917, Heft 1 (1917–1918): 130–51.

Richardson, James T. "Definitions of Cult: From Sociological-Technical to Popular-Negative." *Review of Religious Research* 34, no. 4 (June 1993): 348–56.

Riley, D. W. "Tegg V. Everett: The Publication of the Second Edition of Adam Clarke's Commentary." *Proceedings of the Wesley Historical Society* 44 (September 1984): 145–50.

Roche, John A. *The Life of John Price Durbin, D.D., LL.D., with an Analysis of His Homiletic Skill and Sacred Oratory.* New York: Phillips & Hunt; Cranston & Stowe, 1889.

Rosenberg, Bruce A. *Can These Bones Live? The Art of the American Folk Preacher.* Urbana: University of Illinois Press, 1988. First published 1970 by Oxford University Press.

Rust, Richard Dilworth. *Feasting on the Word: The Literary Testimony of the Book of Mormon.* Salt Lake City, UT: Deseret Book and Foundation for Ancient Research and Mormon Studies, 1997.

Scherer, Mark A. *The Journey of a People: The Era of Restoration, 1820 to 1844.* Independence, MO: Community of Christ Seminary Press, 2013.

Scot, Reginald. *Scot's Discovery of Witchcraft.* London: R. C. and Giles Calvert, 1651.

Silverman, Kenneth, ed. *Benjamin Franklin: The Autobiography and Other Writings.* Harmondsworth, UK: Viking Penguin, 2003. First published 1986 by Penguin Books.

Simeon, Charles. *Helps to Composition; or, Six Hundred Skeletons of Sermons.* 1st American ed. 5 vols. Philadelphia: William W. Woodward, 1810–11.

Skousen, Royal, ed. *Analysis of Textual Variants of the Book of Mormon: Part One, 1 Nephi 1 - 2 Nephi 10.* Vol. 4 of *The Critical Text of the Book of Mormon.* Provo, UT: Foundation for Ancient Research and Mormon Studies, 2004.

———, ed. *The Book of Mormon: The Earliest Text.* New Haven, CT: Yale University Press, 2009.

———. "How Joseph Smith Translated the Book of Mormon: Evidence from the Original Manuscript." *Journal of Book of Mormon Studies* 7, no. 1 (1998): 22–31.

———. "The Original Language of the Book of Mormon: Upstate New York Dialect, King James English, or Hebrew?" *Journal of Book of Mormon Studies* 3, no. 1 (1994): 28–38.

———, ed. *The Original Manuscript of the Book of Mormon: Typographical Facsimile of the Extant Text.* Provo, UT: Foundation for Ancient Research and Mormon Studies and Brigham Young University, 2001.

Skousen, W. Cleon. *Isaiah Speaks to Modern Times.* Salt Lake City, UT: Ensign Publishing, 1984.

Smith, Calvin. "A Critical Analysis of the Public Speaking of Joseph Smith, First President of the Church of Jesus Christ of Latter-Day Saints." PhD diss., Purdue University, 1965. (Purdue Doc. No. 66-5304).

Smith, Joseph. *The Book of Mormon.* Palmyra, NY: E. B. Grandin, 1830.

———. *The Doctrine and Covenants of the Church of Jesus Christ of Latter-day Saints.* Salt Lake City, UT: Church of Jesus Christ of Latter-day Saints, 1991.

———. *History of the Church of Jesus Christ of Latter-Day Saints,* edited by B. H. Roberts. 7 vols. Salt Lake City, UT: Church of Jesus Christ of Latter-day Saints, 1902–32.

Smith III, Joseph. "Last Testimony of Sister Emma." *The Saints' Herald* 26, no. 19 (October 1879): [289]–90.

Smith, William V. "Joseph Smith's Sermons and the Early Mormon Documentary Record." In *Foundational Texts of Mormonism: Examining Major Early Sources*, edited by Mark Ashurst-McGee, Robin Scott Jensen, and Sharalyn D. Howcroft, 190–230. New York: Oxford University Press, 2018.

Sondrup, Steven P. "The Psalm of Nephi: A Lyric Reading." *BYU Studies* 21, no. 3 (1981): 357–72.

Spencer, Stan. "Seers and Stones: The Translation of the Book of Mormon as Divine Visions of an Old-Time Seer." *Interpreter* 24 (2017): 27–98.

Sprague, William Buell, ed. *Annals of the American Pulpit; or, Commemorative Notices of Distinguished American Clergyman of Various Denominations.* 9 vols. New York: Robert Carter & Brothers, 1856–69.

Stoddard, Solomon. *The Defects of Preachers Reproved in a Sermon Preached at Northampton, May 19th, 1723.* New London, CT: T. Green, 1724.

Stott, Graham St. John. "The Seer Stone Controversy: Writing the 'Book of Mormon.'" *Mosaic: An Interdisciplinary Critical Journal* 19, no. 3, Literature and Altered States of Consciousness, Part I (Summer 1986): 35–53.

Stout, Harry S. *The Divine Dramatist: George Whitefield and the Rise of Modern Evangelicalism.* Grand Rapids, MI: W. B. Eerdmans, 1991.

———. *The New England Soul: Preaching and Religious Culture in Colonial New England.* New York: Oxford University Press, 1986.

———. "New Lights." In *Dictionary of Christianity in America*, edited by Daniel G. Reid, Robert D. Linder, Bruce L. Shelley, and Harry S. Stout. Downers Grove, IL: InterVarsity Press, 1990.

———. "Old Lights." In *Dictionary of Christianity in America*, edited by Daniel G. Reid, Robert D. Linder, Bruce L. Shelley, and Harry S. Stout. Downers Grove, IL: InterVarsity Press, 1990.

Swain, Joseph. "Lo, He Comes, Array'd in Veng'ance (The Coming of Christ to Judgment)." In *A New Selection of Seven Hundred Evangelical Hymns, for Private, Family, and Public Worship*, edited by John Dobell. Morristown, NJ: Peter A. Johnson, 1810.

Taves, Ann. *Fits, Trances & Visions: Experiencing Religion and Explaining Experience from Wesley to James.* Princeton, NJ: Princeton University Press, 1999.

———. *Revelatory Events: Three Case Studies of the Emergence of New Spiritual Paths.* Princeton, NJ: Princeton University Press, 2016.

Taylor, Alan. "The Early Republic's Supernatural Economy: Treasure Seeking in the American Northeast, 1780–1830." *American Quarterly* 38, no. 1 (1986): 6–34.

Thomas, Keith. *Religion and the Decline of Magic.* London: Penguin Books, 1991. First published 1971 by Weidenfeld & Nicolson.

Thomas, Mark D. *Digging in Cumorah: Reclaiming Book of Mormon Narratives.* Salt Lake City, UT: Signature Books, 2003.

———. "The Meaning of Revival Language in the Book of Mormon." *Sunstone* 8, no. 3 (May–June 1983): 19–25.

Tillett, Wilbur F. "Part First." In *The Doctrines and Polity of the Methodist Episcopal Church, South*, edited by Wilbur F. Tillett and James Atkins, 1–90. Nashville, TN: Methodist Episcopal Church, South, 1905.

Towle, Nancy. *Vicissitudes Illustrated, in the Experience of Nancy Towle, in Europe and America*. 2nd ed. Portsmouth, NH: Nancy Towle, 1833.

Turner, Orsamus. *History of the Pioneer Settlement of Phelps & Gorham's Purchase*. Rochester, NY: William Alling, 1852.

Turner, William. *The History of All Religions in the World: From the Creation Down to This Present Time*. London: John Dunton, 1695.

Tvedtnes, John A. "Colophons in the Book of Mormon." In *Rediscovering the Book of Mormon*, edited by John L. Sorenson and Melvin J. Thorne, 32–37. Salt Lake City, UT: Deseret Book and Foundation for Ancient Research and Mormon Studies, 1991.

Van Dyke, Blair G., and Loyd Isao Ericson, eds. *Perspectives on Mormon Theology: Apologetics*. Salt Lake City, UT: Greg Kofford Books, 2017.

Van Wagoner, Richard, and Steve Walker. "Joseph Smith: 'The Gift of Seeing.'" *Dialogue: A Journal of Mormon Thought* 15, no. 2 (1982): 48–68.

Versluis, Arthur. *Magic and Mysticism: An Introduction to Western Esotericism*. Lanham, MA: Rowman & Littlefield, 2007.

Vogel, Dan, ed. *Early Mormon Documents*. 5 vols. Salt Lake City, UT: Signature Books, 1996–2003.

———. *Joseph Smith: The Making of a Prophet*. Salt Lake City, UT: Signature Books, 2004.

———. "The Locations of Joseph Smith's Early Treasure Quests." *Dialogue: A Journal of Mormon Thought* 27, no. 3 (1994): 197–231.

———. *Religious Seekers and the Advent of Mormonism*. Salt Lake City, UT: Signature Books, 1988.

Walker, John. *A Rhetorical Grammar: In Which the Common Improprieties in Reading and Speaking Are Detected*. 3rd ed. London: John Walker, 1801.

———. *The Teacher's Assistant in English Composition*. Boston: J. T. Buckingham, 1810.

Walker, Samuel. *The Christian: Being a Course of Practical Sermons*. 3rd ed. London: Edward Dilly and Barnabas Thorn, 1759.

Ware, Henry. *Hints on Extemporaneous Preaching*. Boston: Cummings and Hilliard, 1824.

Watson, J. R. "Olivers, Thomas (Bap. 1725, D. 1799), Methodist Preacher and Hymn Writer." In *Oxford Dictionary of National Biography*. Oxford: Oxford University Press, 2004. http://www.oxforddnb.com/view/10.1093/ref:odnb/9780198614128.001.0001/odnb-9780198614128-e-20738.

Watts, Isaac. *An Extract from the Works of the Pious, and Laborious, Isaac Watts, D. D.* New Brunswick, NJ: A. Blauvelt, 1812.

———. *A Guide to Prayer; or, a Free and Rational Account of the Gift, Grace and Spirit of Prayer*. Aberdeen: J. Boyle, 1792. First published 1716 (London).

Welch, John W. "Documents of the Translation of the Book of Mormon." In *Opening the Heavens: Accounts of Divine Manifestations, 1820–1844*, edited by John Welch, 126–227. Provo, UT: Brigham Young University Press and Deseret Book, 2017.

———. "How Long Did It Take Joseph Smith to Translate the Book of Mormon?" *Ensign* 20, no. 1 (January 1988). https://www.lds.org/study/ensign/1988/01/i-have-a-question/how-long-did-it-take-joseph-smith-to-translate-the-book-of-mormon?lang=eng.

———. "Timing the Translation of the Book of Mormon." *BYU Studies Quarterly* 57, no. 4 (2018): [10]–50.

Welch, John W., and Tim Rathbone. "Book of Mormon Translation by Joseph Smith." In *Encyclopedia of Mormonism*, edited by Daniel H. Ludlow, 210–13. New York: Macmillan, 1992.

———. "How Long Did It Take to Translate the Book of Mormon?" In *Reexploring the Book of Mormon*, edited by John W. Welch, 1–5. Salt Lake City, UT: Deseret Book and the Foundation for Ancient Research and Mormon Studies, 1992.

Welch, John W., and Miriam A. Smith. "Joseph Smith: 'Author and Proprietor.'" In *Reexploring the Book of Mormon*, edited by John W. Welch, 154–57. Provo, UT: Deseret Book and the Foundation for Ancient Research and Mormon Studies, 1992.

Wenzel, Siegfried. *Medieval Artes Praedicandi: A Synthesis of Scholastic Sermon Structure.* Toronto: Medieval Academy of America, University of Toronto Press, 2015.

Wesley, John. *Directions Concerning Pronunciation and Gesture.* Bristol: William Pine, 1770.

———. *Sermons on Several Occasions.* Vol. 1. London: W. Strahan, printer; T. Trye, bookseller, 1746.

———. *Sermons on Several Occasions.* Vol. 1. Philadelphia: J. Crukshank; John Dickins, 1794.

———. *Sermons on Several Occasions.* 5th ed. Vol. 4. London: G. Whitfield, 1796–99.

———. *Sermons, on Several Occasions.* Vol. 1. New York: The Methodist Connection in the United States, 1810.

Whitefield, George. *A Letter to the Rev. The President, and Professors, Tutors, and Hebrew Instructor, of Harvard-College in Cambridge.* Boston: S. Kneeland and T. Green, 1745.

———. *Letters of George Whitefield: For the Period 1734–1742.* Chatham, UK: The Banner of Truth Trust, 1976.

Whitmer, David. *An Address to All Believers in Christ.* Richmond, MO: David Whitmer, 1887.

Wilkins, John. *Ecclesiastes: Or, a Discourse Concerning the Gift of Preaching.* 6th ed. London: Samuel Gellibrand, 1675.

Williamson, David. *Reflections on the Four Principal Religions.* Vol. 2. London: John Richardson, 1824.

Wilson, Haley, and Thomas Wayment. "A Recently Recovered Source: Rethinking Joseph Smith's Bible Translation." *Journal of Undergraduate Research* [Brigham Young University] (March 2017). http://jur.byu.edu/?p=21296.

Wilson, Lynne Savage Hilton. "Joseph Smith's Doctrine of the Holy Spirit Contrasted with Cartwright, Campbell, Hodge, and Finney." PhD diss., Marquette University, 2010. ProQuest (Order No. 3398997).

Woodward, Walter W. *Prospero's America: John Winthrop, Jr., Alchemy, and the Creation of New England Culture, 1606–1676.* Chapel Hill: The Omohundro Institute of Early American History and Culture and the University of North Carolina Press, 2010.

Wright, David P. "Isaiah in the Book of Mormon: Or Joseph Smith in Isaiah." In *American Apocrypha: Essays on the Book of Mormon*, edited by Dan Vogel and Brent Lee Metcalfe, 157–234. Salt Lake City, UT: Signature Books, 2002.

———. "Joseph Smith's Interpretation of Isaiah in the Book of Mormon." *Dialogue: A Journal of Mormon Thought* 31, no. 4 (1998): 181–206.

Index

CPSIA information can be obtained
at www.ICGtesting.com
Printed in the USA
LVHW112000220420
654207LV00003B/371